✣

CATARINA THE WISE

and Other Wondrous

SICILIAN

FOLK & FAIRY

TALES

T0308917

Catarina replied boldly, "Fine. I'll be cooler down there."

❖

CATARINA
THE WISE

and Other Wondrous

SICILIAN

FOLK & FAIRY

TALES

by

GIUSEPPE PITRÈ

Translated and Edited by
JACK ZIPES

Illustrated by Adeetje Bouma

◆

The University of Chicago Press
Chicago and London

The University of Chicago Press, Chicago 60637

The University of Chicago Press, Ltd., London

© 2017 by Jack Zipes

All rights reserved.

Published 2017.

Printed in the United States of America

Portions of this book were previously published in an earlier form in *The Collected Sicilian Folk and Fairy Tales of Giuseppe Pitrè* translated by Jack Zipes and Joseph Russo 2009 by Routledge © 2009 Taylor & Francis

26 25 24 23 22 21 20 19 18 17   1 2 3 4 5

ISBN-13: 978-0-226-46279-0 (paper)

ISBN-13: 978-0-226-46282-0 (e-book)

DOI: 10.7208/chicago/978022646820.001.0001

Library of Congress Cataloging-in-Publication Data

Names: Pitrè, Giuseppe, 1841–1916, author. | Zipes, Jack, 1937– translator, editor. | Bouma, Adeetje, illustrator.

Title: Catarina the Wise and other wondrous Sicilian folk and fairy tales / by Giuseppe Pitrè ; translated and edited by Jack Zipes ; illustrated by Adeetje Bouma.

Description: Chicago ; London : The University of Chicago Press, 2017. | Includes bibliographical references and index.

Identifiers: LCCN 2016043309 | ISBN 9780226462790 (pbk. : alk. paper) | ISBN 9780226462820 (e-book)

Subjects: LCSH: Tales—Italy—Sicily. | Folklore—Italy—Sicily.

Classification: LCC GR177.S5 P42413 2017 | DDC 398.209458—dc23 LC record available at https://lccn.loc.gov/2016043309

♾ This paper meets the requirements of ANSI/NISO Z39.48–1992 (Permanence of Paper).

To Joe Russo
in memory of our wonderful collaboration
and with gratitude

Contents

Illustrations appear on pages ii, 14, 40, 58, 70, 77, 89, 137, 174, and 240.

Preface

Giuseppe Pitrè, a tiny man, barely more than five feet tall, was actually a great man, whose stature as a folklorist exceeded all the great European folklorists of the nineteenth century including the Brothers Grimm. His work, however, has not received its due recognition, and, therefore, in honor of the hundredth year since his death in 1916, I have joined with the University of Chicago Press to celebrate Pitrè's unique and extraordinary career with this small sample of his astonishing achievement.

What is startling about Pitrè's tales, which were really not *his* tales but oral tales spoken by diverse Sicilian storytellers, largely from the lower classes, is their brusque, lively, and imaginative style. While it is extremely difficult to capture the tone and meaning of tales told in a foreign dialect, Joseph Russo and I have tried to remain faithful to the different styles of the storytellers and to recapture some of the melodic quality of the tales. My selection of fifty tales out of more than 400 is geared to feature the diverse manner in which Sicilian storytellers re-created well-known, so-called classical tales with astonishing results. Most of the tales were told to Pitrè and his informants by women ranging from twelve to seventy years of age. Unlike the tales in the Grimms' collections, there is a strong "feminist" touch to all the well-known classical fairy tales that changes their meanings. The first ten tales in this present selection are highly original and provocative versions of "Rapunzel," "Cinderella," "Sleeping Beauty," "Donkey Skin," and "Puss in Boots," and their concerns are articulated in a manner that still speaks to the conflicts of our present day.

The tales in this collection, first published in 2008 by Rout-ledge as *The Collected Sicilian Folk and Fairy Tales of Giuseppe Pitrè*, were translated by Joseph Russo and myself. They were based on Pitrè's famous four-volume edition of *Sicilian Fables, Stories, and Folktales* (*Fiabe, novelle e racconti popolari siciliani*, 1875) in Sicilian di-alect. The present volume includes forty-four tales from the En-glish edition of more than 400 tales that I translated with Joseph Russo and six newly translated tales from Pitrè's *Popular Sicilian Fables and Legends* (*Fiabe e Leggende popolari siciliane*, 1888) and *Studi di Leggende popolari in Sicilia* (*Sudies of Popular Legends in Sicilia*, 1904) that I have translated alone. In fact, I have revised and honed all the tales in this new volume, often changing titles, phrasing, and style, in an attempt to come closer to Pitrè's original stories. I have also included four "Cola Pesce" legends, which are especially rel-evant for understanding Sicilian culture.

To conclude, I want to express my deep gratitude to Marga-ret Hivnor, who provided me with an abundance of good advice and careful editing, and Alan Thomas, who initiated the project. I would also like to thank Elizabeth Ellingboe and Trevor Perri for their thorough copyediting. Furthermore, here is a good place to show my appreciation to Bianca Lazzaro and Carmine Donzelli, who have been a driving spiritual force behind my work on Pitrè for the past six years. I am greatly indebted to them. Finally, I should like to state how grateful I am to Erica Wetter and Rout-ledge Press for granting me the rights for this paperback edition.

Introduction

THE EXTRAORDINARY GIUSEPPE PITRÈ

Jack Zipes

The people who were the slowest and most reluctant to be persuaded about the extraordinary if not unique merits of Giuseppe Pitrè were not the common Sicilians, but the cultivated people. For some time it seemed to cultured Italians that the good doctor of Palermo, also a folklorist, had damaged the dignity of scholarship, humiliating himself by collecting scattered little stories that formed the domestic and traditional lore of the Sicilian people. . . . But through the determination, persistence, and seriousness of Pitrè's studies, he ended by inspiring all Sicilians with an appreciation for his various works. Gradually, this appreciation reached the university, where Pitrè brought about a new science of comparative psychology of popular customs and traditions. Thanks to Pitrè's merits, this new field of study was designated a place of honor in academia. ANGELO DE GUBERNATIS, *Italia illustre. Giuseppe Pitrè* (1911)

If one were to name the greatest European folklorists of the nineteenth century, one might begin with the Brothers Grimm and move through the ranks of the enterprising British, German, Italian, and French pioneers and probably end with the illustrious names of James George Frazier, Theodor Benfrey, Edward Tylor, Paul Sébillot, and Andrew Lang. Probably no one would list Giuseppe Pitrè, the versatile and brilliant Sicilian, whose works are totally neglected in the English-speaking world. Yet, Pitrè, more than the Grimms or any other folklorist of the nineteenth century, made greater contributions to laying the solid groundwork for major developments in collecting and preserving oral tales, songs, legends, anecdotes, and proverbs than any other scholar of his time.

Who, Then, Was Giuseppe Pitrè? Why Was He Neglected?

Well, he was certainly not neglected in his time. In an obituary published in *The Nation* soon after Pitrè's death in 1916, the renowned American scholar Thomas Frederick Crane, a gifted folklorist in his own right, made this comment in comparing Pitrè to the Grimms:

> Wide as the scope of their [the Grimms'] labors, it did not equal in extent the field cultivated by Pitrè, and after the *Kinder- und Hausmärchen* (*Children and Household Tales*) and the *Deutsche Sagen* (*German Legends*) the interests of the brothers became almost exclusively linguistic and lexicographical. Pitrè, on the other hand, was all his life a practicing physician, and took a prominent part in the civic affairs of Palermo, being Syndic, or Mayor, for many years. The Grimms were chiefly concerned with the tales and legends of Germany and its medieval literature: Pitrè throughout his long life devoted himself to every branch of folk-lore—popular tales, legends, songs, children's games, proverbs, riddles, customs, etc.—and collected himself an astounding mass of material, only a part of which is represented in the twenty-five volumes of the *Biblioteca delle tradizioni popolari siciliani*. (The *Library of Sicilian Folklore*, Palermo, 1871–1914)[1]

Born in Borgo, a lower-class district in Palermo, on December 22, 1841, Pitrè came from a family with a strong maritime tradition. His father Salvatore was a sailor and worked on trans-

1 Thomas Frederick Crane, "Giuseppe Pitrè and Sicilian Folk-Lore," *The Nation* 103/262 (1916): 234.

atlantic ships, and his mother, Maria Stabile, was the daughter of a seafaring family. Unfortunately, Pitrè's father died in 1847 from yellow fever while he was in New Orleans, and Pitrè and his younger brother Antonio were compelled to move into their maternal grandfather's house in Borgo. This early death brought the young Pitrè closer to his grandfather Giuseppe Stabile, and it also strengthened his mother's desire to further her son's education and keep him away from the sea. Thanks to the support of her tightly knit extended family and the help of a priest, she was able to provide educational opportunities and security for both her sons. Especially for Giuseppe Pitrè, these close and warm relations among his relatives and friends in the Borgo district stamped his positive attitude toward the common people his entire life.

Already, as a young boy, Pitrè began collecting proverbs, maritime expressions, and songs, and it soon became clear that he had a literary bent and was especially curious about the history of Sicilian customs and beliefs. When he turned thirteen, he began attending a Jesuit seminary, San Francisco di Paola, where he received a rigorous classical education, but when the Italian insurrection against the Austrians erupted, he was inspired to fight for an independent and united Italy, which was to include a liberated Sicily. Consequently, he left school in 1860 to enlist in Garibaldi's navy. Throughout the spring of that same year, he sailed to different port cities such as Marseilles, Genoa, and Naples. This was the only time he ever left the island of Sicily, and, fortunately for the future of Sicilian folklore, he was not involved in any battles. When the uprising was quelled and the Italians defeated, he returned to Sicily to finish his studies and enrolled as student of medicine at the University of Palermo in 1861.

When Pitrè completed his studies in 1866 and could not find work as a doctor, he began teaching Italian literature at a high school in Palermo. However, he lost this teaching position (due to a dispute with a vindictive official, who was later punished for indiscriminate behavior), and started practicing as a private doctor.

That year a major cholera epidemic spread throughout Sicily. For the next two years Pitrè helped hundreds of people stricken with cholera, and he came to realize how important it was to continue practicing medicine, and also that he could pursue his interest in folklore at the same time. Indeed, he put this realization to work: as he walked or traveled by horse and buggy to his patients, and their relatives and friends, he collected and wrote down songs, proverbs, and tales.

From this point on until his death, Pitrè became widely known in Palermo as "the little doctor," who took notes and even wrote entire books while riding in his horse and buggy. Nobody dared disturb him while he concentrated on his work. In a revealing reminiscence of a visit with Pitrè, the Swiss folklorist, Walter Keller wrote:

And so we went down the stairs where his servant was already waiting for us in front of the house with an old-fashioned coach drawn by a single horse. "Please allow me to introduce my *traveling study*," Pitrè said to me and asked me to climb in.

"Padrone," the servant said to the doctor, "I've put the mail on the table in the coach for you."

Indeed he had! The inside of the coach had been transformed into a small study with a desk, and the walls contained all kinds of shafts, secret folders, and invisible pockets from which Pitrè took out manuscripts, books, magazines, and letters.

"You see," he explained to me, "for years I've taken care of almost all my correspondence in this traveling study."

"Aha!" I thought. "That's why the handwriting of his letters is so unclear and shaky."

"And it's inside here that I've written a good part of my books, always on the way from one sick person to the next. I can't conceive of how I could have otherwise completed my large collections and wrapped up everything during my lifetime. This coach bounces softly, as you can see, and Old Fritz, my faithful horse, doesn't trot very fast so that I can work here very nicely. You can get used to anything."[1]

And Pitrè always seemed to get used to everything. By 1868, he had gathered enough folk songs to publish his first major book, *Sicilian Popular Songs*. This collection became the first in his twenty-five volume series, *The Library of Sicilian Folklore*, 1871–1913, supported by Luigi Pedone Lauriel, one the first great publishers in Palermo dedicated to Sicilian history and folklore. When Pitrè began his serious work in the field of folklore, journalists and educators ridiculed him at first. The four volumes of *Fiabe, novelle e racconti popolari siciliani* (*Sicilian Fairy Tales, Folk Tales and Stories*, 1875) were dismissed as vulgar, indecent, and trivial by critics and academics alike, especially since the tales and stories were published in Sicilian dialect. But it was precisely Pitrè's dedication to the neglected "authentic" traditions of the Sicilian people that made and make his work so valuable. Unlike many of his predecessors in Europe, Pitrè endeavored to provide accurate renditions of the spoken word and also wrote historical studies about the customs and belief systems of the Sicilian people to provide a cultural and historical context for his work. Not only did Pitrè collect materials from his patients and friends, but he also recruited his own family to work with him and began corresponding with interested scholars on the island and on the Continent. Many of them sent him tales or information that he included in various collections.

At the same time that he carried out his extensive folklore research and worked as a medical doctor, he was gradually drawn into politics. Pitrè never joined a party, but remained an independent politician, disposed to support the causes of the common people. They, in turn, had great trust in Pitrè, who had always prided himself on being frank and honest. Consequently, he was

---

1 Walter Keller, "Zum Andenken an Giuseppe Pitrè," *SAVk* 21 (1917): 94–96.

"drafted" as a candidate and elected as an independent councilor (consigliere) of the Comune di Palermo and was soon regarded as one of the most beloved representatives of the people in his district. (Eventually, in 1915, he became a senator.) His major passion, however, remained the study of folklore. In 1909 he established the first folklore museum, Il Museo Etnografico Siciliano, in a former convent on the outskirts of Palermo, to house all the tools, costumes, pottery, etchings, and other artifacts that Pitrè had personally collected over the years. Finally, in 1911, thanks to Pitrè's work, the University of Palermo established the first chair in folklore. Yet, despite all his accomplishments and all the honors, Pitrè's latter years were devastated by personal tragedies. His youngest daughter Rosina perished in the Messina earthquake of 1908. His son Salvatore, who had graduated from the University of Palermo in 1911 and had become a medical doctor, died from food poisoning in 1912. Only his eldest daughter, Maria d'Alia Pitrè, who had assisted him in his research and had left Sicily in 1904 to live in Brazil, would live to survive him.

. . .

When Pitrè began to collect songs, proverbs, and tales, he was a young man in his twenties, and he did not have a clearly defined method or concept of folklore. His approach to collecting evolved as he realized that the preservation of oral storytelling entailed a combination of meticulous research and a deep theoretical understanding of the problems involved in the transformation of the oral to a written text. It was clear from the beginning, however, that Pitrè wanted to give voice to humble and neglected narrators, who were, so to speak, the curators of Sicilian history.

In the district of Borgo, Pitrè was aided by two informants, Agatuzza Messia, whom he knew as a child, and Rosa Brusca, who worked as a weaver and eventually became blind. He had also met another important narrator, Elisabetta Sanfratello, who worked as a servant in Vallelunga. About sixty percent or more of the tales he collected were narrated by women. Consequently, Pitrè's collection is more balanced than Laura Gonzenbach's *Sicilianische Märchen* (*Sicilian Folk Tales*, 1870), which consisted of tales almost entirely told by women and represented a particular feminine view of Sicilian culture from a small region. Since the tales told by men tended to be different in style and content, Pitrè's collection allows readers to compare and contrast the manner in which women and men narrated their versions of well-known tales, legends, and proverbs. Pitrè's informants were also from diverse regions on the island, and he always gave credit to the storytellers at the end of each tale. Therefore, we can see that the styles and shaping of the tales tend to be gender specific and stamped by the region in which the tale was told.

Pitrè generally took notes when he heard a tale told in dialect, and based on a hearing and possibly two or three, he reconstructed the tale using a method that enabled him to keep the phonetic sounds while at the same time shaping the dialect to make it as accessible as possible to a reading audience. In other words, Pitrè favored the Palermo Sicilian dialect as his standard in terms of spelling and grammar. However, when colleagues, friends, and relatives brought him or sent him tales in different Sicilian dialects from all parts of the island, he tried to remain as faithful to other unusual dialects and would explain the differences in his footnotes that often included several variants. Because he regarded the tales as ethnological, historical, and social relics, Pitrè was scrupulous about providing variants in his notes. By the time he put together the four volumes of his Sicilian collection, he could refer to variants in all parts of Europe and the Middle East and could trace the history of certain tales to the Greco-Roman period, often working like a detective to explain the derivation and deviation of a particular tale. Those critics who have asserted that Pitrè eliminated scatological references, brutality, and sexual innuendoes from the tales have clearly not read the entire collection. Not only did Pitrè allow for "vulgar" language and stories with risqué and comical scenes, for instance, one in which fairies make a woman out of manure, and one in which a young woman seduces a prince while he is asleep, but he also explained the metaphorical references to sex in his notes. In many of the tales the ogres devour humans, and brutality is not uncommon. Indeed, there are few signs of censorship in Pitrè's collections of Sicilian tales, whether they were told by women or men.

Pitrè's collections constitute one of the richest sources of European folk tales in the nineteenth century, if not the richest. Pitrè was fully aware of just how fertile the diverse stories were for understanding how European tales originated and were cross-fertilized, so to speak. After all, Sicily had been a country that had been constantly attacked, invaded, and occupied by the Greeks, Romans, Arabs, Turks, French, and Spanish for long and short periods of times. All of these occupations left their imprint on Sicilian culture, and numerous tales can be traced to storytelling traditions of these other cultures. Many are even set in Spain and Portugal, often criticizing Spanish and Portuguese rulers, responsible for the oppression of the Sicilian people.

Sicilian storytellers of the nineteenth century, no matter how much magic, fantasy, transformation, and humor were contained in their tales, always brought their listeners back to reality at the end of their telling. These endings or codas reveal how the storytellers were well aware of their own condition and the impossibility of realizing their fantasies. The verses vary, but the messages are similar.

And so they lived on as husband and wife,
While we toil away without a life.

Now they are happy and content,
While we sit here without a cent.

My tale's been written, my tale's been told,
Now you tell yours, because mine is old.

They remained happy and content,
While we still can't pay the rent.

Happiness was a fiction. Happiness was a wish that was bound *not* to be fulfilled in the lives of most of the storytellers and their listeners. However, the stories were in and of themselves a fulfillment. The art of storytelling and listening enabled both tellers and listeners to extract meaning, "revenge," joy, and important knowledge from the narratives, just as storytelling continues to enable people today to confront their everyday vicissitudes. Though Pitrè may have edited many of the tales in his collection, he did not negate the essential mode of thinking and talking that characterized traditional Sicilian storytelling about work, sex, religion, magic, law, other ethnic groups, money, and power.

One only has to read several of the Sicilian versions of "classical fairy tales" such as "Cinderella," "Donkey-Skin," "Rapunzel," "Beauty and the Beast," and "Puss in Boots" to grasp how Pitrè respected the narrators' voices, and styles, and how he endeavored to record them as "authentically" as possible. Since most of these tales were told by women, they tend to be candid and stark depictions of extraordinary young women who cleverly shape their own destinies, in contrast to the male literary versions of Straparola, Basile, Perrault, and the Brothers Grimm. For instance, in "Caterina the Wise," a young educated woman magically sails from city to city to assert her will and teach a prince a lesson in humility. In "The Magical Little Date Tree," the sprightly Ninetta (Cinderella) teases the prince in his garden until he falls desperately in love with her. She evades him after, not one, but three different balls until he is at his wits' end. In "Pilusedda," a version of "Donkey-Skin," a clever young woman escapes her father's lecherous desires and uses three gifts from the fairies to entice a prince to marry her. In "The Old Hag's Garden" ("Rapunzel"), a young girl is abandoned by her mother and is treated brutally by an ogress; but instead of running away

with a prince, she shoves the ogress into an oven and makes peace
with her mother. There are several beast bridegroom tales such
as "The King of Love," and in each one of the stories a young
woman is put to severe tests to rescue an enchanted prince or to
tame a beast. Life was hard and cruel for most of the people from
the lower classes, and the "relics" of the past that surface trans-
parently in all the tales reveal the hopes and wishes for wealth,
food, revenge, and power.

Perhaps the most biting and humorous stories concern two
"folk heroes," Firrazzanu and Giufà, who stem from two different traditions connected to the character of the wise fool Hodja
Nasreddin. Firrazzanu generally profits from the pranks he plays,
while the Giufà character evolved from tales first told about a noble protagonist in the Arabic folk tradition of the medieval period. He understands the world in a literal sense that leads him to
do very brutal things. Giufà is clearly a fool, but he is not a wise
fool. He is laughable because he always brings out the superstitions, amorality, and injustice in Sicilian society.

Pitrè's collection includes legends, stories based on proverbs,
and animal tales that tend to be more realistic and historical than
the fairy tales. The legends are blunt but intriguing stories about
secular heroes and religious saints as well as about occupation
and survival. The most significant is the legend about Cola Pesce,
who became a national hero. In the three, which I have included
from Pitrè's *Leggende popolari in Sicilia* (1904), the tales concern
a common fisherman who could swim like a fish and sacrificed
himself to learn about the columns that support Sicily. There is
something heroic about the common fisherman, Colapesce, who
exposes the wiles of oppressors and sacrifices his life to support
the columns beneath the sea. In contrast, there is no heroism in
the animal tales which emphasize the theme of cunning. They
owe a debt to Aesop. However, the tales such as "Brancaliuni"
and "Friend Wolf and Friend Fox" exceed Aesop's fables in their

depiction of life and death struggles, often ending on a tragic note or with hard justice.

In my estimation, the four volumes that constitute *Fiabe, novelle e racconti popolari siciliani* are more important than the Grimms' tales because there are over five hundred texts, originally in Sicilian dialect, that cover a wide range of tale types often told in a brusque and disjointed style. As a result, some of the tales are jarring because they lack description and are crude. However, for the most part, they have a charming earthy quality and reflect the customs, beliefs and superstitions of the common people in Sicily more clearly than most nineteenth-century European collections portray the experiences of common people in their respective countries. As a result, they expose just how *literary* the Grimms' tales are. Like most of the dedicated folklorists of the nineteenth century, Pitrè admired the simplicity, honesty, and candor of the common people, and he was intent on preserving their stories as they told them because they were filled with unvarnished "truths" that still spoke to the conditions in his day and age. As tales of survival that are centuries old, they have a unique quality, for they depict the world as it was without questioning the magic and impossibility of the events. Pitrè listened carefully to the words of his storytellers and kept their simple, frank words in Sicilian dialect and, ironically, felt compelled to instruct the educated on how to grasp what the "popolo" said and did. Though much is lost in an English translation, these tales can still offer insights into the power of the spoken word and can preserve to a certain degree a great heritage that deserves to be known throughout the world.

❖

FAIRY TALES

Free Schooling for Whoever Wants to Study with Catarina
the Wise. *Children began coming, and Catarina had them sit on
benches alongside one other with no rank or class distinction.*

1

CATARINA THE WISE

Well, gentlemen, here's a tale that people have told time and again.

In Palermo, there was once a great merchant, who was married and had a remarkable daughter. From the moment she was weaned, she was so wise that she understood everything that happened in the house and could comment on it. Because of this talent, her father called her "Catarina the Wise." Indeed, she grew up studying all sorts of languages, reading all sorts of books, and displaying abilities and talents unmatched by anyone.

When the maiden turned sixteen, her mother died. In her grief, Catarina locked herself in her room and refused to come out. She decided to eat and to sleep in her room and gave up taking walks, going to the theater, or enjoying any other diversions. Her father was very unhappy that his only daughter denied herself from having any pleasure in life. Therefore, he decided to call together the leading men of the city to seek their advice. Of course, as a merchant, he generally knew all the best people.

"Gentlemen, you know very well that I have a daughter who is the apple of my eye. But ever since her mother died, she keeps herself shut indoors like a cat and won't even stick her nose out the door."

The councilors replied, "Your daughter is famous throughout the entire world for her exceptional wisdom. Why don't you start and organize a college? Perhaps by teaching young people, your daughter will be able to lift this burden from her mind."

"What a good idea!" the father exclaimed.

Therefore, he called Catarina and said, "Listen, my child. Since you've been unable to find anything to interest you, I've thought of starting a college and placing you in charge of it. What do you think of this plan?"

Well, she liked it very much and took charge of organizing all the teachers for the college. The girl had brains to spare! Once the college was organized, they put up a sign: *Free Schooling for Whoever Wants to Study with Catarina the Wise.*

Consequently, children began coming to the school, both boys and girls, and Catarina had them sit on benches alongside one other with no rank or class distinction. Someone objected and cried out, "He's the son of a coal merchant!" But it made no difference: the son of the coal merchant had to sit next to the daughter of the prince. As the proverb says, "First come, first served." And that's how this school began. Catarina taught everyone equally, and those students who failed to do their assignments got a lick of the cat-o'-nine-tails.

The school's reputation spread as far as the palace so that even the prince wanted to attend. He put on his most regal outfit and went and found a seat. When it was his turn, Catarina asked him a difficult question, and he didn't know the answer. *Whack!* She gave him such a hard smack that I think his cheek must still be burning. The prince returned to the palace very upset and went straight to his father.

"May it please your Majesty, I want to get married, and the one I want for my wife is Catarina the Wise."

So the king sent for Catarina's father, and as soon as the merchant arrived, he said:

"Majesty, I am at your service."

"You may rise, and you might as well know that my son is infatuated with your daughter. So, I think he should marry her."

"As your Majesty wishes, but I'm a merchant, while your son is of royal blood."

"No matter. She is the one my son desires."

When the merchant returned home, he said, "Catarina, I've learned that the prince wants you for his wife. What do you say?"

"I accept."

Within a week everything was ready. (Incidentally, don't imagine these people lacked wool for the mattresses, or chests of drawers!) Catarina had twelve bridesmaids, and when they opened the royal chapel, the marriage took place.

After the ceremony, the queen told the bridesmaids to carry out their task of undressing the princess for bed, but the prince said, "No, I don't want anybody to undress her or dress her, or any guards outside our door!"

Then, as soon as they were alone, he said, "Catarina, do you recall that slap you gave me at school? Are you sorry for it now?"

"Why should I be sorry? I'll give you another if you want!"

"You mean you have no regrets?"

"Not in the least."

"And you're not going to apologize?"

"Why should I?"

"So that's how it is, is it? Well, I'll teach you a lesson!"

Consequently, he prepared a rope to drop her through a trapdoor down into a pit, but before dropping her, he declared one more time: "Catarina, either you apologize, or I'll drop you down through this trapdoor."

The maiden replied boldly, "Fine. I'll be cooler down there."

Consequently, without further ado, he dropped her down into the pit with nothing but a small table and chair, a jug of water, and a piece of bread.

The next morning the king and queen came to visit the newlyweds and wish them the customary "good morning."

"Nobody may enter," stated the prince. "Catarina isn't feeling well." Then he opened the trapdoor and asked,

"How was it last night?"

"Just fine, nice and cool."

"Have you thought about that slap you gave me?"

"You should be thinking about the next one I'll be giving you."

After two days had passed, she began to feel terrible hunger pangs and couldn't think of anything to do. Then she pulled one of the stays out of her corset and began digging a hole in the wall. She dug and dug, and after twenty-four hours, she saw a glimmer of daylight that gave her hope. Consequently, she widened the opening and looked out. It just so happened that her father's clerk, Don Tommaso, was walking past that spot, and she called out, "Don Tommaso, Don Tommaso!"

The man couldn't figure out how a voice could emanate from a wall.

"It's me, Catarina! Tell my father that I need to speak to him as soon as possible!"

So Don Tommaso came back with her father (who couldn't have found the place by himself), and she called out:

"Father, unfortunately my husband has lowered me into this underground pit. Have a tunnel dug from the cellar of our house all the way to this spot here. Make sure that there are supporting arches and a lantern every twenty feet. Then leave the rest to me."

While they were carrying this out, her father sent her food every day: chickens and all kinds of good dishes. Three times a day the prince would come and call down the trapdoor, "Catarina, are you sorry for that slap you gave me?"

"Not at all. I'm thinking about the next one I'll be giving you."

Once the workers had completed building the tunnel with arches and lanterns every twenty feet, Catarina would wait until the prince closed the trapdoor and then go to her father's house. After a few days, the prince grew frustrated with this game. He opened the trapdoor and called down,

"Catarina, I've decided to go to Naples. Do you have anything to say to me?"

"Have a nice trip, and don't forget to write. And by the way, you know that old saying, 'See Naples and die?' Please don't take it literally!"

"So then, I should leave?"

"I can't believe that you're still here."

Consequently, the prince departed.

As soon as the trapdoor was closed, Catarina ran to her father.

"Father, father, I really need your help now. Get me a brigantine ready to sail, some servants and a housekeeper, and a supply of fancy gowns, and send them all to Naples. Rent me a house that faces the royal palace, and wait for me there."

Her father loaded the brigantine and sent it off. In the meantime, the prince had prepared a fine frigate and sailed away on it. When Catarina saw the prince depart from her father's balcony, she got on another brigantine and arrived in Naples before he did. (Small boats travel faster than large ones.) Once she arrived, she dressed herself in her finest gown and went out on her balcony. For a week she paraded opposite the royal palace in her finest gowns. Finally, the prince, having fallen in love with her, sent a messenger to her palace.

"My lady, if it pleases you, the prince would like to pay you a visit."

"At my lord's service," she replied.

And so the prince arrived, dressed all in his finest. After the usual compliments and conversation, he asked,

"Are you married or single?"

"Single," she replied, "And you?"

"I, too, am single. And do you know what? You bear a great resemblance to a lady I was in love with in Palermo. I'd like to have you as my wife."

"I accept," she said.

And within a week they were married.

Soon she was pregnant—time passes quickly in a story—and after nine months Catarina gave birth to a handsome baby boy. The prince came to her bedside and asked, "What shall we name him?"

"Naples," she answered, and so the boy was named Naples.

Two years passed, and the prince wanted to leave. Despite his wife's protests, he insisted on it. He left a document with her, declaring that the boy was his firstborn and heir to the throne. Then he went off to Genova.

As soon as he was gone, Catarina wrote to her father asking him to have a brigantine loaded with furniture, servants, and a housekeeper to be sent to Genova. She also asked him to rent a house opposite the royal palace and to wait for her there. As soon as the prince departed, Catarina took another ship, arrived there before the prince did, and set herself up in the new house. When the prince saw this beautiful woman with all her jewels, wealth, and royal coiffure, he couldn't help but exclaiming, "Holy Mary, she looks just like Catarina the Wise!" and he sent a messenger to ask if he could pay a visit. She accepted, and after he met her, they began conversing, and he asked, "Are you single?"

"I'm a widow," she replied.

"I, too, am a widower," he said, "with a little boy. Do you know, by the way, that you bear a great resemblance to a lady I knew in Palermo?"

"How remarkable! But you know the old saying: 'you can't tell a book by its cover.'"

To make it brief, within a week they were married. Catarina got pregnant, and in nine months—time goes by quickly in a story—she gave birth to another baby boy, even handsomer than the first. You can imagine how happy the prince was!

"My princess, what shall we name him?"

"Genova," she replied. And so the child was baptized Genova.

Two months passed, and the prince felt the urge to travel again.

"How can you do this and leave me with the baby?" Catarina asked.

"Don't worry," he said. "I'll leave you a document saying that he is my son and a young prince."

And so he did.

While the prince was readying his departure for Venice, Catarina wrote to her father in Palermo and had him send a brigantine to Venice loaded with servants, a housekeeper, furniture, new clothes, and many other things. The prince departed, and so did Catarina. Since large ships take more time than small ones,

Catarina arrived and took up residence first. The prince arrived, moved in, and where do you think he cast his eye? On Catarina's window, of course.

"Oh my God!" he exclaimed. "This woman is the very image of Catarina the Wise! Also the lady in Naples! Also the lady in Genova! But that simply can't be, because Catarina is down in a pit, and the one lady is in Naples, and the other is in Genova. But I'll be damned if she doesn't look exactly like her!"

He sent a messenger and arranged a visit, and his first words were:

"Excuse me, madam, but I must say it's amazing how much you resemble a lady I met in Palermo, and in Naples, and in Genova."

"How remarkable! But you know the old saying: 'you can't tell a book by its cover.'"

Then they proceeded to carry on the usual conversation.

"Are you single?"

"No, I'm a widow."

"I, too, am a widower, with two little boys."

By the end of the week, they were married. She grew pregnant, the months passed—time goes quickly in a story—her labor pains came, and she delivered a baby girl, as beautiful as the sun and the moon.

"What shall we name her?" asked the prince.

"Venezia."

And so they baptized her Venezia.

Two years went by.

"I'm thinking," the prince said to Catarina, "that I've done enough traveling, and it's time for me to go back to Palermo. But here's what I'll do: Before I go, I'll give you a document stating that this girl is my daughter and a royal princess."

Upon doing this, he departed, and so did Catarina. She went right to her father's house and through the passageway back to her place under the trapdoor. The prince arrived and went immediately to open the trapdoor.

"Catarina, how are you doing?"

"Just fine."

"Are you sorry now for the slap that you gave me?"

"Not at all. I'm thinking about the next one I'll be giving you."

"Listen, Catarina, I'm planning to get married."

"So what's holding you back?"

"Well, if you're willing to say you're sorry, you can still be my wife."

"No way."

The prince was stymied. Then he decided on a plan: He announced that his wife had died, and he was looking to re-marry. Afterward, he wrote to request portraits of all the eligible princesses. The portraits arrived, and the one he liked best was the daughter of the King of England. Consequently, he declared that he had chosen his new bride, and he sent for her and told her to come with her mother.

They arrived in Sicily with the King of England and went straight to the palace since the wedding was to be the very next day. Meanwhile, Catarina had three gorgeous royal outfits made for her children Naples, Genova, and Venezia. As for herself, she was adorned as the queen that she was, and then she took Naples dressed as the crown prince and Genova and Venezia dressed like a little prince and princess, climbed into a luxurious carriage, and drove to the palace. Along the way, she told her children,

"When I give you the word, go up to your father and kiss his hand."

Inside the palace, they found the prince sitting on his throne.

"Naples, Genova, Venezia, go and kiss your father's hand."

As they did this, the prince practically died of shock.

"So this is the next slap!" he exclaimed, coming down and embracing his children. The princess from England was left in the lurch, and the next morning she departed.

Now Catarina explained to her husband how she had managed the whole business, and he begged her forgiveness for all the suffering he had caused her. From that day forward, they loved each other dearly.

And so they lived on, in contentment and peace,
While we just sit here, grinding our teeth.

―――――――――

Told by Agazuzza Messia in Palermo

2

SNOW WHITE, BLAZING RED

There was once a king and a queen who didn't have any children. They continually made vows and swore that, if they were somehow blessed and could give birth to a son or even a daughter, they would have two fountains built for a seven-year period, one flowing with wine and the other with oil. Once they uttered this vow, the queen became pregnant and gave birth to a handsome baby boy.

Soon after the birth, the king and queen had two fountains built, and all the people in the realm came and obtained their oil and wine there. At the end of seven years, the fountains began to dry up, and a Mamma-draga, an old ogress, wanted to gather those final few drops that were still trickling. She approached one of the fountains with a sponge and a pitcher to soak up and squeeze out what she could—soaking and squeezing, soaking and squeezing. After she worked very hard to fill her pitcher, the king's son, a mere boy, who had been playing with his bocce balls, picked up one and, as a whim, hurled it at the pitcher. As soon as the pitcher shattered, the old woman realized what he had done and said to him, "Listen, even though I can't lay a finger on you because you're the king's son, I can lay this curse on you: may you never marry until you find Snow White, Blazing Red!"

Since the prince was a clever boy, he picked up a piece of paper, wrote down the woman's words, and stored the paper in a drawer without ever telling anyone about it. When he reached the age of eighteen, the king and queen were eager for him to marry. However, he remembered the old woman's curse, and after he fetched the piece of paper and showed it to them, he said, "Unfortunately, unless I can find Snow White, Blazing Red, I can't get married!"

Once the king and queen read the paper, he took leave of his parents and began traveling all by himself. He walked and walked. Months passed without him meeting anybody. Then one fine evening, as it was growing dark, he found himself in the countryside, tired and discouraged. Nearby there was a large house, and at daybreak, he saw a frightfully big, fat Mamma-draga, who had arrived and began crying out,

"Snow White, Blazing Red, let down your hair so I can climb up!"

When he heard these words, he took heart and said to himself, "She's there!"

Snow White, Blazing Red let down her hair that was so very long that it never seemed to end, and the Mamma-draga took hold of it and climbed up. Then she ate a good meal, while the prince waited outside, beneath a tree. The next day the ogress descended, and after the prince watched her depart, he came out from under the tree and called loudly, "Snow White, Blazing Red, let down your hair so I can climb up."

Believing it was her mother—because she was used to calling the Mamma-draga her mother—she loosened her hair, and the young prince boldly climbed up. As soon as he arrived, he announced, "Ah, my sweetheart, how hard I've worked to get here and find you!"

Then he told her all about the curse the old woman had put on him when he was only seven years old. After she helped him refresh himself and gave him something to eat, she said, "Look, the Mamma-draga is coming! If she finds you here, she'll eat you. Hide yourself."

Fortunately, the prince was able to hide himself just before the Mamma-draga arrived.

"Snow White, Blazing Red, let down your hair!" the Mamma-draga cried out.

"I'm coming. I'm coming, mother!" and Snow White, Blazing Red ran to pull her up with care. She let down her hair, and the Mamma-draga climbed up and found the dinner ready for her. She ate, and after she ate, Snow White, Blazing Red gave her something to drink that caused her to become drowsy. When Snow White, Blazing Red saw that the old woman had finished her meal, she said, "Mother, what must I do to get out of here? Of course, I don't want to leave. I want to stay with you. But I'd like to know just out of curiosity."

"What must you do to get out of here?" the Mamma-draga said. "You'd have to enchant everything here in such a way that I'd lose time. So, if I were to call out to the chair, the table, and the drawer, they would have to respond for you. Then, if you didn't appear, I'd have to manage to climb up here by myself. However, before this, you'd have to take the seven balls of yarn that I've been keeping here, and when I come and don't find you, I'd begin pursuing you. When you see me chasing you, you'd have to throw down the balls one after another, but I'd keep trying to catch you until you threw the last ball . . ."

The maiden listened to all that the Mamma-draga told her and stored it in her head until the time was ripe. The next day the Mamma-draga left, and Snow White, Blazing Red and the prince did what they had to do. She went through the entire house speaking to the different objects: "Table, if my mother comes, you're to respond by saying such and such. Chair, if she comes, you're to respond this way. Drawer, if my mother comes, you're to respond that way."

And so, she enchanted the entire house and left with the prince in such a hurry that they seemed to fly. When the Mamma-draga returned, she called out, "Snow White, Blazing Red, let down your hair so I can climb up!"

The table responded, "Come, mamma, come."

She waited a little while, but when no one appeared to pull her up, she repeated, "Snow White, Blazing Red, let down your hair so I can climb up!"

The chair responded, "Come, mamma, come."

She waited a little while more and no one appeared. Once again she called, and the drawer responded, "Come, mamma, come."

Meanwhile, Snow White, Blazing Red and the prince kept running. When no one at all responded to the Mamma-draga the next time, she screamed, "I've been tricked! I've been tricked!"

She immediately grabbed a ladder and climbed up. However, when she reached the top, she couldn't see or find anyone, not even the balls of yarn.

"Ah, you wretch! I'll drink your blood!"

She sniffed and sniffed, and then all at once, after she had their scent, she began to pursue them. As soon as she saw them from a distance, she cried out, "Snow White, Blazing Red, turn around so I can see you!"

(Well, she didn't dare turn around; otherwise, she would have been enchanted.)

When Mamma-draga drew near, Snow White, Blazing Red threw the first ball of yarn, and suddenly a very high mountain appeared. But Mamma-draga would not let herself be deterred. She climbed over the mountain and kept going until she was once again very close to Snow White, Blazing Red and the prince. Consequently, the maiden threw the second ball of yarn, and all at once, a plain of razors, sharp as knives appeared. The old woman was now completely cut and sliced up, but she continued to run after them dripping with blood. When Snow White, Blazing Red saw her close by again, she threw the third ball, and a large and tumultuous river appeared. Despite it all, Mamma-draga threw herself into the river, and when she emerged on the other side, she was more dead than alive. Then Snow White, Blazing Red threw another ball, and a fountain with many vipers and other horrible things appeared. When the last ball had been thrown, Mamma-draga was worn out and couldn't continue anymore. Therefore, she stopped and uttered a curse at Snow White, Blazing Red:

"May the prince forget you as soon as his mother the queen gives him a kiss!"

Indeed, this was the Mamma-draga's last breath, and she dropped dead.

Meanwhile, Snow White, Blazing Red and the prince continued running until they reached a village near the royal palace, where the prince stopped and said to Snow White, Blazing Red, "Listen to me. It's best if you stay here because your clothes are dirty and ragged. I'm going to go and get some things for you so you'll make a better impression on my father and mother."

Then he left her there, and soon after, when his mother saw him appear, she threw her arms around his neck to kiss him.

"Mother," her son said, "I took a vow not to let myself be kissed. It's a vow that I must keep."

His poor mother became petrified. That night, while her son was sleeping, she couldn't contain her burning desire to kiss him and went to his room. As soon as she kissed her son, the prince lost all memory of Snow White, Blazing Red.

Now let's leave the prince with his mother and turn to the poor maiden who was in the middle of nowhere. An old woman came by and saw the poor maiden, who was as beautiful as the sun and was weeping.

"What's wrong, my daughter?"

"What's not wrong? I don't know what I'm doing here!"

"My daughter, don't get upset. Come with me."

And she took Snow White, Blazing Red to her home. Since the maiden was good with her hands and could work wonders, she made various things, and the old woman sold them. This is how they made a living. Then, one day Snow White, Blazing Red said to the old woman that she wanted two old pieces of cloth from the royal palace for a thing that she had to make. Therefore, the old woman went to the palace and asked for these pieces. Indeed, she kept on asking for them until they gave them to her. Now, the old woman had two doves, one male and the other female, and Snow White, Blazing Red, dressed the doves in these pieces so elegantly that they were a marvel to behold. The maiden picked up the two doves and whispered in their ears, "You are the prince, and you are Snow White, Blazing Red. When the king sits down at the table to eat, I want you to fly there and tell him everything that has happened."

Later, when the king, queen, prince, and everyone else were eating at the table, the two doves flew there and landed on the table.

"How beautiful they are!"

Everyone began to rejoice. Then the dove, pretending to be Snow White, Blazing Red began to speak:

"Do you remember, when you were little, your father promised to build a fountain of oil and another fountain of wine so that you would be born?"

And the other dove replied, "Yes, I remember."

"Do you remember the old woman whose pitcher you broke? Do you remember?"

"Yes, I remember," the dove said.

"And do you remember the curse that she uttered and how she said that you'd never be able to marry until you found Snow White, Blazing Red?"

"I remember," the dove said.

In short, the dove began to recall everything that had happened in the past. Finally, the female dove asked, "And do you remember how the Mamma-draga almost caught you and then uttered a curse that you would forget Snow White, Blazing Red as soon as your mother gave you a kiss?"

When they had reached the point concerning the kiss, the prince remembered every single thing, while the king and queen were flabbergasted when they heard the doves speaking. Immediately after the doves finished their conversation, the birds made a beautiful bow and flew away.

"Hey there! Hey there! Watch where the doves are going! Watch where they are going!"

The servants rushed to the windows and saw that the doves had flown to a small country house nearby and had perched on the roof. The prince rushed to this house and found Snow White, Blazing Red. When he saw her, he threw his arms around her.

"Ah! My darling, how you've suffered because of me!"

Then he quickly had her dressed in clean clothes and took her to the palace. When the queen saw her, she said, "Oh! How beautiful!"

Then they prepared a feast, exchanged vows and rings, and were married.

They remained happy and in peace,
While we still sit here picking our teeth.

———————

Told by Rosa Brusca in Palermo

3

THE OLD HAG'S GARDEN

Once upon a time there was a cabbage garden. The crops each year were becoming more and more scarce, and when two women began talking, one of them said:

"My friend, let's go and pick some cabbages."

"How are we to know whether anyone's there?" said the other.

"All right. I'll go and see if someone's keeping guard," the neighbor said.

She went and looked.

"There's no one. Let's go!"

They entered the garden, gathered two good batches of cabbage, and left. Then they cheerfully ate the cabbages. The next morning they returned, but one of the women was afraid that the gardener might be there. However, since they didn't see anyone, they entered. Once again, they gathered two good batches of cabbage and ate them all.

Now let us leave them eating the cabbages and turn to the old hag who owned the garden. When she entered her garden, she cried out, "Jesus! Someone's eaten my cabbages. Well, I'm going to take care of this . . . I'll get a dog and tie him to the gate at the entrance. When the thieves come, the dog will know what to do."

Now, let us leave the old hag, who fetched a dog to guard the garden, and return to the two women. On the third day, one of them said to the other:

"Let's go and pick some cabbages."

"No, my friend, there's a dog there."

"Not a problem! We'll buy some dry bread with our money and feed it to the dog. Then we can do whatever we want."

So they bought some bread, and before the dog could bark, they threw it some large crumbs. As soon as the dog became silent, they quickly gathered the cabbages and left. Later on, the old hag arrived, and when she saw the damage, she cried out, "Ahh! So, you let them gather the cabbages! What a lousy guard dog you are! Out you go!"

Now the old hag took a cat to guard the garden and hid herself in the house. As soon as the cat screeched *meow! meow!* she intended to grab the thieves by their throats.

The next day one of the women said, "Friend, let's go and pick some cabbages."

"No. There's a cat guarding the garden, and this means trouble for us."

"I don't think so. Let's go."

When they saw the cat, they took out some fish they had bought, and before the cat could *meow*, they threw the fish, and the cat didn't utter a sound. Consequently, the women gathered some cabbage and left. When the cat finished eating the fish, it went *meow, meow!* The old hag came running but didn't see anyone. So, she picked up the cat and cut off its head. Then she said, "Now I'm going to have the cock keep guard, and when it crows, I'll come running and kill those thieves."

The next day the two women began talking with one another.

"Let's go and pick some cabbage."

"No, my friend, there's the cock."

"Doesn't matter," her friend said. "We'll take some grain with us and throw it to the cock so it won't make a sound."

And this is what they did. While the cock ate the grain, they picked the cabbages and left. When the cock finished eating the grain, it crowed: "*Cock-a-doodle-do!*" Immediately, the old hag came running and saw that more cabbages had been stolen. Therefore, she picked up the cock, wrung its neck, cooked it, and ate it. Then she called a farmer and said, "I want you to dig a hole just my size."

Later, she hid herself in the long hole, but one of her ears stuck outside. The next morning, the women came to the garden and didn't see a soul. The old hag had asked the farmer to dig the hole along the path that the women would have to pass, and when they came by, they didn't notice a thing. They passed the hole and collected some cabbages, and on their return, one of the women, who was pregnant, looked at the ground and saw a mushroom which was actually the old hag's ear.

"Look at this beautiful mushroom!" the pregnant woman exclaimed.

She knelt down and tugged at it. She pulled and pulled, and finally, she yanked the old hag with all her might, and out she came!

"Ahh!" the old woman exclaimed. "You're the ones who've been picking my cabbage! Just wait and see what I'm going to do to you!"

She grabbed hold of the pregnant woman, while the other scampered away as fast as her legs could carry her.

"Now I'm going to eat you alive!" the old hag said to the pregnant woman, who was in her clutches.

"No! Listen to me! When I give birth, and my child is sixteen years old, I promise that, whether boy or girl, I'll send the child to you, and I'll keep my promise."

"All right," the old hag said. "Pick all the cabbages you want, and then leave. But remember the promise you've made."

The poor pregnant woman was more dead than alive when she returned home.

"Ah, friend," she said to her neighbor. "You managed to escape, and I'm still in trouble. I promised the old hag that I'd give her my first-born when the child turns sixteen."

"And what do you want me to do?"

After two months, the Lord blessed the pregnant woman with a baby girl.

"Ahh, my daughter!" she said to the baby. "I'll raise you, give you my breast, but then someone is going to eat you!"

And the poor mother wept. Now, when the girl turned sixteen, she went out to buy some oil for her mother. The old hag saw her and said, "Whose daughter are you, my girl?"

"My mother's name is Sabedda,"[1] she replied.

"Well, tell your mother to remember her promise. You've become a beautiful maiden. You're nice and tasty," she said as she caressed her. "Here, take some of these figs and bring them to your mother."

The maiden went to her mother and reported what had happened.

"The old hag told me to remind you of your promise."

---

1 Here the storyteller, Elisabetta (Sabedda) Sanfratello, interjects that she has given the mother in the story her own name, as a name "for example," and then feels compelled to add that, of course, she herself was not present for the actions of the story.

"Why did I promise her?" the mother began to cry.

"Why are you crying, mamma?"

But her mother said nothing. After weeping for some time, she said to her daughter, "If you meet the old hag, you're to say: 'She's still too young . . .'"

The next evening the maiden went again to get some oil and encountered the old hag who did the same thing as she had done the day before.

Meanwhile, her mother thought, "It's now or in the course of two years that I'll have to give up my daughter." So she said to her daughter, "If you meet the old hag, tell her, 'when you see her, take her, and the promise is kept.'"

Then the old hag soon appeared and asked, "What did your mother say?"

"When you see her, take her."

"Well then, come with your grandma, for I'm going to give you many things."

She took the maiden with her, and when they arrived at the old hag's house, she locked the maiden in a closet and said, "Eat whatever you find there."

After a fair amount of time had passed, the old hag said, "I want to see if you've gotten fatter."

There was a little hole in the door.

"Show me, little one. Stick out your finger."

The maiden was clever. A mouse had come by, and she had cut off its tail and showed it to the old hag.

"Ahh! How thin you are, my daughter. You've got to eat for your grandma. You're so thin, and you've got to eat."

Some more time passed.

"Come out, my daughter, so I can see you."

The maiden came out.

"Ahh! You've become nice and fat. Let's go and knead some bread."

"Yes, grandma. I know how to do it."

When they finished kneading the bread, the old hag had her heat up the oven.

"Light it for your grandma."

The maiden began to clear it out to heat the oven.

"Come on. Do it for grandma," the old hag said. "Let's put the bread in the oven."

"But, grandma, I don't know how to put the bread into the oven. I know how to do everything else, but I don't know how to put the bread into the oven."

"Well then," said the old hag, "I'll put the bread into the oven. You just have to pass it to me."

The maiden took the bread and gave it to the old hag who said, "Pick up the iron slab that closes the oven."

"But grandma, I don't have the strength to pick up the slab."

"Well then, I'll pick it up."

When the old hag kneeled down, the maiden grabbed her from behind and shoved her into the oven. Then she picked up the slab and used it to close the oven.

"Now there's nothing more to do here. So, I'll find out where my mother is."

When she went outside, a neighbor caught sight of her.

"My, you're alive!"

"Why do you ask? Should I be dead? Now, listen to what I'm going to tell you. I want you to look for my mother. I want her to come here."

The neighbor went away and called her mother, who soon arrived at the old hag's house. When her daughter told her everything that had happened, she became very happy, and they took charge of everything in the house.

They remained happy and content,
While we still don't have a cent.

———

Told by Elisabetta (Sabedda) Sanfratello in Vallelunga

4

THE MAGICAL LITTLE DATE TREE

Once upon a time there was a merchant who had three grown-up daughters: the eldest was called Rosa, the middle daughter, Giovannina, and the youngest, Ninetta, who was also the most beautiful of them all.

One day, this merchant went and purchased a great deal of goods, but when he returned home, he appeared to be very disturbed.

"What's wrong, father?" his daughters asked.

"Nothing, my daughters, I purchased some excellent merchandise, but I can't do anything with the goods because I can't leave you by yourselves."

"Why are you getting so upset, my lord?" the eldest daughter asked. "Just leave enough provisions here for the time you are gone. Then, have the doors sealed, and if it's God's will, we shall see you again."

So, this is what the father did. He stored a great quantity of food and ordered one of his servants to appear on the street below their window every morning. He was to call out to the eldest daughter and run errands for whatever his daughters wanted. Before the merchant took his leave, he said, "Rosa, what do want me to bring you?"

"Three dresses with different colors," she said.

"And you Giovannina?"

"Whatever your lordship wants to bring me."

"And you Ninetta?"

"I want a beautiful little tree of dates. And if you forget this tree with dates, may your ship be prevented from moving forward or backward."

"Oh, you shameful creature!" her sisters said. "What kind of bad spell are you casting on our father?"

"It's nothing," the father responded. "Don't take her seriously. She's still young, and we need to indulge her."

Finally, the merchant took his leave and journeyed to the country of his destination where he carried out his business and then bought three beautiful dresses for Rosa and three for Giovannina. But what did he forget? Indeed, it was the little tree of dates for Ninetta! Later, after he boarded his ship, a terrible storm broke out in the middle of the sea—lightning, flashes, thunderbolts, rain, and huge waves—and the ship was unable to move forward or backward.

The captain became desperate and said, "Where did this bad weather come from?"

Then the merchant remembered his daughter's spell and replied, "Captain, I forgot to buy something. My advice is that we turn around and see what happens."

And, it was a miracle! As soon as they turned around, the weather changed, and they sailed with a fair wind. The merchant went ashore, bought a little tree with dates, and went back on board the ship. The sailors unfurled the sails, and after three days, they reached their country in favorable weather.

After he arrived, the merchant had the doors of his house unsealed, opened the windows, and gave the gifts to all his daughters, the dresses to Rosa and Giovannina and the little tree with dates to Ninetta.

Ah, excuse me. I almost forgot the best part of my tale!

While the merchant was on his journey, the eldest daughter began sewing by the well in the courtyard. Indeed, their father had made this well for them so they would not lack any water. Well, one time she accidentally dropped her thimble into this well, and Ninetta said to her sisters, "Don't worry. Lower me down into the well, and I'll fetch the thimble."

"Are you joking?" the eldest sister said.

"No, I want to go down and fetch it."

They said, no. She said, yes. Back and forth they went. Finally, they had to lower her down into the well. As soon as she touched the water, she grabbed the thimble. However, when she pulled her hand out of the water, she noticed some light coming from a hole in the wall off to the side. When she removed some stones, she saw a marvelous garden through the hole, an exquisite garden, for there were all kinds of flowers, trees, and fruit. At once, she slipped inside and began gathering the most beautiful flowers, fruit, and other fine things. After she had an apron full, she returned to the well without making a sound, replaced the stones, and cried out, "Pull me up!" And she reappeared fresh as a rose.

When her sisters saw the apron full of fine things, they said, "Where did you get these beautiful things?"

"What does it matter to you? Tomorrow, you'll lower me back down, and I'll get the rest."

Now, the garden belonged to the son of the King of Portugal, and when he discovered that someone had damaged his garden, he began scolding the poor gardener, who told him that he didn't have the slightest clue about what caused the damage. So the prince ordered him to pay more attention in the future, otherwise he'd be in trouble.

The next day Ninetta prepared to descend into the well again in order to explore the garden.

"Sisters, lower me down!"

"Are you crazy or drunk?"

"I'm neither crazy nor drunk. Lower me down!"

They told her, no, and she told them, yes. Back and forth they went. Finally, they had to lower her down. Again, she removed some stones from the wall and entered the garden. After she gathered an apron full of flowers and fruit, she had her sisters pull her up.

The prince, who had been watching from a window, saw her in the middle of the garden as she was slipping away. Immediately, he ran down from the palace, but he couldn't find anyone. So, he called the gardener.

"Where did that young woman come from?"

"What young woman, your majesty?"

"The one who was gathering flowers and fruit in my garden."

"I didn't see a thing, your majesty!" and he began to swear on his life that he hadn't seen a single thing. The prince realized he was innocent and retired to his rooms. However, the next day he personally kept watch and muttered to himself, "If you return, you won't escape."

On the third day Ninetta insisted again and told her sisters to lower her into the well. She had enjoyed the adventure of the previous day. They kept saying, no, and she kept saying, yes, until they had to lower her down. She removed some stones from the wall, slipped into the garden, and gathered some wonderful things, better than the day before, until she had an apron full without realizing that the prince was lying in wait for her. As soon as she heard some noise, she turned and saw that the prince was heading her way and about to grab her. However, in one leap, she made it back through the hole, closed it with the stones, and got away.

After this encounter, the poor prince couldn't find any peace of mind, and he became grief-stricken because the maiden seemed to him to be a real fairy. None of the doctors in the kingdom were able to cure him, and once the king realized that his son was losing his senses, he called all the wise men and philosophers of his kingdom together to discuss the prince's illness. First this one spoke, then another, until an old sage with a long white beard said, "Your majesty, try to find out whether your son has fallen in love with a young maiden, and then we might approach this differently."

The king called his son to him and questioned him. In response, his son told him the entire story and concluded by saying that he'd never be cured unless he found this maiden. Consequently, the sage said, "Your majesty, I advise you to hold a festive ball for three consecutive days at your palace and issue a proclamation that all the mothers and fathers from all social classes must bring their daughters under pain of death."

The king agreed and issued the proclamation.

Now let us return to the merchant's daughters. When they had the dresses that their father had brought to them, they began decorating them for the first night of the ball. On the other hand, Ninetta retired to her room with her little tree and dismissed the festive ball as something trivial. Her father and sisters could barely put up with her. Finally, they were convinced that she was somewhat crazy and let her do what she wanted. However, they expected Ninetta to attend the ball and reminded her that, when the king had issued the proclamation, the father had reported, "The king is going to hold three days of festivities at his palace, and he wants every father and mother to bring their daughters. Whoever keeps a daughter away will be condemned to death."

Nevertheless, Ninetta shrugged her shoulders and said, "You three go. As for me, I don't want to attend the festivities."

"No, my daughter," her father said. "I'll be punished by death if you don't go, and you don't joke with death!"

"It doesn't matter to me. Besides, who knows that you have three daughters? Pretend that you only have two."

"You must go."

"No, I'm not going."

They argued back and forth until Ninetta won and remained at home with her little tree of dates which were her delight.

However, as soon as her father and sisters had departed, she turned to the tree and said:

"Oh date, oh little date tree,
Open please, and let them out!
Let them dress me,
Let me be
More beautiful than anyone has ever seen."

Well, what do you think came out of the dates? Suddenly, many fairies appeared carrying unique dresses and jewels. They washed

Within minutes, she was completely covered with
a necklace, diamonds, and precious stones.

her, combed her hair, and dressed her—and within minutes, she was completely covered with a necklace, diamonds, and precious stones. Indeed, in the end, she looked like gold. Then, she got into a carriage and arrived at the royal palace. When she entered, everyone looked at her in astonishment. The prince recognized her and told this to the king. Then he approached her, took her by the arm, and asked, "My lady, how are you?"

"Like the winter," she replied.

"What do you call yourself?"

"By a name."

"Where do you live?"

"In a house with a door."

"In what street?"

"In the street with a cloud of dust."

"How strange you are! You will be the death of me."

"May you bite the dust!"

They danced together the entire night. The prince got tired, but Ninetta remained lively because she was enchanted. Finally, she sat down near her sisters. When the party was over, the king secretly ordered his servants to follow her to find out where she lived. She left the palace and got into her carriage. However, as soon as she became aware that the servants were following her, she shook her golden braids and let pearls and precious stones fall onto the road. When the servants saw this, they threw themselves upon them like chickens pecking grain. And good-bye, lady! She ordered the horses to be spurred on, and she was back at her home in a flash. As soon as she arrived, she said:

"Oh dates, magical dates,
Come and undress Ninetta.
Make her as she was before."

Within seconds, she found herself in the clothes that she wore around the house.

Now, let us turn to her sisters who soon arrived home.

"Ninetta, Ninetta, what a beautiful ball! There was a lady there who looked just like you! If we hadn't known that you were here, we would have said that it was you!"

"What are you saying?" Ninetta said. "I stayed here with my little tree of dates."

"But tomorrow evening, you should come, you know!"

Let us now turn to the king who was waiting for his servants. When they came back to the palace, they threw themselves at his feet and told him what had happened. Then the king said, "Worthless people! Won over by money! If you do the same thing tomorrow, you'll be in trouble!"

The next evening the sisters insisted that Ninetta go with them, but she didn't want to hear anything about this. Finally, her father ended the discussion by saying, "Don't you see that she's lost her mind over this little tree of dates? Who knows but I'll get into some trouble because of it . . . No matter, let's go!" And they left.

As soon as they departed, Ninetta approached the little date tree:

"Oh date, oh little date tree,
Open please, and let them out!
Let them dress me.
Let me be
More beautiful than anyone has ever seen."

Immediately many fairies emerged from the tree. They combed her hair and dressed her in garments more splendid than before and covered her with all sorts of jewels. After she was completely dressed, she got into a carriage and went to the royal palace. When she appeared, everyone was astounded, especially her sisters and her father. The prince approached her and was very content.

"My lady, how are you?"

"Like the winter," she replied again.

"What are you called?"

"By a name."

"Where do you live?"

"In a house with a door."

"In what street?"

"In the street with a cloud of dust."

"How strange you are! You will be the death of me."

"May you bite the dust!"

But he paid no attention to what she said and invited her to dance. And they danced the entire evening. Afterward, she went and sat down next to her sisters.

"Madonna!" one of them said. "She looks exactly like Ninetta."

When the ball was over, Ninetta was among the first to leave. As the king accompanied her to the door, he made a signal to the servants. However, Ninetta noticed this, and after she got into her carriage, she saw them approaching. Therefore, she took out a number of sacks with gold coins that she had in the carriage and threw them in the face of the servants, who broke each other's noses and hit one another in the eyes to get at the gold. As a result, the servants could not follow the carriage and had to crawl back to the palace like whipped dogs.

When the king saw them, he took pity on them and said, "It doesn't matter! Tomorrow is the last evening, and in one way or another I'll get to the bottom of this."

Let us turn now to Ninetta, who just arrived at her home and said to the little tree:

"Oh dates, magical dates,
Come and undress Ninetta
And make her as she was before."

Within seconds, her clothes were changed, and she was wearing the dress she usually wore around the house. When her sisters arrived, they said, "Ninetta, Ninetta, what a beautiful ball! The lady who looked exactly like you returned. She was your spitting image—the eyes, the hair, the mouth, everything, even the way she talked. She was wearing a dress that we've never seen before. And she had jewels and precious stones that sparkled like a mirror!"

"Why are you telling me?" responded Ninetta. "I've had fun with my tree, and I don't care about attending either balls or parties."

"All right, but tomorrow you should go!"

"Really! As if it's the only thing I can think about!"

After she ate, she went to bed.

The next evening Rosa and Giovannina wore the best dresses that their father had brought them, and they went to the party.

Ninetta refused to attend. However, as soon as they left, she ran to the little tree and said:

"Oh date, oh little date tree,
Open please, and let them out!
Let them dress me.
Let me be
More beautiful than anyone has ever seen."

Immediately numerous fairies appeared. They combed her hair, washed her, and dressed her. Afterward they put her into the carriage. At the palace, she was so radiant, the people were dazzled, and she was wearing a dress and jewels that nobody had ever seen in their lives.

The prince was waiting for her, and as soon as she saw her, he asked, "My lady, how are you?"

"Like the winter."

"How are you called?"

And they had the same conversation as they had before.

They danced and danced, for it was the last night. Finally, she sat down near her father and her sisters, who continued to speak among themselves.

"She is the exact image of Ninetta," they kept saying.

The king and his son also kept looking at her, and at a certain point the king took her by the arm with the excuse that he wanted to bring her into another room to give her something. When they were alone, Ninetta wanted to take her leave so she could return home, but the king was resolved to finish everything right then and there and said, "For two nights you've led me in circles. But you won't succeed on the third night!"

"What's the meaning of this, your majesty?"

"The meaning is that I know who you are. You are the beautiful young lady who has driven my son crazy. You must become his wife!"

"For a favor, your majesty."

"What favor do you want?"

"I'm not free. I'm obliged to my father and two sisters."[1]

"You have nothing to fear," the king said, and he immediately summoned her father.

The summons of a king is not always a good sign, so they say. The father broke out into a cold sweat because he had committed a few illegal acts and didn't have a clear conscience. However, the king told him how things stood and that he would pardon anything he had done if he allowed Ninetta to become the prince's wife.

Indeed, the next day the royal chapel was opened, and the prince and Ninetta were wed.

Well, they remained content and in peace,
While we still sit here and pick our teeth.

Told by Agatuzza Messia in Palermo

1 The youngest sister in a family was generally not allowed to marry before her elder sisters had found husbands.

5

PILUSEDDA

Once upon a time there was a king and queen, and they had a daughter who was extremely beautiful. When the girl reached fifteen years of age, her mother fell seriously ill, and realizing that her end was near, she called her husband and said to him, "Husband, my life is done, but you are still young and can marry again. Therefore, I am leaving you this ring. Whoever tries it on and finds that the ring fits, she will be the one you should take as your bride."

Soon the wife died, and after some time the husband decided to re-marry. There were many women available, and he offered marriage only to the one whose finger fit the ring. However, it turned out that the ring was too loose on some and too tight on others. "It's fated not to be," he said. "Let's forget it for now." And he kept the ring.

One day his daughter was cleaning a room in the palace, and she found the ring in a drawer of a cupboard. She tried it on and then found she couldn't get it off. "What will I do about my father?" she said to herself.

And so what did she do? She took a piece of black cloth and wrapped it around her finger. When her father saw her finger, he asked, "My daughter, what's wrong?"

"Nothing, father, I just scraped my finger."

But after a few days had passed, her father insisted on seeing the finger, and after he unwrapped it and saw the ring, he exclaimed, "Ah, it's you who must be my wife!"

Yet, inside the girl, she kept saying to herself, "I can't marry my father! I'd rather die!"

Not knowing what to do, she went to a wise man and told him her story.

"Here's how to solve your problem," he said. "Tell your father that you want a wedding dress, a special dress the color of the sky, embroidered in gold and precious stones shaped like the sun and the moon and all the planets."

When the girl went to her father and asked for such a dress, he replied, "Where in the world can I find such a dress?"

He pondered this for a while and then went out into the fields and called upon his cousin, who was a demon, and told him the entire story. His cousin replied, "If I find you such a dress, what will you give me for it?"

"I'll give you my soul."

"Just wait here."

And in a half hour he was back with this marvelous dress and gave it to the man.

The girl told the wise man what had happened, and he had another idea. "Ask him for a dress of sea-green, decorated with all the houses that are in the countryside."

So, she went to her father and said, "Father, that was the wedding dress, but now I need another one for the civil ceremony."

Once again, the king went to his cousin, who brought him a second dress in less time than it takes to tell. When the girl had the second dress, she asked for a week's delay. At the end of a week, she went to the wise man, who told her, "Now ask him for a dress for the first day that you are a married woman. And this must be a rose-colored dress, ornamented with four rows of bangles and tiny golden bells."

She did this, and her father, as usual, turned to his cousin. When the dress was ready, the father said, "Now, my daughter, we have no more time to lose. A week from today we shall be married."

The poor girl was utterly distraught and went to the wise man.

"There's no way out for you now," he said. "Take this walnut, this chestnut, and this hazelnut, and make use of them when you need them. Right now what you must do is find yourself a horse's hide, and have everything removed except the outer skin.

Have this skin cleaned and salted, and put it on like a garment so you can pass for a horse."

The maiden did all this. Then she gathered her clothes, and all the money, rings, and jewels in the house. When the evening came before she was to be married, she told her father that she wanted to take a bath. (This was the ancient custom, to bathe before a wedding ceremony.) Then what did that clever maiden do? To give the impression she was bathing, she put a dove inside a basin full of water, and outside she had a second dove tied by its feet to the first dove. Whenever the dove on the outside moved, it pulled the one inside the basin, and so they kept fluttering around and making splashing noises like a person washing herself. Meanwhile, the maiden went into the bathroom, slipped on her horse-skin, and escaped.

Her father waited for some time, but she didn't come out of the bath. Finally, he opened the door and found that no one was there. "I've been tricked and betrayed!" he shouted, and batted his head against the wall so hard that he dropped dead on the spot. Down came the Evil One and took him away.

Now let us return to the maiden. She had already walked a great distance, and where do you think she found herself? In a preserve where all kinds of animals were kept. And who do you think was the owner of this preserve? The son of a king.

The next morning the royal gamekeeper saw a strange horse, walking with its front legs in the air, and his first impulse was to shoot it. However, fortunately the king's son came along, forbade him to shoot it, and went up close to the creature and caressed it. For her part, she rubbed against him affectionately, and this pleased him so much that he had her brought to the palace. At the foot of the stairs, there was a room where she was enclosed, and the prince ordered food brought to her. Curious as to what kind of creature she was, he asked, "What sort of animal are you?"

"I am Pilusedda," she replied.[1]

---

1 The name Pilusedda may be translated as "little shaggy one."

They soon became good friends, and the prince's greatest delight was only to spend time with Pilusedda. However, this was very troubling to the prince's mother, who couldn't stand to see such a friendship developing.

One day Pilusedda said to the prince, "O prince, please give me a bit of dough. I'd like to make a loaf of bread."

The prince had it brought at once. When Pilusedda was alone, she made a loaf and put her father's watch inside it. When the prince returned, she asked him to have the loaf baked, and it was baked together with the royal bread. The royal bread ended up scorched, while Pilusedda's loaf came out looking like a masterpiece. So, what did the bakers do? They sent the good bread to the prince, and nothing to Pilusedda.

When the prince broke open the bread and saw the watch, he was astonished. The following day Pilusedda again asked the prince for dough, made another loaf, and this time she put her father's tiepin inside. The prince sent it to the oven where the royal bread was also being baked, and again the royal bread came out scorched, while her loaf was done to perfection. The bakers were perplexed, and again they sent the good bread to the prince and the bad bread to Pilusedda. The prince found the pin and was astonished, while poor Pilusedda could only lament.

Now the third day arrived. When Pilusedda made her loaf, she put in a beautiful, shining ring, unique of its kind. When they baked the loaves, the same thing happened: the good loaf went to the prince, the scorched bread to Pilusedda. Breaking open the loaf, the prince found the ring and said, "If this loaf comes from Pilusedda, she cannot be an animal—she must be something else."

Now at this time, a holiday was drawing near, and the prince said to Pilusedda, "Would you like to come with me to the Royal Chapel?"

"How could I possibly go there?" she replied.

Consequently, the prince had to go and leave her behind. Meanwhile, she decided to crack open the walnut, and what do you imagine was inside? There were fairies, and they had clothing, jewels, and carriages for her. She slipped out of the animal skin and into the rose-colored dress her father had made for the day she was to become a woman. She got into a carriage—so elaborate that it had twelve shutters and outrider wheels—and she arrived at the Royal Chapel. The minute the prince saw her, he was transfixed and forgot all about the Royal Chapel. Later, when she left, he called to his servants,

"Go find out where this lady lives, and come back and tell me," he ordered.

Since Pilusedda realized the servants were following her, she shook out her hair, scattering pearls and diamonds. The servants, dazzled by such riches, had to give up and go back to the prince. "Your Majesty, this woman's wealth blinded us. We beg your pardon."

"Ah, you scoundrels, letting money blind your vision!"

Pilusedda went back into her room, placed the two halves of the nutshell together, and immediately all the fairies, carriages, and everything else disappeared. When the prince arrived there, he said to her, "Oh Pilusedda, if only you had come! There was a lady there who was unbelievably beautiful!"

"And what's that got to do with me? All I want is to eat!"

The next week it so happened that there was another festival at the Royal Chapel. The prince told Pilusedda, but she said she wanted nothing to do with it. When he was gone, she opened the chestnut. Within seconds, the fairies were busy again, this time dressing her as the sovereign she really was—in the sea-green outfit that she had requested for the civil ceremony. When she came to the Royal Chapel, and the prince laid eyes on her, he called his servants and said, "This time open your eyes and find out who the lady is. If you fail, you are finished."

When she left and got into her carriage, the servants were right behind her. However, she flung down gold and silver, and—goodbye servants! They returned to the prince, saying, "Majesty, do what you will with us, but just see what she threw at us!"

"All right, we'll talk about it some other day."

Pilusedda returned home, closed the chestnut, and the fairies disappeared. Days passed, and there was another Royal Chapel event. The prince told Pilusedda, but once again, she said she wasn't interested. All she wanted to do was to eat. After the prince had gone, she cracked open the hazelnut, and the fairies began dressing her in the dress her father gave her for her engagement: sky-colored, embroidered with gold and precious pearls, with the sun, the moon, and all the planets. When she went to the Royal Chapel and the prince saw her, he said to his servants, "Prepare my carriage."

After Pilusedda left the festivities, the prince was right behind her. She got into her carriage, and he followed in his.

"Where is that carriage going?" he asked.

"To the palace," he was told.

She darted into her room, but he was right behind her and grabbed hold of her. "Oh you little schemer! It turns out I was right when I said to myself that you were fooling me. Now explain to me how you can be a horse but can also turn into such a beautiful woman?"

And so, she finally told him her whole story.

The prince called the king and queen and told them that he wished to marry, and that his bride would be this gorgeous young maiden. The king and queen were happy, because they saw that the bride was stunningly beautiful. And once they gave their approval, the couple were wed.

Thus they lived on, in contentment and peace,
While we just sit here, picking our teeth.

———————

Told by Agatuzza Messia in Palermo

6

THE EMPRESS ROSINA

I've heard tell that there once was a merchant who had three daughters. The youngest was the best of them, and she was called Rosina. However, her sisters called her "Stable Girl," and they always treated her with disdain. When the father's fortunes fell due to a shipwreck, he retired to the country with his daughters. Some time thereafter he received news that one of his merchant ships had been saved and the merchandise recovered, and he got ready to depart for the city.

"Father, when you return, bring me a beautiful dress!" his oldest daughter said.

"Me, too," said the second.

However, the third remarked, "Father, I only want a rose."

Soon the father set out on this way, but when he received the money for his goods, there were so many debts to pay that he didn't have a cent left to his name. Therefore, he remained in debt. When he began his journey home, he saw a rose bush on the road and said to himself, "Though I can't bring the dresses to my two eldest daughters, I'll bring a rose to Rosina." So he picked one, but when he picked it, he found himself face to face with a monster

"How dare you pick this rose?"

The merchant told him what had happened and that his daughter Rosina asked him to bring back a rose.

"Listen," said the monster, "I'll give you a full week to bring me your daughter Rosina, and she will make you rich."

Then he took the merchant into the palace, and there was a sumptuous well-furnished table, and after they ate, there was a beautiful well-made bed, and the merchant went to sleep. Upon waking the next day, the merchant found a goodly sum of money on the table. Then he left the palace, got on his horse, and departed. When he arrived at his home, he gave the rose to Rosina.

"And nothing for us?" the two elder sisters asked.

"Nothing, my daughters, because we don't have any more money!"

"Well, just look! You thought about Stable Girl, but you didn't think about us at all!"

Then the father had them look at the money and told them the story about the monster.

"Do you want to go to the monster's place, Rosina?"

"Yes, you take her there!" the two sisters responded.

"Let's go, father!" Rosina was content, and they departed.

When they arrived, they were taken care of by servants who took the horses to the stable. At the palace, they found the table covered with dishes of luscious food, and they ate and went to bed. The father had one bed, and the daughter another. The father stayed three days, and at the end of this time, he took his leave from his daughter and departed with bags filled with gold coins. The monster was at the head of the stairs and said to him: "Thank you for bringing me your daughter. Don't worry about how she'll be treated."

Rosina was glad to be in the palace. She opened some books and read "The Empress Rosina." She opened the wardrobe closet and found written there, too: "The Empress Rosina." Then she took a beautiful dress that was also stamped with the name: "The Empress Rosina." Always "The Empress Rosina!" In the evening, a small door opened, and the monster appeared.

"Beautiful Rosina," he asked, "do you need anything?"

"Nothing," she responded with grace. "I only want to thank you."

Each evening the monster showed up, and they conversed a little.

One time, he said, "You don't know this, Rosina, but your eldest sister is about to get married. Would you like to attend the wedding?"

"Yes, I'd like to go there."

"I'll send you there, but only on the condition that, after you see her, you'll return here."

The next day the chambermaids and servants dressed and groomed her. Then she departed in a grand carriage accompanied by ladies of the court. When the sisters saw this lady arrive with such an entourage, they were amazed. Rosina did not reveal who she was. She attended the wedding, and at the end, she got back into the carriage and returned to the monster's palace. Meanwhile, her sisters remained curious and wanted to learn who the unknown lady was.

Upon her return, the monster appeared in the evening and asked, "Did you enjoy yourself, Rosina?"

"Very much!"

And after some days: "Rosina, do you know that your middle sister is going to marry. Would you like to go there?"

"Yes, if you send me."

The monster had another dress made for her, more beautiful than the first one. After the chambermaids dressed her, she got into a carriage and arrived at her father's home. Everyone was amazed to see such a fine lady, and they showered her with honors, bowing and paying respects. When the party finished, she returned home.

That night the monster appeared and asked her, "Did you enjoy yourself, Rosina?"

"Very much."

However, one day the monster spoke frankly to her: "Rosina, do you want to marry me?"

"Listen, I want you for a friend, not for a husband . . .

But then she thought to herself, "How can you be this way? He helped my family out of a miserable situation, gives me everything I need, and loves me very much. And I spoke to him that way? Why shouldn't I take him for my husband?" Then she looked at him and realized how ugly he was.

One evening the monster sighed.

"Why are you sighing?"

"Why should I tell you? You would feel as if you had been stabbed."

"No, if that's the reason, I want to know."

The monster turned to her and said, "Your father is sick. Would you like to go and see him?"

"If you want to send me there."

"Yes, I'm going to send you there. Take this ring. If you don't return at the end of nine days, I'll start to die. When you look at the ring and see that it is black and you don't return, I shall die."

Then he picked up the ring with the tip of a cane. After he gave it to her, she placed it on her finger. The next morning Rosina found the carriage ready for her departure. As soon as she arrived at home, she found her father more dead than alive. Poor girl, she couldn't restrain herself from crying out, "Oh, my father!"

When her sisters heard this, they exclaimed, "Ah, you're our sister!" and they embraced her.

After two days, her father recovered, but her sisters didn't want her to leave anymore. Yet, Rosina insisted that she had to depart while they continued to argue against her. That night—she had been absent from the palace for nine days—after she went to bed, she looked at the ring and saw that it was as black as spades. Consequently, she jumped out of bed, dressed herself, and left. The carriage was ready, and she departed. After she arrived at the palace, she found the monster entangled in the branches of the rose bush. Rosina turned pale. With the patience of a saint, she began pulling the thorns out of his back so that he wouldn't suffer any more. Then she took a certain ointment and spread it on his body. Afterward she began to weep like Maria Our Lady in Sorrow. She did the same thing the next day, and for the four days that followed.

On the fourth day, the monster reappeared at her door.

"You see, Rosina, because of you I almost died. Now, do you want me for your husband?"

And she replied without catching a breath and said, "No, my lord."

One evening the monster reappeared and said the same thing: "Rosina, do you want me for your husband?"

"No. I want you for a friend, not for a husband."

He closed the door and went away. However, right after the door reopened, a handsome young man appeared and said, "Rosina, do you want me for a husband?"

"No, between you and the monster, who has done so much for me, I would prefer to take the monster who has been so good to me and not you!"

"But I'm a handsome man, and he's ugly . . ."

"No. I won't pick you. Between the two of you, I would pick him."

"No? Well then, good evening!" He closed the door and went away.

Then the monster reappeared.

"Let me be," Rosina said. "Just a moment ago, a handsome young man came and asked: 'Would you like to take me for your husband?' And I responded, 'Get out of here. Between the two of you, I would prefer to take the monster.'"

"Are you telling the truth, Rosina? How did he look? Handsome?"

"Yes, my lord. Handsome!"

"Did he look like me?"

"No. He was a handsome young man. You're ugly."

"If you were to see him again, would you recognize him?"

"Yes, my lord, I would recognize him. But I wouldn't pick him."

"So then, you would take me?"

"Now we are courting! So, I would take you!"

"Truly? You'll take me for your husband?"

"Yes, truly, I'll take you for my husband!"

No sooner did she utter these words than he began to shed the skin of the monster and immediately became a handsome young man, more handsome than the man who had appeared before. All at once, a great number of servants, lords, cavaliers, and ladies of the court gathered there. The palace was completely illuminated, for it was the palace of the emperor, and the monster was the emperor in person. The royal chapel was opened, and they were married. Then the emperor and empress began their regime and thus

> They remained happy and in peace,
> while we're still here picking our teeth.

———————

Told by a woman in the home of Pardi in Palermo

7

THE LITTLE MOUSE *with the* STINKY TAIL

Once upon a time, so they say, there was a king, who had a beautiful daughter, more beautiful than words can describe. She received marriage proposals from many monarchs and emperors, but her father was unwilling to give her to anyone because he heard a voice every night that said:

"Do not allow your daughter to marry!"

Every day the princess looked at herself in the mirror and said, "How can it be that I am so very beautiful and yet cannot marry?"—and she continued to be bothered by this.

One day, when they all were dining, the princess said to her father:

"Father, how is it that I am so very beautiful and yet cannot marry? Let me speak my mind clearly: I *want* to get married!"

"My daughter, do you think I can simply *order* people to marry you?"

"Well, father, let me say this: I'll give you two days to find a husband for me. If you can't do it within two days, I'll kill myself."

The king explained to his guests why the mouse was there, and they all laughed and said, "You're right! That's right! The little mouse should marry the princess!"

"Since it's come to this," the king said, "listen to what you must do. Dress yourself today in your finest outfit and sit at the window. Whoever's the first to pass by and look at you will be the one you are to marry."

The princess did exactly what he said, and when she was seated at the window, along came a little mouse with a tail very long and very stinky. As he passed by, he looked at her. When the princess realized what he was doing, she ran into the palace screaming.

"Father, do you know what happened? Just now a mouse passed by and looked at me. Is this the one I must marry?"

"Yes, my daughter, isn't that what I told you? The first one who passes by is the one you must marry."

Well, back and forth they went, she saying "no," and he saying "yes," until it was dawn. Then the king wrote to all the princes and people of nobility, inviting them to a great wedding feast to celebrate his daughter's marriage. Soon the guests arrived and took seats at the table. At the height of the festivities, they heard a tapping at the door, and who do you think it was?

The mouse with the stinky tail.

A servant went to open the door, and when he saw a mouse, he said, "What do *you* want here?"

"Go and tell the king that the mouse has come to marry his daughter."

The servant went to inform the king, laughing scornfully, but the king ordered him to admit the creature. Once inside, the mouse ran and took a seat right next to the princess.

Poor girl! When she saw him next to her, she shrank away from him in disgust, but the little mouse just pressed himself closer and closer to her, as if he didn't have a seat of his own. The king explained to his guests why the mouse was there, and they all laughed and said, "You're right! That's right! The little mouse should marry the princess!"

The next day there was another great banquet, and at the height of things, *presto!* The mouse appeared again and took his seat next to the princess. At this point, the guests all began laughing up their sleeves. When the little mouse saw this, he went up to the king and gave him a warning: everyone at the table had better stop their laughing, otherwise there was going to be trouble!

The little mouse was so short that he couldn't reach the table from his chair. Consequently, in order to eat, he had to climb up onto the middle of the table, and no one dared to say anything. However, at this banquet there was one rather fastidious lady. When the first course came, the mouse began to run around to all the plates, and this lady suffered in silence. The same thing happened with the second course. When it happened with the third course, she lost control and heaped all kinds of abuse on the mouse. In turn, the mouse became furious at being treated so harshly and began leaping at the faces of all the guests. At the height of this turmoil, the table vanished, along with the guests and the palace and everything else, and they all found themselves scattered here and there in the valley.

Now let us leave them and return to the princess.

Finding herself alone in the valley, she began to weep and repeat over and over,

"Oh my little mouse, at first I didn't want you, but now I long for you!"

Then she set out walking, trusting to God and to fortune, and eventually she met a hermit, who asked her, "What are you doing here, my fine young lady, alone amongst all these animals? You should be careful, lest you meet up with Mamma-draga the ogress or with a lion, and then, poor you!"

"That's not what I'm worried about. What I need is to find my little mouse. At first I didn't want him, but now I long for him. Oh, my dear little mouse, where did you go?"

"Do you want my advice?" the hermit asked. "Turn around and go back, otherwise your life will be in danger."

"What choice do I have? Whether I live or die, I have to find the little mouse."

"Oh my child, in order to find him you'll have to journey far and wide. So, here's what you must do: go further, and you'll find another hermit, older than I am. He'll be able to tell you where to search."

Upon hearing this, the princess said good-bye to him and went onward, singing the same song repeatedly: "Oh my little mouse, where in the world can you be?"

As she walked along, she met an old man with a white beard, so long that it reached his feet. She was afraid, but he said, "Don't be afraid, my child. I am a human being, the same as you. Tell me, where are you going?"

"I am looking for the little mouse with the stinky tail."

"Then here's what you must do. Dig a hole in the ground as large as yourself, go down the hole, and then it's up to you to see what happens."

The poor girl had no way of digging such a hole. Then she thought of taking out her hairpin and using that, and so she began to dig. Eventually, she had dug a very large hole, and she disappeared down into it. She found a large underground chamber and began to walk along in the dark.

"Here's to luck and good fortune!" she said to herself.

She had to pass through so many spider-webs that they clung to her pretty face and made it dark as smoke. For every cobweb she pulled from her face, a hundred others attached themselves. After she had walked for an entire day, she heard the rustling sound of water. Drawing closer, she saw a pond full of water. She wanted to cross it, but the pond was too deep. Therefore, she began to cry and to repeat:

"Oh my little mouse, how I long for you!
Oh my little mouse, where in the world can you be?"

There was no way she could go forward, and there was no turning back because the hole had closed up again. All she could do was to weep.

At this moment, a shower of water began pouring down on her from above. "What can I do now?" she asked. "If I haven't died by this time, surely I'm going to die now."

As she said this, she heard a voice that said, "Why all this whimpering? You're hurting my ears! Just throw yourself into this pond, and see what happens."

The girl had no choice but to throw herself into the water. All at once, she found herself inside a huge marvelous palace. She entered the first room, and it was all made of glass. She entered the second room, and it was all velvet. She entered the third, and it was all gold and sequins with immense couches and lamps, such as she had never seen before.

She walked so far that she was unable find the spot where she had entered, and now she was lost—that's how huge the palace was. Feeling completely lost, she cried out, "Oh, my little mouse, what should I do?"

Then a voice answered, "Just utter a command."

"My command," she said, "is for something to eat."

Suddenly a beautiful table appeared before her, and it was completely set with a big plate of pasta and so many other dishes that even someone with no appetite would have wanted to eat. The poor girl began eating with gusto. However, the strange thing was, she didn't see anybody, and the dishes came and went of their own accord with no one carrying them.

Next, she found herself inside a carriage in the middle of a garden. She saw many lovely things there, but couldn't detect where they were coming from. When evening arrived, she found a beautiful bed and lay down in it. At midnight, she heard a rustling noise. When she looked, she saw a little mouse approaching her bed. The poor girl was terrified and trembling like a leaf because she didn't know who he was. She prayed to God for help, reciting a string of Our Fathers and Hail Mary's.

At dawn, not a soul could be seen. "What strange things happened last night!" she said to herself, as she went on with her day. Evening came, and when she went to bed, she heard the rustling noise again. "Who could it possibly be?" She had no way of knowing. The third night came, and precisely at midnight, the mouse appeared. "*Pi-ti-pi-ti, pi-ti-pi-ti,*" the mouse was dancing.

"Oh blessed Mary, all this commotion again?" she said. "Tell me, who in the world are you to be making such a racket?"

"Who am I? Just light the lamp, and you'll see who I am."

So, she quickly got off the bed and lit the lamp, and all at once, she stood gazing at a handsome young man!

"I was the little mouse with the stinky tail, turned into a mouse by a wicked spell. The only way I could be set free from the spell was if a maiden fell in love with me and suffered all the terrible things you have suffered. Once you came all the way here without feeling disgusted by me, I was able to turn back into a man."

Well, you can imagine the joy the princess felt! The two of them made their way out of the underground place and at once were engaged and married.

And so they lived on, in contentment and peace,
While we just sit here, cleaning our teeth.

———————

Told by a young girl named Maria Giuliano in Palermo

8

SUN, PEARL, AND ANNA

Gentlemen, there was once a childless king and a queen who longed to have either a son or a daughter. At a certain point, the Lord took pity on them, and the queen became pregnant. During those times there were astrologers. Therefore, the king called an astrologer and said to him, "What can you tell me about the queen?"

After examining the queen, the astrologer declared, "The queen will have a daughter, but . . ."

And he stopped with "but." So, the king said, "What's the meaning of this *but*?"

"Your majesty, when your daughter turns seven and touches a spindle, she will be cast under a spell."

Upon hearing this, the king said, "Quick! I want a house built beneath the ground."

Meanwhile the queen began preparations for giving birth, for the time had come. Indeed, she brought forth a beautiful daughter, and you can just imagine the happiness in the palace! Soon afterward they called for a wet-nurse and sent her with the baby beneath the ground so that they could see neither the sky nor anything else above. In short, the little girl grew up in another world, not seeing anything at all. She had already turned seven when, one day, it seemed to the nurse that the girl was sleeping, and she said to herself, "I'd like to entertain myself a bit."

Thinking that the girl was in a deep sleep, she took a spindle and began spinning. But what did she do? Well, she soon had a desire to drink a glass of water in another room. Therefore, she put the spindle and the distaff on top of a chair and went off. Well, guess who woke up? The girl, of course. She got up from the bed, saw the spindle, and it seemed like such a new thing that she took it into her hand, and all at once, she was enchanted.

Now let us return to the nurse.

When she re-entered the room, she saw the enchanted girl, who seemed as if she were dead.

"My girl! My girl! What am I going to do?" She began to shout. Her screams were heard above the ground, causing the king and queen to descend. When they saw their daughter, she seemed to be dead. The king burst into tears and immediately took the girl and had three dresses made for her, one more beautiful than the other, and then he had her dressed in them one on top of the other.

"These are the dresses that I would have made for your wedding, my daughter!"

Then he ordered his servants to bring her to a small cottage in the country where he had a beautiful coffin built for her. After that, he had her sealed in the cottage, which was not to be opened.

Now, years later, there was a prince who went into the forest to hunt, and it started to rain very hard. The poor man couldn't find any shelter and ran toward the cottage. At that time there was a ladder of silk on the side of the cottage, and once he arrived there, he ordered his valet to climb the ladder. After the valet reached the balcony, he opened the windows to a room and saw a beautiful maiden, just as beautiful as the sun (for the girl of seven had continued to grow). The valet went back down the ladder and said to the king, "Your majesty, what a luscious catch we've made!"

They went inside together, and the prince climbed the stairs and saw the beautiful creature just as she was—alive and breathing with a rosy complexion and the spindle in her hand. In all the confusion, no one had ever thought of taking away the spindle. The prince approached her, looked at her, and said, "Oh! My daughter, I pity you . . . What's that you have in your hands?"

As soon as he took the spindle from her hands, the maiden came to life. However, she was afraid, and he said to her, "You have nothing to fear. You've found a father, a brother."

He gave her something to eat, restored her health, and did everything he could for her. Then he said, "I've got to go now, but you can count on my returning here tomorrow."

So, he went back home with his valet, and the prince's mother said to him, "Why are you so late?"

"Mother," he said, "I really enjoyed the hunting today."

The next day he returned to the hunt and went to the maiden's cottage. Her name was Anna.

"How are you, Anna?"

"Very well. And you, prince?"

"I'm fine."

To be brief, by the end of nine months the maiden became very pregnant. She gave birth to a handsome baby boy and named him Sun.

Now, let us turn to the old queen who worried about her son because he was rarely at the palace any more, and she wondered what he was doing. Indeed, the queen racked her brains, for she wanted to know where her son was spending his time, and since she couldn't discover anything, she said to him, "You've got to tell me whether you're spending your time with some maiden."

And, without knowing her, the queen felt a great anger toward poor Anna. Meanwhile, the poor prince went and enjoyed his time with Sun and was crazy about him. As the boy grew, Anna became pregnant again. In nine months she gave birth to a baby girl and named her Pearl.

Now, the old queen continued to suspect something and would say, "My son, you're doing something deceitful! What are you thinking? . . . The entire realm is falling to pieces . . ."

Soon the prince happened to become sick and had to stay in bed. His mother was afraid that he might die. Clearly he had become sick because he missed being with Anna! The poor prince secretly wrote a letter to her and told her not to worry about him because his sickness was nothing, and he wanted to know how the children were doing because he was thinking about them.

However, he went from bad to worse and was overcome by fever. In his delirium he said, "Sun, Pearl, and Anna, you've taken my heart and soul."

When his mother heard this, she said, "Ahh! That whore has destroyed my son!" After she uttered many insults, she said, "Be quiet, my son, because tonight I'm going to have you eat with Sun!"

Meanwhile, she called her son's valet, his faithful servant, and said to him, "Tell me the truth, or I'll cut off your head. What has my son been doing?"

She was so furious with the valet that his legs trembled, and he told her everything from the beginning to the end,

"Ahh! That wicked woman!" the queen said. "Wait till I get my hands on her! Well, I want you to bring me Sun, and if his mother doesn't want to give him to you, tell her that my son wants to see him."

On official orders, the valet went to the prince's wife, and Anna asked, "How is the prince?"

"Better," the valet responded, "but today he wants to see Sun."

The mother took Sun, dressed him nicely, washed him, and gave him to the valet.

"Make sure to take care of him. Is there a risk of some treachery?"

The poor maiden's heart was speaking to her. However, the valet departed without saying anything, and when the old queen saw the spitting image of her son, she said to the boy, "Ahh! You're wicked, more wicked than your father!"

She took the boy by the arm and said to the cook, "Take him and slaughter him. Then I want you to cook him for me."

Instead of killing the boy, the cook took him to his home and hid him. Then he made a dish of meat to please the queen. At noon, he carried it to her.

"This is Sun."

"Ahh, come! Come here. I'm going to have you eat with your father who's made me suffer and almost die from the pain."

Then she went to her son with the dish and said, "Take this, my son. Eat this here. It's Sun."

The next day the vile queen said to the valet, "Now you've got to bring me Pearl so that I can have her eat with her father."

The valet went to the princess, who asked him, "How is my son doing?"

"Very well."

"And my husband?"

"Better, but he wants Pearl so that they can eat together."

The princess asked him, "Is there a risk of some treachery?" It was as if she sensed something in her heart.

"What kind of treachery could there be?" the valet responded.

She dressed the little girl. The valet took her away in a coach, and after they arrived at the palace, the old queen said, "Ahh! You're more wicked than your father, and now I'll show you how to amuse yourself."

She called the cook,

"Take this little girl, and prepare her for me."

The cook took the little girl, hid her, and made a dish of meat that pleased the queen. She took it to her son who continued to be delirious because of the fever.

"Here," she said. "This is Pearl. Eat with Pearl, and tomorrow I'll have you eat with Anna."

The next day she said to the valet, "Tell the princess that the prince is much better and wants to see her at the palace."

The valet departed and said to the princess, "The queen wants your majesty at the palace. They are all well. The prince is almost better and would like you to be there to enjoy some peace and quiet."

The princess dressed herself with the three dresses that her father had put on her, and she got into the coach. The old queen was at the window and kept looking at the road. When Anna appeared, the queen went out and approached her. As soon the queen was next to her, she grabbed Anna and dragged her by the hair, insulting her and accusing Anna of being a harlot. Yelling and bawling, she took her into the palace and forced her into a room where there was a kettle of boiling oil. She brought her to the kettle and said, "Get undressed!"

Anna took off the first dress and cried out in distress, "Sun!" The dress clattered and sounded like church bells. The prince heard the great tumult from his room and began to listen more attentively. Anna took off the other dress and cried out even more loudly, "Pearl," and the dress clattered again.

"Ahh!" the prince said. "That sounds like Anna crying out for our children!"

While the old queen made Anna take off the third dress, the prince got up deliriously and crawled on all fours to see what was happening. Anna took off the third dress and screamed in fright, "Anna!" The prince crawled on all fours into the room and found his mother who had grabbed hold of Anna and was about to shove her into the kettle. He couldn't believe his eyes, the poor prince!

Immediately, he seized the queen from behind and threw her into the kettle. Then he embraced Anna and kissed her. When they searched for their children, the cook delivered them unharmed and full of life. Little by little, they made preparations for a wedding and were soon married. The cook received great compliments, and

> They remained happy and in peace
> While we sit here picking our teeth.

Told by Rosalia Varrica in Palermo

9

COUNT JOSEPH PEAR

There were once three brothers who owned a pear tree and lived off their pears. At a certain time, one of the brothers went to pick some pears and saw that some had been taken.

"My brothers! What shall we do? Somebody's picked our pears!"

Indeed, they had been stolen, and that night the eldest went to the garden to guard the pear tree. However, he fell asleep, and

*"Don't shoot!" cried the fox. "Please don't shoot me. I shall call you Count
Joseph Pear, and I'll see to it that you'll marry the king's daughter."*

the next morning the middle brother came and said, "What were you doing, brother? Now look at what's happened! More pears have been picked. Well, tonight I'm going to stand guard."

So, that night the second brother was on the lookout. The next morning the youngest brother went to the garden and saw that more of the pears had been picked.

"And you said you were going to keep close watch over everything!" he said to his brother. "Get out of here! Now I'm going to spend the night guarding the tree, and we'll see whether the thief can pull the wool over my eyes!"

That night, to keep himself awake, the youngest brother began to play and dance under the pear tree. After he stopped for a moment, a female fox, who thought the young man had gone to sleep, came out of a hiding place, climbed the tree, and picked the rest of the pears. As she was coming down the tree, the young man quickly aimed his gun at her and was about to shoot.

"Don't shoot!" cried the fox. "Please don't shoot me, Count Joseph. Yes, I shall call you Count Joseph Pear from now on, and I'll see to it that you'll marry the king's daughter."

"But if I let you go, I'll probably never see you again. Besides, as soon as the king sees you, he'll kick you out and make you disappear."

Despite saying all these things, Count Joseph Pear took pity on the fox and let her go. As soon as she went to the forest, the fox caught all sorts of game—squirrels, rabbits, and pheasants—and carried them to the king, who was quite pleased by the gift.

"Your majesty," said the fox, "it is Count Joseph Pear, who asked me to bring you this game that he caught."

"Listen, little fox," the king replied, "I'll take this game you brought, even though I've never heard of your Count Joseph Pear before."

The fox left the game there and returned to Count Joseph.

"Listen, Count Joseph, I've taken the first step," the fox reported. "I went to the king with a gift, and he took it."

A week later the fox went to the forest, caught some more animals—squirrels, rabbits, birds—and told Count Joseph he wanted to take them to the king, and this is what he did.

"Your majesty, Count Joseph Pear sent me to offer you another gift," the fox said.

"Oh, my little fox," the king replied, "I don't know who this Count Joseph Pear is. I'm afraid your count's been sending you to the wrong king. However, I'll tell you what we'll do: you bring Count Joseph Pear here so I can at least make his acquaintance."

The fox left the game there and said, "I'm not mistaken, your majesty. My master sent me here, and in exchange for his generosity, he would like to wed your daughter, the princess."

The little fox returned to Count Joseph and said to him, "Listen, things are going well. After I see the king one more time, the matter will be settled."

"I won't believe you until I have my wife," Count Joseph responded.

Now the fox went back into the forest to Mamma-draga the ogress and said, "My friend, my friend, isn't it time for us to divide our money and put the gold coins with the gold and the silver with the silver?"

"Certainly," the ogress said to the fox. "Go fetch a scale so we can weigh and put the gold with the gold and the silver with the silver."

The little fox went to the king, but she didn't say, "The ogress wants to borrow your scale." Instead, she said, "Count Joseph Pear wants to borrow your scale to weigh and divide his gold and silver."

"How did Count Joseph Pear become so wealthy? Is he richer than I am?"

The king gave the fox the scale. When he was alone with his daughter, they talked and talked, and he said to her, "I see that this Count Joseph Pear is very rich because he's weighing and dividing his gold and silver."

In the meantime, the fox carried the scale to the ogress, who began to weigh and divide the gold and silver. After she was finished, the fox went to Count Joseph Pear and dressed him in new clothes and gave him a watch with diamonds, some rings, and an engagement ring for the princess, and everything that was needed for the marriage.

"Listen to me, Count Joseph Pear," the fox said. "I'm going out before you to prepare the way. You are to go to the king, fetch your bride, and go to the church."

Therefore, Count Joseph went to the king and got his bride. Then they went to the church together. After they were married, the princess got into the carriage, and the bridegroom mounted his horse. The fox made a sign to Count Joseph and cried out, "I'll ride ahead, and you follow me. Let the carriages and horses follow me."

On their way, they came to a sheep farm which belonged to the ogress. When the shepherd, who was tending the sheep, saw the fox approach, he threw a rock at her. The fox began to weep.

"Now I'll have to have you killed!" she said to the shepherd. "Do you see those horsemen behind me? They are mine, and I'll have you killed!"

The shepherd was frightened and said, "If you don't harm me, I won't throw stones at you anymore."

The fox turned and responded, "This is what you must do if you don't want to be killed," the fox replied. "When the king passes by and asks you who the owner of the sheep farm is, you must tell him that the farm belongs to Count Joseph Pear. He's the king's son-in-law, and the king will reward you."

Soon the cavalcade passed by, and the king asked the shepherd, "Who is the owner of this sheep farm?"

"Count Joseph Pear," the shepherd replied, whereupon the king gave him some money.

The fox kept about ten feet in front of Count Joseph, who turned to her and whispered, "Where are you taking me, fox?

How can you make them believe that I'm rich? Where are we going?"

"Listen to me," replied the fox. "Leave everything to me."

They went on and on, and the fox saw another farm of cattle with a herdsman. The same thing happened there as with the shepherd. The herdsman threw a stone, and the fox threatened him. The king passed by and asked, "Herdsman, who owns all these fields?"

"Count Joseph Pear," the herdsman responded, and the king, astonished at his son-in-law's wealth, gave the herdsman a piece of gold.

On the one hand, Count Joseph was pleased, but on the other, he was confused and wasn't sure how things would end. When the fox turned around, Count Joseph said, "Where are you taking me, fox? You are going to be the ruin of me."

The fox kept on as if she hadn't heard a thing. Then she came to a horse farm, and the boy who was tending the stallions and mares threw a stone at the fox, who, in turn, frightened him with a threat just as she had done with the others. When the boy saw the king, he said that the farm belonged to Count Joseph Pear.

They kept on traveling, and soon the fox came to a well. The ogress was sitting next to it. The fox began to run and pretended to be tremendously afraid of some rogues.

"Friend! Friend!" she cried out to the ogress. "Do you see them coming after me? Those horsemen will kill us! Quick, let's hide down inside the well."

"Yes, let's do it, friend!" the ogress responded in fear. "We've got to save ourselves."

"Shall I throw you down first?" the fox asked.

"Certainly, friend," the ogress said, and that was her death sentence.

So, the fox threw the ogress down the well and then entered her palace. Count Joseph Pear followed the fox with his wife, father-in-law, and all the horsemen. The fox showed them through the apartments, displaying all the riches. Of course, Count Joseph was happy because he had found his fortune, and the king was even happier because his daughter had married a very rich man. There was a celebration for a few days, and then the king, who was most satisfied, returned to his own castle, and his daughter remained with her husband.

One day soon after the king's departure, the fox was looking out the window, and Joseph and his wife were going up to the terrace. Joseph took some dirt and threw it at the fox's head. The fox raised her eyes.

"What's the meaning of this?" she said to Count Joseph. "You're disgusting! Why are you doing this after all the good things that I've done for you? Watch out, or I'll talk!"

"What does the fox have to talk about?" the wife said to Count Joseph.

"Nothing," he said to his wife. "I threw a little dirt at her, and she got angry."

Then Joseph picked up some more dirt and threw it at the fox's head.

The fox became angry and cried out, "Well, little Joey, now I'm going to talk and tell everyone that you're just the common owner of a pear tree."

Count Joseph became very frightened because the little fox began to tell his wife everything. As the fox was doing this, he picked up a vase and threw it at the little fox's head, and the vase crushed her skull. This was how Count Joseph repaid her kindness, and he continued to enjoy all his wealth with his wife.

And those who tell this tale and whoever caused it to be told
Will not die a terrible death whenever they get old.

————————

Told by Angela Smiraglia, eighteen-years-old, a villager, in Capa

10

MAMMA-DRAGA THE OGRESS

Once upon a time there was a mother who had a daughter called Rosetta. One day she said to her, "Rosetta, my Rosetta, take the garbage pail and throw out the trash."

So, the girl took the garbage pail and went to dump the trash down a nearby well. However, when she dumped it, she also let the pail fall in.

Now it was rumored that an ogress lived in this well. Therefore, the girl called out to her saying, "Oh ogress, Mamma-draga, please give me back my garbage pail."

"Come down yourself and get it," answered Mamma-draga.

"Oh no, you'll surely eat me!" said the girl.

"Oh no, I promise not to eat you. I swear it by the soul of my son Cola."

"And how am I supposed to get down there?"

"Just put one foot here, the other foot there, and down you'll come."

Well, the girl was afraid her mother would beat her if she came back without the pail, so down she went.

When Mamma-draga the ogress saw her face to face, she exclaimed, "Oh my, Rosetta, how lovely you are, how lovely! Sweep my house for me."

Without protesting, the girl began to sweep.

"Well, what have you uncovered in this house?"

"A bit of dirt, a bit of earth, just like any person's house."

"Now examine my head, and tell me what you find on it."

The girl began to examine the ogress's head and said, "A few lice and a few nits, just like any person's head."

"Now examine this bed, and tell me what you find in it."

"A few bedbugs, a few fleas, just like any person's bed."

The girl began to examine the ogress's head and said, "A few lice and a few nits, just like any person's head."

"Rosetta, you are truly beautiful. Now a star will grow on your forehead, and it will be so dazzling that all the people will have to bow their heads when they look at you. And how lovely your hair is! Your hair on your head will grow in golden threads, and when you comb it, one side will gush with pearls and diamonds, and the other side, with wheat and barley!"

Then the ogress took her to a room that contained old clothing and new clothing. She picked up the stockings, which had a good pair and a shoddy pair.

"Which of these do you want?"

Rosetta said she'd take the shoddy ones.

"But I'm going to give you the good ones," said Mamma-draga.

The same thing happened with blouses and dresses. Rosetta chose the old, worn-out ones, but Mamma-draga gave her the new ones. And so it continued, until Rosetta was dressed in a completely new outfit from head to toe, so beautiful that she looked like a German doll. Then the ogress gave her a pocket full of money and sent her back up the well.

When Rosetta's mother saw her, she exclaimed, "Oh, how beautiful you look! What happened to you?"

Then Rosetta told her the whole story. Well, you know how things are in a neighborhood. A woman who knew Rosetta's mother began asking her questions, and her mother told the woman everything that had happened. Now this woman also had a daughter, a girl as ugly as sin.

"Now pay attention to your mother," she said to her daughter. "Do you see how many gifts Rosetta got from Mamma-draga the ogress? I want you to take our trash and dump it. But be sure to let the garbage pail fall into the well, and then ask the ogress to give it back."

So, the girl did this, and let the garbage pail fall into the well.

"Mamma-draga, Mamma-draga, give me back my garbage pail!"

"Come down yourself and get it."

The girl didn't have to ask a second time but climbed right down. The ogress made her sweep the house and then asked,

"Well, what have you uncovered in this house?"

"Terrible dust and too much dirt," the girl answered. "Just like a messy person's house."

"Now examine my head, and tell me what you find in it."

"Dreadful lice, big fat nits, just like a messy person's head."

"Now make up my bed, and tell me what you find on it."

"Awful bedbugs, dreadful fleas, just like a messy person's bed."

"Oh, what an ugly girl you are!" said Mamma-draga. "A stinking horn will grow on your forehead, and dung will shower down from your hair on one side and smelly horse-manure on the other!"

Well, you can imagine how enjoyable this was for the girl!

Then the ogress took her into the room with the old clothing and the new clothing. She showed her the stockings and said, "Which of these do you want?"

"The good ones!"

"Well, I'm giving you the old ones."

Then she showed her the blouses, and the girl asked for new ones and also for new dresses. However, each time she received only the old ones. In the end, the girl came away looking like a shabbily dressed servant. Finally, the ogress dismissed her with a slap.

"Get out of here!" she ordered, and the poor girl had to climb back up the well.

When her mother saw her, she exclaimed, "Oh my child, what in the world happened to you?"

"It was Mamma-draga the ogress who did this!"

Well, the two women were never on good terms after that, but Rosetta's mother became wealthy, while the other became wretched and ugly. That's the way the good Lord punishes envious people.

Collected from Rosa Brusca in Palermo

11

PRETTY POOR GIRL; *or,* POVIRA-BEDDA

Once upon a time, so the story goes, there was an old woman with a beautiful granddaughter. They were so poor that their survival depended on whatever people were willing to give them. The girl was called Povira-Bedda, "Pretty Poor Girl."

One day a fortune-teller came along, one of those charlatans, who travels about and offers to tell the fortune of any woman who'll believe him, just to make some money. He was so insistent that Povira-Bedda agreed to have her fortune told. The poor child had no money to give him, but he had noticed a little bed quilt spread out in the sun outside the house, and he agreed to take this as payment.

Therefore, he began making the usual sign of the cross in the girl's palm, and then he predicted that she would win a king for her husband. Povira-Bedda's first reaction was to laugh, but the idea stayed in her head, and she began to think about it.

Well, it so happened that Povira-Bedda's house stood just below the king's palace. At the very moment the fortune-teller was reciting her future, the young prince happened to be looking out and listening. He was very amused, and as he laughed, he called out to her:

"You lost the little quilt from your bed,
But a prince like me you'll never wed!"

Povira-Bedda answered him:

"Why should I worry?
There's one above and one below,
And I'll be the prince's wife, I know.
Since I trust in the Lord and things divine,
The son of the king is sure to be mine.

Since I trust in God and the saints alone,
The prince will soon be my very own."

The prince chuckled at hearing this, but inside him, a little love wound had opened and would never heal.

Now let us turn to the old woman, who came back home and found her little quilt missing. She screamed and howled and tore her hair so much that the prince had one of his own quilts sent over to appease her. But then, as the days passed, the prince found that he couldn't take his mind off Povira-Bedda and thought of ways to keep teasing her and reciting the same taunt. Deep in his heart, the flame of his love for her was burning more brightly every day.

The prince's mother, the queen, was fully aware of what was happening to her son. Therefore, she made the shrewd decision to ease his soul by having him marry. When she suggested this, he answered that he would marry only when she brought him a young woman who was the exact image of Povira-Bedda. Upon hearing this, the queen felt like someone caught in a thorn-bush, but she quickly thought of a way to disentangle herself and came up with the following plan.

She arranged to have her son marry a certain princess and had her brought to the palace. Then she summoned the old grandmother and told her that she wanted Povira-Bedda to come and be her son's bride, in place of the intended spouse, since the prince insisted that he would only marry a girl who was the exact image of Povira-Bedda.

When the old woman told this to her granddaughter, the girl didn't need any persuading! The following evening Povira-Bedda, all dressed up as you can imagine, presented herself to the prince. At the sight of her, he was at a loss for words, and he married her on the spot. However, Povira-Bedda did not dare get into the marriage-bed. The queen, you see, had ordered her to hide beneath the bed so that the bride that she had selected for her son could lie in the bed. The prince, of course, did not understand what was happening.

In the wink of an eye, Povira-Bedda vanished under the bed and—zoom!—the princess slipped in between the bed-sheets.

Well, there is a proverb about such tricks: "The devil creates them, and the devil exposes them." So, when the prince realized what had been done to him, he became enraged.

"I've been tricked! I've been betrayed!" he kept shouting, until all the palace servants came running.

Now the queen had to admit that her plan had completely backfired, and she had no choice but to give her blessing to her son's marriage with a poor but pretty girl. And that's the way Povira-Bedda won the king's son as her very own.

Collected by Mattia Di Martino from an anonymous storyteller at Noto

12

THE POT OF BASIL

Once upon a time there was a father who had a daughter called Rusidda. Since there was no one at home to educate her, he sent her to live at school with a teacher. Now this teacher had a terrace that faced the king's residence, and the king had a son who frequently looked out from his own terrace. One day Rusidda was looking out and singing a song that went: "*Oh, oh, oh, the things that I know.*" The king's son was passing by, and he called out to her:

"Rusidda, Rusidda, how much do you know?
How many leaves does the basil plant show?"

Rusidda, not knowing how to answer, went to ask her teacher for help.

"What's the problem?" asked the teacher, and Rusidda answered, "The king's son said to me:

Rusidda, Rusidda, how much do you know?
How many leaves does the basil plant show?"

"If he asks you again," the teacher replied, "say to him:

And you, with your royal crown of gold,
How many stars does the dark sky hold?"

The next morning Rusidda went out again on the terrace and across the way, the king's son appeared on his terrace and said:

"Rusidda, Rusidda, how much do you know?
How many leaves does the basil plant show?"

And she answered:

"And you, with your royal crown of gold,
How many stars does the dark sky hold?"

Now it was the young prince who was unable to respond. He was filled with resentment and vowed to get back at her. Therefore, he went and made a deal with her teacher.

"Allow me to spend one night under Rusidda's bed, and I'll give you a fine gift in return."

The teacher agreed. When the hour came, and Rusidda went to bed, the prince took a pointed tool and kept poking her through the mattress. The next morning, Rusidda was miserable. Her teacher noticed and asked, "Rusidda, what happened to you?"

"Oh teacher, what terrible fleas, what terrible bed bugs!"

The next morning there was another confrontation: Rusidda went out on the same terrace, and the two of them began taunting each other:

"Rusidda, Rusidda, how much do you know?
How many leaves does the basil plant show?"

"And you, with your royal crown of gold,
How many stars does the dark sky hold?"

"Rusidda, what keeps you from sleeping at night?
'Oh teacher, these bed bugs and fleas can bite!'"

Rusidda went to her teacher and said, "Teacher, you've betrayed me!" and then she left.

When she returned home to her father, he asked why she didn't want to stay with the teacher any longer.

"It's all because this young prince keeps pestering me. The minute I appear on the terrace, he says to me, 'Rusidda, Rusidda, how much do you know? How many leaves does the basil plant show?' and I answer him: 'And you, with your royal crown of gold, how many stars does the dark sky hold?' Last night I slept at my teacher's house, and all night long I was tossing and turning, imagining there were bed bugs and fleas. However, it turned out to be the prince who was poking me."

"Calm down, my daughter," said her father, "and let me figure out what to do next."

Soon thereafter, Russida's father went and bought the best horse there was, and then he had a belt made entirely of gold.

"Take this belt," he said. "Mount the horse, and tomorrow go riding in front of the king's palace."

So the next morning Rusidda did this, and as she rode in front of the palace with the belt in her hand, she cried out:

"Whoever kisses this horse's ass and shows he's bold
Will win this belt made entirely of gold!"

The prince called out to her, "If you bring the horse here, I'll kiss it myself," and he kissed the horse's behind. However, Rusidda, who was on her own horse, gave the stallion a sharp goad with the spur, and the horse took off, leaving the prince standing there after having kissed the horse's rear end. Meanwhile, Rusidda still held the belt in her hand and called out:

"My horse's behind you kissed and smelt,
But you didn't get the golden belt!"

And she rode away.

The next morning Rusidda went back to her teacher, who asked,

"Rusidda, are you here again?"

"Yes, Ma'am, my father insists that I come."

Rusidda went out on the terrace again, and the prince appeared on his.

"Ah, Rusidda, my little rose, it's been a while since we've seen each other."

"I haven't been able to come, I've been terribly busy."

"Do you know what I have to say to you?" said the prince.

"Rusidda, Rusidda, how much do you know?
How many leaves does the basil plant show?"

(and they continued)

"And you, with your royal crown of gold,
How many stars does the dark sky hold?"

"Rusidda, what keeps you from sleeping at night?
'O teacher, these bedbugs and fleas can bite!'"

"My horse's behind you kissed and smelt,
But you didn't get the golden belt!"

The prince became angry all over again.

"All right, I'll get my revenge, you'll see!"

The next morning he dressed up like a sailor, picked up a basket of fish, and went hawking the fish through the streets of the town: "I've got fish, fresh fish for sale!"

"O teacher, please buy me some fish!" Russida cried out.

"How much do you want for them?" the teacher asked him.

"I don't sell fish for money. I sell them for kisses," he replied.

"Are you telling me the truth? I've never heard of fish being sold for kisses before. How strange!"

"Yes, I'm telling you the truth.

If you'll just give me a lovely kiss,
I'll give you back a lovely fish."

The teacher told this to Rusidda, who foolishly fell for the prince's deception. So, she went and gave him a kiss. However, the prince ran off, taking all his fish with him. As soon as he was home, he took off his sailor's clothes, went out on his terrace, and resumed the exchange.

"Rusidda, Rusidda, how much do you know?
How many leaves does the basil plant show?"

"And you, with your royal crown of gold,
How many stars does the dark sky hold?"

"Rusidda, what keeps you from sleeping at night?
'O teacher, these bedbugs and fleas can bite!'"

"My horse's behind you kissed and smelt,
But you didn't get the golden belt!"

"But I got you to give me that little kiss,
And you didn't taste one morsel of fish!"

"I'll make you pay for this," said Rusidda, who went straight to her father and told him the whole story. "My daughter, the only way we can put an end to this is to stop sending you to that teacher."

Therefore, he did just that.

Now the prince went a long time without seeing Rusidda. Consequently, he fell seriously ill, and his father became concerned.

"My son," he said, "tell me what's wrong. What are you suffering from?"

"I'm sick and feel terrible. Call all the doctors."

Therefore, an entire medical staff was called upon to treat him. However, the prince's condition kept growing worse the longer he was unable to see Rusidda.

Meanwhile, Rusidda dressed herself up like a foreign doctor and entered the palace, where she met a servant. "Take this message to the king," she said. "Tell him that a doctor has come from abroad, who can make his son well again."

Of course, the king invited her into his throne room at once, hoping that this doctor would cure his son.

"Your Majesty, before I look at this case," Rusidda disguised as the doctor announced, "there is one thing I must warn you about: There is no need to come running, if you hear a loud cry. This is just a sign that the cure is beginning. You must close the door to the room with me inside alone with your son. Then I shall work on him in the dark."

Eager to have his son well again, the king granted her every wish. So, into the prince's room she went, and she began to shout in a loud voice: "Death is coming on her crooked haunches! She's come to claim the king's son."[1]

When Rusidda left the prince's chamber, the king asked this "doctor" to explain what had happened.

"No problem, your highness, your son is cured. He simply needs to be placed on the terrace first thing tomorrow morning. He told me that his illness is a desire for a young woman called Rusidda. Therefore, I'll go to her and her teacher and arrange for her to appear on the teacher's terrace. Then the prince will be well again."

"Doctor, I'll have everything done exactly as you say," answered the king. "I love my son, and I wouldn't know what else to do but follow your instructions."

The next morning Rusidda went to her teacher.

"Rusidda, what brings you here?"

[1] Death is generally a female in Sicily and Italy.

"I've come for some pleasant distraction. It's been so long since I spent some time on your terrace, and I'd love to take a little air there."

Meanwhile the king's first thought was to bring his son to the terrace that very morning. When Rusidda looked out, the king's son was already there. He began sighing and said:

"Rusidda, Rusidda, how much do you know?
How many leaves does the basil plant show?"

"Even though you're practically dead, you still want to play games?" Rusidda asked, and yet, she continued:

"And you, with your royal crown of gold,
How many stars does the dark sky hold?"

"Rusidda, what keeps you from sleeping at night?
'O teacher, these bedbugs and fleas can bite!'"

"My horse's behind you kissed and smelt,
But you didn't get the golden belt!"

"But I got you to give me a little kiss,
And you didn't taste one morsel of fish!"

"Death is coming on her crooked haunches,
She's come to claim the son of the king."

Upon hearing this, the king ordered his men not to let Rusidda get away from the house and to bring her to the palace.

"You owe me an explanation! What is this all about?"

"Your Majesty, my mother died, my father sent me to a teacher to be educated. When I went out on her terrace, your son, the prince, made fun of me." —And here she proceeded to tell him everything that had taken place. —"So, now I ask your Majesty's permission to allow me to return to my house."

"What do you mean, 'return to your house,' when your mischief has almost cost me the life of my son?"

*"Oh, how sweet my wife's blood is! Oh, please, somebody, stop me,
because I feel like killing myself for having lost such a sweet wife!"*

"Nevertheless, I want to go home!"

And she made such a fuss that the king had no choice but to let her go.

Now the prince declared that he had to have this woman as his wife. Consequently, the king and the queen, even though they were royalty, decided to pay a visit to the girl's father and ask for her hand in marriage.

"Yes, I'll give my daughter in marriage, but you must allow my daughter a forty days' waiting period."

Meanwhile, Rusidda had her servants bring her a sack of flour, a large jug of honey, and a carafe, and she shaped these materials into a puppet doll that was her own size. When the nuptial night arrived, and she was about to get into bed with the prince, she said, "I'm a little embarrassed to undress in front of you. So, won't you please go into the other room a minute, while I take off my clothes and get into bed?"

After the prince went out, she set up the doll in her place in bed, took the puppet strings in her hands, and hid beneath the bed. When her husband came back, he asked, "Rusidda, do you recall when I said to you:

Rusidda, Rusidda, how much do you know?
How many leaves does the basil plant show?"

Then the puppet, controlled by Russida, nodded her head.

"Do you remember when I came and sold you fish in exchange for kisses?"

And, once again, the puppet nodded her head, while the prince continued reciting a whole list of questions, and at the end he asked her: "And are you sorry now for all that you did to me?"

Here the puppet shook her head, signaling, "No."

When the prince saw this, he drew his sword and shoved it into the doll's neck. The blow broke the carafe that was at the neck, and the honey began flowing out. In his rage, the prince licked his sword. "Oh, how sweet my wife's blood is! Oh, please, somebody, stop me, because I feel like killing myself for having lost such a sweet wife!"

As soon as he said this, Rusidda came out from under the bed shouting, "I'm alive! I'm alive!"

Immediately, Rusidda and the prince embraced one another.

And what became of the puppet so sweet?
The couple ate it as their wedding treat.

Told by a daughter of Giuseppa Furia at Ficarazzi

13

THE COUNT'S SISTER

Here's a tale that people like to tell. Once there was a count, as rich as the ocean, and he had a young sister, beautiful beyond words. She was just eighteen years old, and the count was so jealous and possessive that he kept her locked away in a small room of the palace. No one had ever seen her, and no one knew her.

Now the wall of the count's palace was next to the prince's palace. The lovely little countess, confined and guarded like a dog, was no longer able to endure her condition. Therefore, during the night, she began digging, softly, softly, and made a hole in the wall of her room, behind a beautiful big picture that was hanging in her room. Well, this hole turned out to be connected to the prince's bedroom, and its opening was behind a picture he had hanging there. Therefore, the hole could not be seen on the prince's side.

One night, the countess gave the picture a nudge and peered into the prince's room, and when she saw a precious, illuminated lamp, she addressed it with these words:

"Lamp of gold, lamp of silver, burning bright,
Is your prince sleeping or awake this night?"

And the lamp answered,

"My lady, you're welcome to come in here,
The prince is sleeping, have no fear."

Consequently, she entered the room, and as she climbed into bed alongside the prince, he woke up. After he embraced her and kissed her, he asked,

"Where do you live, my lady? Where are you from?
Is there some state that you call your home?"

And she laughed with her little golden mouth and replied,

"Prince, what are you saying, what are you asking?
Just keep quiet, and enjoy what you're doing!"

When the prince woke up later and saw that the divine creature was no longer at his side, he quickly dressed and summoned his councilors. When they arrived, he told them about all that had happened and asked,

"What do I have to do to make her stay with me?"

"Oh, your royal majesty," they answered, "when you are embracing, you must tie her hair to your arm so that you'll wake up as soon as she tries to leave."

The next evening the countess repeated her refrain:

"Lamp of gold, lamp of silver, burning bright,
Is your prince sleeping or awake this night?"

And the lamp answered again,

"My lady, you're welcome to come in here,
The prince is sleeping, have no fear."

She went in and again climbed into the prince's bed.

"Where do you live, my lady? Where are you from?
Is there some state that you call your home?"

"Prince, what are you saying, what are you asking?
Just keep quiet, and enjoy what you're doing!"

Gradually, they fell asleep, and although the prince managed to tie the countess's lovely hair to his arm, the countess took some scissors, cut the hair, and disappeared while he was asleep. When the prince woke up, he called out, "Councilors, councilors, the divine creature has vanished!"

The councilors answered, "Oh majesty, next time you must take the end of the little gold chain she wears around her neck and tie it to your own neck."

The following night the little countess peered into the room and said,

"Lamp of gold, lamp of silver, burning bright,
Is your prince sleeping or awake this night?"

And the lamp answered,

"My lady, you're welcome to come in here,
The prince is sleeping, have no fear."

When the prince had her in his arms, he asked his usual question.

"Where do you live, my lady? Where are you from?
Is there some state that you call your home?"

And she gave her usual answer:

"Prince, what are you saying, what are you asking?
Just keep quiet, and enjoy what you're doing!"

The prince managed to tie her little chain around his neck, but when he fell asleep, she cut the chain and disappeared. In the morning, the prince called for his councilors and told them what had happened. "Oh, your majesty," they replied, "take a wash basin filled with saffron water and set it under your bed. When she takes off her blouse, grab it and throw it into the basin to soak in the saffron. That way, when she puts it on and leaves, she will leave a trail that you can follow."

That evening the prince prepared a small basin with the saffron water and went to bed. Midnight came, and the countess said to the lamp,

"Lamp of gold, lamp of silver, burning bright,
Is your prince sleeping or awake this night?"

And the lamp answered,

"My lady, you're welcome to come in here,
The prince is sleeping, have no fear."

When the prince saw her, he asked his usual question:

"Where do you live, my lady? Where are you from?
Is there some state that you call your home?"

And she gave her usual answer:

"Prince, what are you saying, what are you asking
Just keep quiet, and enjoy what you're doing!"

When the prince began to snore, she got up and began to tiptoe away, but she found her blouse all soaked in the basin with the saffron. Without uttering a peep, she wrung it and squeezed it until it was clean and escaped without leaving a trace.

From that night on, the prince waited for his divine creature to come, but he waited in vain and eventually fell into deep despair. However, exactly nine months later, he woke up one morning to find a beautiful baby boy sleeping next to him, and he looked just like an angel. It took the prince just seconds to get dressed and begin shouting, "Councilors! My councilors!"

When they arrived, the prince showed them the boy.

"This is my son!" he said. "But how can I ever find out who his mother is?"

The councilors answered, "Oh, your royal majesty, you must pretend that the child has died. Then place him in the middle of the church and order all the women in town to come and weep for him. The one who weeps best of all will be his mother!"

Consequently, the prince did just what they said, and all kinds of women came.

"My son! My son!" they cried out, and they left the way they came. At last, the countess arrived. She was already in tears, and once she saw the baby, she began wailing, tearing her hair, and crying out:

"O son of mine, O my son!
In trying to get you too much good,
I cut my braids as best I could.
In looking for more beauty than I can pay,
I had to give my gold chain away.
And for carrying vanity much too far,
A saffron blouse I was forced to wear!"

Now the prince, his councilors, and everyone who was there began to shout: "She's the mother! She's the mother!"

Suddenly the count arrived to redress his sister's shame. He drew out his sword and pointed it at his sister. However, the prince threw himself between them and said:

"My count, hold back! No shame can this woman bring.
She's been sister to a count, but now she's wife to a king!!"

And so the two of them were married right then and there.

They continued to live in contentment and peace,
While we just sit here, picking our teeth.

Told by Francesca Leto to Salvatore Salomone-Marino in Borsetto

14

THE TALKING BELLY

I've heard tell, gentlemen, that there was once a king and queen, who had an only son. When he turned eighteen, his father wanted him to marry, but his son said, "Your majesty, it's too soon."

The father kept insisting, and his son always responded, "Your majesty, it's too soon."

One day, so as not to be bothered anymore, he told his father, "All right, I'll marry, but only if I find a maiden whose belly talks."

The king ordered all the bells to be rung and summoned his councilors. As soon as they were gathered together, he said, "I need your advice. My son has told me that he'll only marry a maiden whose belly talks. But I don't want to give my realm to just anyone."

A wise old councilor stood up and said, "Your majesty, I think you should call for twelve courtiers. Then give each of them a painter and send them on a journey throughout the entire world—Portugal, Brazil, Spain, and France. Whoever finds the maiden whose belly talks is to have a portrait of her drawn and brought to you. If the portrait pleases your son, all will be well. If it doesn't please him, he'll never say a word again about marrying a maiden whose belly talks."

Consequently, the king commanded twelve noblemen to depart from the court and journey all over the map, each one with a painter. One of them, for example, the Duke of Butera, took a superb painter with him, and together with his servant, they traveled far and wide. At one point, a sudden storm erupted, and they couldn't see anything because it was so cloudy. Therefore, they took refuge in a forest. The servant found shelter in one part, the prince and the painter in another part. Later, when they made their way to the end of the forest, they saw an old man tilling the soil.

"I greet you, man of the soil," the duke cried out.

And the old man responded, "Welcome, man of war."

"Are you still standing on your own two feet?"

"I'll soon have three feet."[1]

"Do you still see well?"

"I can tie my shoes."[2]

"Is there snow on the mountains?"

"There's still time for me."[3]

The good old man stood up and invited the duke and the painter into his home where they found a maiden sitting and weaving. When the duke entered, he said, "Oh, young lady, what is that cloth that you're stretching out?"

"Oh, cavalier, watch what you're doing with your sword!"[4]

Then her father turned and asked her, "And your mother?"

"She's gone to help someone see the world who's never seen it before."[5]

"And you, what are you doing?"

"I'm making things dance without a sound."[6]

"And your grandma?"

"She's gone to honor someone who cannot be honored anymore."[7]

The father turned to the duke and said, "Gentlemen, please make yourselves at home, and I'll get you something to eat."

In the meantime, the grandmother and mother arrived, and they all sat down to dinner. While they were all eating, the duke said to the painter in a low voice, "If her belly talks, this maiden will become the prince's wife. She doesn't have one defect."

1 Implied here is that he will be walking with a cane.

2 Implied is that he can see quite well.

3 The duke has indicated that the old man is indeed very old and has white hair on his head (the mountains), and the old man responds that he still has time to live.

4 The expression in Sicilian is: "O Cavalieri, vidi chi ti penni." Pitrè makes clear that this is a reference to the duke's sword. The implication is that he is poking his nose into something that doesn't concern him. There is also a sexual inuendo.

5 This is a way of saying that the mother has gone to help deliver a baby as midwife.

6 Implied is that the water is boiling in the pot, and the pasta is moving about.

7 She has gone to visit someone who has just died.

When it became dark, they all went to bed, and the maiden's mother forgot to prepare a candle for the duke. During the night, he looked for a light. Since he could not find any, he stood up and searched for a candle, and silently he entered the room where the maiden was sleeping. No sooner did he approach her and begin feeling around in the dark than he touched her belly, which said, "Don't touch me because I belong to the prince."

The duke returned to the painter and said, "I've got something to tell you: the maiden's belly is talking in there."

"Well then," replied the painter, "tomorrow I'll draw her portrait, and we'll bring it to the king."

The next day, as soon as they got up, the painter drew the portrait. Then the duke took his leave.

"Farewell," he said. "I'll be seeing you again in a few days."

"It will always be a pleasure to see you," said the old man.

After they reached the first village, the painter finished the portrait. The duke tied it around his neck with a string, and they returned to the court. Meanwhile, the other courtiers began gradually returning with their painters. After they all had gathered at the court, the king held a meeting with his councilors and noblemen, and the king listened to them as they showed their pictures. However, the prince found fault in all the portraits. Then Duke Butera stood up and declared, "Your majesty, if this portrait doesn't please you, you'll never find a wife."

Then he displayed the portrait that he had been carrying around his neck.

"I like this maiden," the prince announced. "But does her belly talk?"

"Yes, your majesty."

"Well then, she will become my wife."

Beautiful garments were prepared for the maiden as well as four coaches and twelve chambermaids. They all got into one of the coaches—the duke, the chambermaids, and the servants— and they departed to fetch the maiden.

When the good old man saw the coaches, he immediately realized they were coming for his daughter. After the coaches arrived and stopped, the duke descended and bowed before the maiden and said to her that the king's son wanted to have her for his wife. The chambermaids bathed her, dressed her, and helped her climb into the coach, all in a grand display. The maiden wept for joy and embraced her father and mother. Then she asked permission to depart and left.

The king, queen, and prince were all at the palace awaiting her. The prince took her by the arm and led her to a grand party in her honor. That night, before she went alone to her bed (for they had not been married yet), the prince said to his mother: "Your majesty, when she is asleep, please enter her room, touch her belly, and see if it talks."

His mother did as he asked. When the maiden was sound asleep that night, she entered the room and touched her belly.

"Don't touch me. I belong to the prince."

She withdrew her hand, and afterward she told her son, "Everything's all right, my son. You've found what you've been looking for."

The next day, as soon as the royal chapel was opened, they were married. However, let us leave them while they are entertaining themselves and turn to another story.

Once upon a time there were two merchants, very good companions. These two friends loved each other as much as they loved their own eyes. One of them had a beautiful mare. Well, one day one of the merchants went to the other and said, "My friend, I must take a trip to Monreale. Would you lend me your mare?"

"Of course, comrade."

So the merchant road on horseback to Monreale. While he was in the town, he put the mare in a stable where it gave birth to a colt. Since the mare had to rest after having the colt, the merchant had to wait two days before returning the horse to its owner. After the two days had passed, the merchant got on the mare and returned to Palermo. Then he went to the stable where he left the mare for his friend, and he took the colt to his own home.

The friend's servant saw that the mare had given birth to a colt and told his master.

"How can that be? How could my friend take the colt and treat me so badly?"

Therefore, he went to his friend's house and said, "How can you do such a thing when we are bound in friendship?"

"What's wrong? The mare gave birth to the colt while it was in my hands. Therefore, the colt's mine."

There was a lawsuit, and they went to a judge, who said the owner was wrong. Consequently, they went to a higher court, and the same thing happened. Enraged, the poor colleague said, "Well, my friend's a rogue, and he's taking advantage of me by using the courts to justify his wrong actions."

Therefore, he went to the king's palace and presented himself before the prince. "I want to thank you, your majesty, for seeing me," and he explained what had happened. However, the prince also told him he was in the wrong and had no right to the colt.

When the merchant left and was descending the stairs, he burst into tears like a baby. The princess saw him and asked, "Why are you crying?"

"Your majesty, let me tell you what's happened," and he told her the entire story.

"Don't despair," she responded. "Just be quiet, and climb those secret stairs over there. Then I'll tell you what you're to do."

The merchant was content and went up the secret stairs. The princess told him that she was the maiden whose belly talks and said, "This evening, at midnight, dress the way you are, and cry out: 'Help! Help!' without ever stopping. You're to continue doing this until the guards come and take you to the prince, who'll ask you, 'What's going on? What's wrong?' Your response will be: 'Your majesty, the fish are coming from the sea and are climbing up the mountain.' 'How is that possible?' the prince will ask you, and you'll know just what to say."

The merchant did as she instructed. When the king's son heard him scream, "Help! Help!" he went down stairs and had him brought up into the palace and asked him, "What's wrong, my poor man? Has something happened to you? Is there something dangerous? Speak!"

"Your majesty, we're lost," he cried out. "The fish are coming from the sea and are climbing up the mountain!"

"How's that possible?" the prince asked. "How is that possible?"

"And how's it possible," the merchant replied, "that you've allowed my colleague to keep my colt?"

Upon hearing these words, the prince said, "Very well, the mare is yours, and the colt is yours as well. Go down to my stable and take the horse you want. But I know that these words did not come from your mouth."

Early the next morning, the prince said to the princess, "Since you've mixed your nose into my affairs, take whatever you want from the palace, whatever appears to be yours and whatever you cherish most, and leave!"

"My prince," she responded, "I would like a month's time to do this."

"Take as long as you want."

And what do you think the princess did? Well, she summoned many artisans—bricklayers, carpenters, painters, and decorators—and said to them: "Within twenty-eight days I want you to build me a palace that's to be the finest imaginable, but it must be completely different from this one, and I want you to build it so that it is facing this one."

On the evening of the twenty-seventh day, the palace was ready with tapestry, sofas, and all sorts of comfort. On the twenty-ninth day, the princess called the prince and said to him that it would give her great pleasure to have dinner with him that night. While they were eating that evening, she put a sleeping potion into his glass of wine. Therefore, when the prince drank it, he soon fell asleep. Then the princess had him dressed in his best clothes and carried over to her palace.

The next morning, as soon as he awoke, the king's son glanced around the room, and he had no idea where he was. So he went back to sleep. Then he awoke again, and he could not believe his eyes. Finally, he cried out, "Hello! Hello! Where are we?"

Then his wife appeared, and the king's son recalled the agreement that he had made with the princess a month ago.

"You're still here?" he said.

"What do you mean 'still here'? You told me that I could take with me whatever I cherish the most. Well, I cherish you the most, and I've taken you with me."

"Everything you've done is right," the prince said. "The first time you showed me you were right was with the mare. Now it's with this palace. Do you know what I say to you? Take this kingdom and rule with your talents in your own way. You have a grand sense of justice, good enough for yourself and for others."

And this is what was done.

To be sure, they lived happy and content,
While we just sit here without a cent.

Told by Agatuzza Messia at Palermo

15

MANDRUNI AND MANDRUNA

Here's a tale that people like to tell. Once there was a king and queen who were married for a long time, but the good Lord refused to give them either a son or a daughter. One day, the queen addressed the almighty Lord and said, "Dear God, if you send me a son or a daughter, I shall proclaim a seven-year holiday."

Well, the good Lord was pleased and made her pregnant. When she was three months pregnant, the king summoned the astrologer, who said that she was carrying a male child and that the boy had to be named Mandruni. So, the king sent this astrologer off with a fine gift.

Months passed—a tale doesn't keep time—and the queen gave birth to a fine baby boy whom she named Mandruni. A wet-nurse was summoned and began giving him milk. Then the royal couple proclaimed a holiday and had the fountain in front of the palace equipped with two pipes that spurted oil and wine. All goods were at bargain price and tax-free, and there was a general feast of abundance for the whole city of Palermo.

The child grew by leaps and bounds, and they made golden balls that he used for play. When he reached the age of seven, he happened to be playing in front of the palace just as the holiday was coming to its end, and only a trickle of oil was coming from the pipe, one drop at a time. At this very moment, an old woman arrived from another town carrying a small glass jug, which she placed there in order to fill it. (Just imagine: seven years had passed without her needing any oil, and it was *exactly* at this moment when the holiday had ended that she felt the need for oil.) Well, the boy noticed her, and while the old woman was waiting for her jug to be filled—*boom!*—he threw one of his balls and shattered the jug. The old woman looked at him and said, "You may have won, but listen to this: *Only when you find Mandruna will you be able to marry!*"

From then on, the boy was haunted by this curse and became obsessed by the thought that he'd never be able to marry if he didn't find Mandruna. When he reached sixteen, he mounted a horse and set off alone into the countryside without a word to anyone. Along the way, he met a farmer gathering crops in front of his cottage, and he asked him, "My good man, would you be willing to do me a favor? Let me have your clothing, and I'll give you mine."

At first, the farmer was reluctant, but once he realized that the exchange was to his advantage, he took off his shoes, work overalls, and cloak and handed them over.

Mandruni continued on to the next city, pretending to be begging for alms. However, underneath he still carried his royal emblem and gold that kept him cheerful. Eventually, he came to a palace, sought out the head coachman, and asked,

"Good sir, would you do me the favor of taking me on as a stable-boy?"

"Come right in and get to work!" said the coachman.

So, Mandruni went in, picked up a broom, and began to sweep. After a few days, the amount of dirt covering his face made him unrecognizable. This suited him well since he didn't want anyone to know who he was, and he made no attempt to wash. However, the coachman kept teasing him:

"Why don't you ever try washing that dirty face of yours? It must be because you're a stable-boy! The good Lord sure loves dirt, said the pig as it returned to the pigsty."

"Well, all right then," said Mandruni, and he finally washed his face.

Being the son of a king, Mandruni naturally had a handsome face, and anyone could see he was no commoner. The princess happened to be visiting the stables and came face to face with this stable-boy. She stared at him, and he stared back at her. Neither one could help staring. Then the princess asked the head coachman,

"Tell me, who is this fellow?"

"Your highness, he's just a poor peasant lad that I took on as stable-boy."

"Oh no, this fellow has to be someone important. Come here, lad, and tell me where you come from."

"I'm from these parts."

"What's your name?"

"Francesco." (He had made up a new name for himself.)

"And your father, what does he do?"

"He's a miller."

"And how is it that you left him?"

"Your Majesty, he wanted to beat me. So, I ran away."

However, these words did not seem very convincing to the princess.

A few days later she called him and said,

"Francesco, I'm thinking of having you removed from the stable and elevated to household service. How would that suit you?"

"As you wish," he answered.

So, the princess spoke to her father, and the king said, "Do as you like."

Now the princess had Mandruni assigned to the kitchen staff. However, she continued to feel very suspicious about him and repeatedly went down to the kitchen to ask him directly,

"Francesco, what's your real name?"

"Haven't I told you already? It's Francesco!"

"No, please tell me the truth. Your name's not really Francesco, and in no way are you a miller."

"But I tell you I *am* a miller."

Back and forth they went, until finally Mandruni had to give in, and he told her his whole story, from the beginning to the present: he was Mandruni, son of the King of Sicily, and he had secretly left his father and mother because an old woman had placed a curse on him so that he couldn't marry until he found a maiden called Mandruna.

"But Mandruna is *my* name!" said the princess, brimming over with joy.

"I didn't realize that."

"Well then, why don't we run off together?"

"Wouldn't everyone recognize you?" he replied.

They pondered this for a while, and finally she came up with a plan.

"Here's what we'll do: tonight you hide yourself in the garden, and at midnight I'll come down, and we'll run off together."

After they made their plan, and the princess came down from the palace at midnight and brought down trunks filled with linens, fine dresses, gold, silver, and abundant clothing. As soon as they mounted horses—dear feet, give me speed!—away they went.

They traveled over long roads, stopping to rest every day, and taking advantage of the barns in the countryside to feed themselves. One day, when they were in open country and had not rested for a long time, they had to lie down. With Mandruna's head resting upon Mandruni's legs, they fell asleep. While they were sleeping, a crow flew down, plucked a ring from Mandruna's hand, and escaped. However, Mandruni heard the flutter of wings, woke up, and saw the crow. Well, what do you think he did? As soon as he got up, he carefully placed Mandruna's head on a little hillock and went off after the crow. He ran, jumped, and climbed up and down—all to no avail. In the end, he realized he had become lost, without either the ring or Mandruna.

Now, let us return to her. She woke up, and finding herself alone and without the ring, she cried out, "You traitor! You said you were taking me away from my home, but only to abandon me! What am I supposed to do now, poor thing that I am?"

While she was in this upset condition, along came a peasant.

"My good man," she said, "would you kindly do me a favor? I'll give you my clothes in exchange for yours."

The man agreed, and taking off his heavy cloak, his shoes, and his cap, he gave them to Mandruna. When the exchange was complete, she set out walking, and where did the path lead her? To the very city where Mandruni was born.

Now, let us return to Mandruni. The poor fellow, lost as he was, could not find any peace of mind and constantly thought about what had happened. "What is Mandruna going to think?" he said to himself. "She'll certainly think that I took her from her home only to abandon her!" In this sorry state, feeling totally abandoned and weak from hunger, Mandruni was forced to beg for a living. So much suffering and heartbreak reduced him to looking like a leper, whose body is like one big sore.

Now, let us return to Mandruna, whom we left as she was entering the city. She asked who was king there, and they told her, "The King of Sicily, and he's in deep mourning over the disappearance of his son Mandruni because he's had no news at all about him."

As she approached the palace, Mandruna found two places for rent, a house and a shop. Therefore, she rented them both and opened a perfume shop and an inn. Then she posted a sign that read: *Whoever takes lodging at the inn near the palace gets three days' free room and meals, if he agrees to tell the innkeeper his whole life story.*

Mandruna was back to dressing like a woman, but she now chose to dress like an old nun. So she drew wrinkles on her face and made herself look sixty-years-old. Of course, every person who encountered her accorded her respect. When poor people came, she would give them three days' lodging. She kept this way of life for seven years, and during this time, she had no news whatsoever of Mandruni.

Finally, in the seventh year, a very poor man came to town. He was a haggard fellow, all sweaty and smelly. The other poor folk said to him, "Why don't you go stay with the old nun whose house is near the palace? She cares for everyone just like a mother."

Consequently, this poor fellow, with his walking stick and his old cape, went to Mandruna and asked for charity. She let him enter, and after she had him cleaned up, she asked him to recount all his travels. As they were sitting there, and Madruna kept looking at him very intently, her heart was telling her that this had to be Mandruni. He was reluctant to speak, but Mandruna urged him, "Tell me what troubles you have experienced. We are put into this world to suffer both the good and the bad. Speak."

"My lady, I am the son of the king of this city"—and here Mandruna pricked up her ears—"To ensure my birth my father proclaimed a seven-year holiday. When I was a child playing with balls, I threw one that smashed an old woman's water jug. Therefore, that old woman put a curse on me so that I couldn't marry until I found someone called Mandruna. At sixteen, I became so obsessed by the curse that I galloped off on horseback, trusting to God and fortune. I met a peasant, changed clothes with him, and then went to the palace of the King of France, who had a daughter called Mandruna. We fell in love at first sight and made plans to run off together, and so we did. As night fell, we came to a forest, and Mandruna fell asleep with her head on my legs and I had my back against a tree. Down came a crow, stole Mandruna's ring, and flew off with it. I went after the crow, and she remained sleeping. I became lost and kept searching for her everywhere, but it has been seven years now, my lady, and I still haven't found her. Oh my Mandruna, who knows into what hands you have fallen! Moreover, I can only imagine what she thought of me! However, I am innocent, innocent as holy Mary herself!"

"Don't worry yourself about this anymore, my son," said the nun. "No need to fear, because this very day Mandruna was taken away by the good Lord. So would you now consider taking me as your wife?"

"But what if she is alive? She is the one that I want."

"But I am telling you that she is dead. Believe me, I know."

"All right, if she is dead then . . . Well, in that case . . . my answer to you is, Yes."

Mandruna asked for a written statement that he was taking her as his wife, and Mandruni had one made. When Mandruna had this document, she covered her head with a great shawl, proceeded to the palace, and began the lament for the deceased:

"Oh Mandruni my love, how can it be that I've lost you? Mandruni my love, how can it be that I've lost you?"

The queen appeared and asked, "Who is doing all that moaning and groaning out there?"

"It's an old nun," said the guards.

"Have her come up to me."

When Mandruna arrived, the queen asked her, "Who are you crying for, my good woman?"

"I am crying for my son, whose name was Mandruni."

"But don't you know that Mandruni was my own son's name?"

"*Your* son, really? Well, your Majesty, if Mandruni was your son, I assure you I can bring him back to you this very day."

"Really? How could you do that?"

"Don't worry. I can definitely bring your son back to you, but on one condition: that you give him to me as my husband."

The queen at first refused. But then, for love of her son, she said, "You can have whatever you want, just so long as you let me see my own son alive again."

Mandruna ran down the palace staircase, hurried back to Mandruni, and told him all that had happened—but still without revealing her identity. She took him by the hand and led him to the queen. No one can possibly describe the joy this mother felt at seeing her son again! Talk led to more talk, and then to the subject of marriage. The queen made a grimace because she couldn't stand the thought of her son marrying this old nun. However, to herself Mandruna was saying, "Since we played your tune, you must pay the piper."

In the end, to cut it short, the old nun and the young prince were to be married. The evening before the ceremony Mandruna went to dress herself, and out she came looking like the princess she was—a beautiful young woman, her charms dazzling beyond compare. Her royal dress had no less than ten flounces and was decorated with chains of gold and diamonds and precious stones. On her head she had placed a star, which was so bright that you couldn't look at it without turning your eyes away. You can imagine why none of the guests could take their eyes off her! Then she described all that had happened to her, from the time she had fled from her home until the present moment. Mandruni burst into tears of happiness. The queen kept kissing Mandruna from one room to the next, while all the guests kept offering her their congratulations and best wishes. Then they sent a courier to her own father, who arrived the very next day. Throughout the whole realm, they celebrated for a week with joy and pleasure. Indeed, nobody had ever seen anything like this before.

So, these folks remained happy and content,
While we here cannot even pay the rent.

———————

Told by Agatuzza Messia in Palermo

16

THE KING OF SPAIN

Gentlemen, this wonderful tale has been told time and again. Once upon a time the son of the King of Spain asked his mother if he could go off and do some hunting with his men.

"Mother, please tell my father the king how much I'd like to go hunting."

"No, my son, you'll get lost!"

"How could I lose my way if I take some troops with me? Give me two regiments of soldiers, and that way there will be nothing to fear."

Thereupon, the queen went to the king and said, "Our son wants to go hunting with his men and wants your permission to go."

"No, my wife," he replied. "He'll get lost if he goes."

However, the queen kept asking until the king called his general, gave him two regiments of soldiers, and said, "Keep your eyes open and watch over my son for a week. If he gets lost, you'll lose your head."

The general took the troops and departed with the prince. When they reached the woods, the prince said, "Now we'll camp here and go to sleep."

While the soldiers slept, the prince left the camp and went on his way. When the soldiers awoke and saw that the prince had left the camp, they cried out, "Ahh, what are we to do! We'll certainly lose our heads!"

They immediately began to spread out looking for the prince in the woods, but they couldn't find him.

"Since we can't find the prince," the general concluded, "we must go and tell the king."

When they returned to the palace, the general said, "Your majesty, you can do with us as you please. The prince disappeared while we were asleep."

"My queen," the king responded, "you see that my words have turned out to be true. So, I'm thinking of cutting off the heads of these poor soldiers."

He decided, however, to pardon them and said, "It's a sign that this is his destiny!"

Now, let us leave the king in his grief and turn to the prince who kept traveling day and night until he came to a cave, where he found a hermit.

"Oh, blessed hermit, I'm lost and would appreciate it if you could tell me where I am."

"Ahh! My son, what's there to tell you?" the hermit replied. "Do you know what you have to do? You must go to my older brother because he can give you better directions than I can."

So, the prince went to the other hermit.

"What do you want here?" the hermit asked him.

And the prince told him everything.

"Don't be discouraged, my handsome lad," he said to him. "There's a house nearby with a magician, who causes trouble to all those who come there. This magician has a daughter. Take this bread and go speak with the daughter who will tell you some secrets that can help you."

The poor young man began to travel once more, and just as the magician's daughter was coming back from fetching water, she saw him.

"Ahh! Handsome lad, what are you doing here?"

The prince recounted everything and asked her to help him get out of there.

"I'll help you," she said to the young man, "but will you marry me if I do?"

"Yes, but what's your name?"

"My name's Bifara. But pay attention. My father's about to come home. My mother's inside the house. I'll take you to my mother for now. When my father comes, he'll say to you: 'Do you want to stay with me? Well, if you do, you must hoe the soil on top of the mountain in an hour, then sow the seeds and reap the harvest, on one side straw and the other side grain.' After my father tells you this, you will travel to the mountain and say: 'Mountain, listen to what you must do now that I am up high. Within an hour everything must be sown and harvested.' Next, my father will say to you, 'Do you see this tree? You're to climb it and collect the little birds in the nest.' After he tells you this, you will climb to the top and say: 'Tree, now that I am up high, here is what you must do in name of the virtuous Bifara.' Now, do you see how large that beautiful oven is? Look carefully, because my father will have you heat it up. When it is very hot, my father will want you to clean it out, and you will say: 'Furnace, when I am inside, you're to become cold in the name of the virtuous Bifara.' Now go, and be on your guard."

She took the young man into the house, and her mother came and said,

"Ahh! I smell some human meat!
When I find the man, he'll be mine to eat."

"Come! Come! Your nose is stuffed," Bifara said to her, "and stop saying such terrible things, mother. I'll tell you the truth. There is a young man who got lost and found his way here. Swear to me that you won't eat him."

If she were to swear, the mother would be obliged not eat anyone. Consequently, when she swore to Biafra, she had to let the young man enter the house. In the meantime the father came and cried out,

"Ahh! I smell some human meat.
When I find the man, he'll be mine to eat."

"Come! Come!" his wife said. "Your nose is stuffed because you've just returned from the woods. We haven't let anyone enter the house."

She gave her husband something to eat, and he kept saying:

"Ahh! I smell some human meat!
When I find the man, he'll be mine to eat."

"Come! Now that you're full, I have something to say to you. I want to tell you the truth. A young man happened to arrive here, and if you'll swear that you won't touch him, I'll let you see him. Neither of us can eat him."

"All right, have him come out."

The prince came out, and the magician said, "Oh, what a nice smell! What's your name?"

"Salvatore."

"Ah! Salvatore! Now you must eat, for tomorrow morning I'll tell you what you must do."

After they gave him something to eat, they all went to bed, and they made up a bed for him. However, Bifara did not lie down. Instead, she went over to him. Toward midnight the magician cried out, "Ahh! Salvatore, Salvatore!"

His old wife responded, "Ahh! Salvatore, Salvatore!"

Then their daughter responded, "And me, too, I want to eat him."

When it turned day, the magician said, "Come, Salvatore, do you see that mountain? Within an hour you have to till the soil, sow the seeds, and reap the harvest with wheat and straw."

The prince took whatever he needed from Bifara and went to the top of the mountain: "Mountain, now that I'm up high, here's what you must do: within an hour you must be hoed and harvested."

After everything had been done, he returned to the magician and his wife.

"Ahh!" the magician said, "You're a talented man! Now, you see that tree?"

"Yes, my lord."

"Do you see how high it is?"

"I see."

"You've got to climb to the top and fetch a nest of little birds."

Salvatore climbed to the top of the tree and said, "Oh tree, high as you are, make yourself low. Do it for the love that Bifara feels for you."

When Salvatore returned with the nest, the magician said, "Ahh! You're a talented man! Now here's what you have to do next. You must heat up that oven over there and make it as hot as possible, and then you have to get inside and clean it out."

"Yes, yes, my lord."

The prince began to heat the oven and then said, "Oh, oven, when I get inside you, you must turn freezing cold, and do it for the love that Biafra feels for you."

Then he got into the oven and cleaned it out. When he came out, the magician said, "You're certainly talented."

After a few days, the magician said that he had to depart and that he and his wife would be away for a week.

"You're to stay with Bifara," he told Salvatore.

When they left, Bifara said to Salvatore, "Now we must leave. My father can smell your scent from a distance of twelve miles, and my mother from ten miles."

So, the two of them fled. After a week passed, the magician returned.

"Bifara!"

Bifara did not respond.

"Ahh! Traitor!" the magician said. "Now I'm going to eat you!"

He left his wife and began running after his daughter and Salvatore. When Bifara saw him, she turned to her lover and said, "Salvatore, my father's coming! Here's what we'll do: I'll turn myself into a gardener and you into broccoli."

When the magician arrived, he found only the gardener and said, "Friend, have you seen a man and woman pass by here?"

"I'm just selling broccoli, cabbage, lettuce, and horseradish."

So, the magician turned around and went home.

"What did you find?" his wife asked.

"One of them became a gardener, and the other a piece of broccoli."

"And why didn't you break them in two!"

"I didn't think of it."

Now the wife pursued them with the intention of killing her daughter.

"Ahh! Salvatore," the maiden said, "my mother's coming. I'll turn myself into a river and you into a fish."

The woman arrived, and instead of going by the river, she tried to catch the fish, but the fish could not be caught. So she cried out, "May you be cursed! Salvatore will forget you!"

Once she uttered this curse, she returned home, and when the magician saw that she hadn't brought back their daughter, he set out again.

"Salvatore," Bifara said, "my father's after us. I'll turn into a church, and you become the sacristan."

When the magician arrived, he said, "Friend, did you see a man and a woman pass by here?"

"Mass will be at one in the afternoon, and if you come at two, there'll be another mass."

"May you be cursed," he said. "Salvatore will forget you forever!" Then he returned home.

"Oh Salvatore," Bifara exclaimed, "you saw how my father cursed me! He'll make you forget me!"

When they arrived near the city, the prince stopped and said he would get a coach from the palace to bring Bifara there in triumph.

"All right," she said to him. "I'll get up on that rock. Be on your guard, because once you're at home, you'll forget about me."

"No, I won't forget about you."

Salvatore went to the palace, and imagine the happiness of his mother. She kissed him all over, and the prince forgot all about Bifara. After a few days passed, Salvatore was going to wed another woman. Bifara knew everything because she had magic powers. Therefore, she took two talking dolls and brought them to the palace, right below Salvatore's window. Then she cried out, "Two talking dolls for sale! Two talking dolls for sale!"

When the prince heard her, he had her summoned up to his room.

"All right," said the prince, "we'd very much like to hear these talking dolls."

All at once, the dolls began to recount everything that had happened to the prince and Bifara. Finally, one of the dolls told all about Bifara's valor, and the prince remembered everything and recognized Bifara. He threw himself at her feet and embraced her. Instead of marrying his bride, he married Bifara.

They remained husband and wife,
And we still don't have a life.

―――――――

Told by Elisabetta Sanfratello at Vallelunga

17

THE KING OF LOVE

Once, so they say, there lived a man, a farmer of wild horse-radish, who had three girls. One day the youngest said to him, "Papa, will you take me with you to pick some horseradish plants?"

"Yes, my girl," and he took her with him. As soon as they arrived at the garden, they began to pick the plants. The maiden caught sight of a beautiful plant some distance away and went there with her father to pull it out. Well, with "I pull" and "You pull," they managed to dig it up. All at once, a Turk appeared and said, "How did you manage to open my master's doorway? Now you must enter so he can decide what your punishment will be."

Consequently, fearing for their lives, they went below, and while they were sitting and waiting, a green bird appeared. They watched him go into a small tub of milk, and then one of water. Afterward he came out, dried himself, and turned into a hand-some young man. Then he turned to the Turk and said, "What do these people want?"

"My Lord, I must tell you that this man and this woman have pulled out the plant and opened up the passage to your under-ground realm."

"How could we know that this was the entrance to your lord-ship's palace?" responded the father. "My daughter saw a beautiful plant, and because she liked it, she pulled it up."

"All right, since this is the case," said the master, "your daugh-ter can stay here and be my wife. Take this little bag of gold coins, and you can go. Whenever you wish to see your daughter, you may come here and feel at home."

So, the farmer took leave of his daughter and departed.

Once the master was alone with the girl, he said to her, "Rusidda (for that was her name), I want you to know that you are the mistress of this place," and he handed her a full set of keys. From that point on, they lived in perfect happiness. One day, however, her two sisters decided to pay her a visit. They knocked and entered. The bird had not yet come back to take his usual bath in milk and water.

"This husband of yours, what is he like?" they asked her.

"I really couldn't say," she answered.

"But how can it be that you spend time with him without knowing who he is and who he isn't?"

"The reason I don't know is that he made me promise that I wouldn't try to find out who he is," Rusidda answered.

"Do you know what you should do? You should pretend that you can't be happy with him unless he tells you who he is."

Eventually, her sisters persuaded Rusidda, and so when the bird returned, took his bath, and turned into a man, she put on an unhappy face for him.

"What's bothering you?" he asked.

"Nothing," she replied.

"It would be better if you told me."

She took a little time to allow him to persuade her and then said, "If you want to know what's bothering me, it's that I want to know what your name is."

"Oh Rusidda, Rusidda, is that really what you want to know, my name?"

"Yes, I want to know it."

"Is that what you really, truly want?"

"Yes, that's what I want."

"All right, if that's really what you want, you must do the following. Take the gold basin and bowl out of the closet and set them on this chair. However, before I even get up on this chair, Rusidda, tell me once more if you really want to know my name. And I warn you, this means trouble for you."

"Yes, that's what I want to know."

So, he got up on the chair, climbed into the basin, and wet his feet.

"Rusidda, do you still want to know my name?"

"Yes."

Now the bird had immersed himself so that the water reached his stomach.

"Rusidda, do you still want to know my name?"

"Yes."

Now the water reached his mouth.

"Rusidda, do you still want to know my name?"

"Yes. Yes. Yes."

"All right then, my name is: *The King of Love!*"

Upon saying that, he vanished. The basin vanished, the palace vanished, and Rusidda found herself out in the middle of a field with not a soul in sight to help her. She called for servants and stewards, but nobody answered. Finally, she said, "Now that he's vanished, I shall have to wander through the world looking for him."

Yet, by this time, she had become pregnant. Nevertheless, she set out on foot, in an advanced state of pregnancy, and walked and walked. She went from one uninhabited region to another, poor thing, so alone that she felt her heart tighten. At a loss for what to do, she cried out:

"Ah, King of Love,
You said it and you did it:
You disappeared from the golden basin,
And who's there forgiving and willing
To take in a poor girl tonight?"

As she began to repeat this, an ogress appeared and said to her, "Oh you miserable creature, how can you be so bold as to search for my nephew? Do you know why I won't eat you on the spot? Well, it is thanks to that little living soul you have in your belly! So come this way, and I'll give you shelter for the night."

So, she took her in and put her to bed. The next morning she gave her a little piece of bread to eat. Then she explained to her,

"We are seven sisters here, each of us is an ogress, and the worst of the lot is your mother-in-law. So be on your toes!"

The girl burst into tears, and when evening came, she set out again on foot. She walked until sunset, and then again, she cried out:

"Ah, King of Love,
You said it and you did it:
You disappeared from the golden basin,
In addition, who's there forgiving and willing
To take in a poor girl tonight?"

As she was crying, another ogress appeared. She was the aunt of the King of Love. First, she gave her a great scolding, but then she offered her shelter for the night in her house. The next morning she gave her a piece of bread and sent her away, telling her the same thing her sister had said.

To be brief, the poor girl walked this way for six more days, and each day an ogress told her the same thing. On the seventh day, she was practically shedding tears of blood and cried even more loudly:

"Ah, King of Love,
You said it and you did it:
You disappeared from the golden basin,
And who's there forgiving and willing
To take in a poor girl tonight?"

Now her sister-in-law appeared, the King of Love's own sister, and she said to her, "Rusidda, Rusidda, since my mother isn't here, come on up."

She lowered her long braids and helped her climb up. Once she had given her something to eat, she said, "Listen, my mother's about to come. She will eat this kneading-trough full of pasta and this entire pig with a whole furnace-load of bread. Afterward, she will drink a whole barrel full of wine. When she is halfway through her meal, you must take her left breast and throw it behind her right side and throw her right breast behind her left side. Then you must grab the ends of her nipples and squeeze so hard that she will almost die. When she cries 'Let go of me, for the love of my son, the King of Spain!' don't let go. Instead, squeeze even harder. When she cries 'Let go of me, for the love of my daughter Rusidda,'[1] don't let go. Then she will shout, 'Let go of me, for the love of my daughter Catarina!' but don't you let go. At last, when she can stand it no longer, she will say 'Let go of me, for the love of my son, The King of Love!'—at that point, let go of her. And now, let me hide you beneath this cup, since my mother is about to arrive."

Consequently, she took her and hid her under a large cup. Meanwhile, Catarina felt a gust of wind, which meant her mother was coming. Sure enough, Mamma-draga the ogress was under the window and began shouting: "Catarina, let down your braids!" So, her daughter looked out the window, loosened her braids, and helped her climb up. As the Mamma-draga entered she said, "Aha!"

"I smell the scent of human meat,
    If I ever find her, she's mine to eat!"

"Oh no, mother, it's because your nostrils are still full of the smell of all the children you have eaten that you imagine that smell is in here. Relax and have your dinner."

Halfway through her meal, Catarina lifted up the cup and let Rusidda out. Rusidda grabbed the ends of Mamma-draga's nipples and squeezed. Feeling herself squeezed like that, the ogress lashed out against her children, but there was nothing she could do. She simply couldn't move, and so she shouted: "Let go of me, for the love of my son, the King of Spain! . . . Let go of me, for the love of my daughter Rusidda! . . . Let go of me, for the love

1 Not to be confused with the protagonist Rusidda; this is a very common Sicilian name.

of my daughter Catarina! . . . Let go of me, for the love of my son, the King of Love!" Suddenly, when she said these last words, Rusidda, who had kept squeezing her, finally let go.

Once she was released, the ogress wanted to devour Rusidda, but her children said to her, "You awful mother! If you devour this innocent child, we'll all run off and leave you completely by yourself!"

"Well if that's the case," she said, "I'm going to write a letter, and you, Rusidda, have to take it to my godmother."

The poor thing, Rusidda, felt uncertain as to what to do when she found herself with this letter. Therefore, she descended into the plain and called out:

> "Ah, King of Love,
> You said it and you did it:
> You disappeared from the golden basin,
> And who's there forgiving and willing
> To take in a poor girl tonight?"

All at once, the King of Love appeared to her and said, "Now do you see? Your own curiosity has brought you to this point."

When the poor girl saw him, she begged his pardon for what she had done, and he took pity and said, "All right, listen to what you must do. You must walk from here until you come to a river of blood. Bend down and scoop up a handful and say, '*What beautiful crystal-clear water! I've never tasted water like this!*' Then you'll come to a garden with a huge amount of fruit. Pick one or two of these, eat them, and say: '*Oh what beautiful pears! Pears like this I've never eaten before!*' As you go on further, you'll come to an oven. Night and day this oven takes in and turns out loaf upon loaf of bread, but nobody ever buys two cents' worth. When you arrive, you must say, '*Oh what beautiful bread! Bread like this I've never eaten before!*' and eat some of it. Further ahead you'll see a doorway, where you'll find two famished dogs. Give them a piece of that bread to eat. Then you'll see an entrance that's all dirty and filled with cobwebs. Take a broom and sweep it all clean. Then go up the stairs, and you'll meet two giants, each with a piece of meat at his side, all dirty. Take a brush and clean them off. As you enter the house, you'll find a razor, scissors, and a knife. Find something to sharpen them with. Once you've done that, you can go in and hand over the letter to my mother's godmother. However, when she tries to get you into the room, snatch up the little casket that you'll see on the table and run away immediately. Make certain you do all the things I've said. If not, you'll pay with your life!"

Rusidda departed, and when she came to the two rivers, she scooped up some blood and drank it and said, "What beautiful, crystal-clear water! I've never tasted water like this!" Then she passed the garden and picked the fruit. In short, she completed all the tasks the King of Love had told her to do. When she went upstairs to the Mamma-draga, she gave her the letter. While that creature was reading it, she snatched the little casket and took off at a run. As soon as the ogress finished reading, she shouted, "Rusidda! Rusidda!" However, Rusidda didn't answer. Realizing she had been tricked, the ogress called out, "Scissors, razor, knife, cut her!"

But they answered, "How long have we been scissors, razor, and knife, and you never bothered to clean us? Rusidda came along and gave us a nice cleaning."

In rage, the Mamma-draga shouted, "Stairway, swallow her!"

"How long have I been a stairway, and you've never bothered to clean me? Along came this girl, and she cleaned me."

Infuriated, the Mamma-draga called out, "Giants, stab her!"

"How long have we been giants, and you've never bothered to sweep away our dirt? Along came this girl, and she swept away our dirt."

"Doorway, swallow her!"

"How long have I been your doorway, and you've never bothered to sweep me? Along came this girl, and she swept me."

"Dogs, devour her!"

"How long have we been your dogs, and you've never bothered to give us a scrap of bread? Along came this girl, and she gave us bread."

"Oven, roast her!"

"How long have I been an oven, and you've never wanted my bread? Along came this girl, and she ate some of my bread."

"Tree, stick her!"

"How long have I been a tree, and you've never picked my fruit? Along came this girl, and she picked some fruit."

"River of mud and river of blood, drown her!"

"And how long have we been river of mud and river of blood, and you've never sampled our water? Along came this girl, and she drank from us."

Meanwhile, Rusidda continued her journey. Finally she couldn't resist the curiosity of seeing what was inside that little casket. She opened it, and out came a company of little dolls, dancing, singing, and playing music. She enjoyed herself for quite some time with these delights, and the dolls had no wish to go back inside the casket. When night fell, and it grew dark, she called out:

"Ah, King of Love,
You said it and you did it:
You disappeared from the golden basin,
And who's there forgiving and willing
To take in this poor girl tonight?"

Now the King of Love himself appeared and said to her, "Ah, so you fell victim to curiosity! As for you, little dolls, I order you back inside at once!"

All the dolls jumped back into the box, and Rusidda continued on her way. Once she reached the Mamma-draga's window, she called to her sisters-in-law, Catarina and Rusidda, who lowered their braids so she could climb up. When the Mamma-draga saw her, she said, "Ah, this success is not your own doing! It comes from my son, the King of Love."

Now the ogress really wanted to eat her, but her daughters restrained her.

"You evil thing! She brought you the little casket, so how can you want to eat her?" they protested.

"All right, but now she must prepare to marry my son, the King of Love. Girl, take these six mattresses and fill them up for me with bird feathers!"

Rusidda picked up the mattress linings, and once outside, she began walking and calling,

"Ah, King of Love,
You said it and you did it:
You disappeared from the golden basin,
And who's there forgiving and willing
To take in this poor girl tonight?"

All at once, he appeared, and she told him the whole story. With a loud whistle, the King of Love summoned the King of Birds.

"Hurry! Have all your birds come here, shed their feathers, and use them to stuff these six mattresses!"

The birds filled the six mattresses, and he ordered them to bring them to his mother's house. When the Mamma-draga saw the six beautifully filled mattresses, she said, "Ah, this gift didn't come from you. It came from my son, the King of Love."

But her daughters said, "What does it matter who it came from, as long as you got your mattresses?"

So, the Mamma-draga made up her son's bed, placing the six mattresses on top of it. The next evening she decided to have him marry the daughter of the King of Portugal. So she called Rusidda and said, "Listen: my son, the King of Love, is getting married, and it's our custom in marriages to have someone at hand kneeling with two lit torches. Therefore, it's your job to hold these lit torches in front of my son's bed."

When the royal couple had gone to bed, it was almost an hour short of midnight. The King of Love said to his bride, "Do you see how weary Rusidda is because of her pregnancy? She can hardly stay on her knees another minute. Why don't you get up just for a bit and take the torches yourself a moment, and let the poor creature lie down?"

The princess got up and let Rusidda lie down. However, the moment the princess had the torches in her hand, the earth opened up and swallowed her, and the King of Love remained happily in bed next to Rusidda.

The next morning Mamma-draga went there, believing that Rusidda was dead. But when she saw her there in the bed, she said, "Oh you wicked creature, sleeping there next to my son! And pregnant, too! My revenge is this: you will not be able to give birth until I take my hands off my head!"

Then she held her hands on top of her head.

When Rusidda began suffering from labor pains, the King of Love was at a loss. So, what did he do? He had a catafalque prepared and lay down on it like someone who had died. Then he had them ring all the bells for the death knell and ordered all the people go about saying, "The King of Love has died!"

The hubbub reached his mother's window. When she heard it, she asked, "What's the meaning of all this noise?"

Her daughters answered, "What do you think it is? Our brother is dead because of you!"

When the Mamma-draga heard this, she lifted her hands from her head and ran about and cried, "Oh, my son, how did he die?"

And as she lifted her hands from her head, Rusidda gave birth. The King of Love got up from his bed and said to her, "Mother, thanks to you, Rusidda has given birth."

When Mamma-draga heard this, she had a heart attack and died on the spot. The King of Love went to get his wife, and afterward he set up a new home with his sisters, and they lived on, happy and content.

> Twiddle dee, twiddle da, now look at me,
> My finger's pointing . . . Who will it be?[1]

———————

Told by the blind Giovanni Patuano at Palermo

18

THE THIRTEEN BANDITS

Once upon a time there was a teacher who had twelve students, and she taught them how to sew in all sorts of ways. The entrance to the teacher's house was inside the city, and the windows faced outside. One day she said to young maidens, "If you hurry up and sew a lot, I'll make you a beautiful dinner with dumplings this Sunday."

The maidens worked hard at their sewing, and on Sunday there was a fine lunch of dumplings. They ate and amused themselves, and there were some dumplings left over for the evening. Then the maidens said to their teacher, "This evening we'll stay here with you, my lady, and later on we'll heat up the rest of the dumplings."

"I have enough beds for all of you," the teacher said. "I'm going to sleep, and you can all enjoy yourselves."

1 Croccu di ccà e croccu di ddà
L'anca di . . . appizata ddà.
Pitrè explains, this is a formula for naming a member of the audience to tell the next story.

Now among the maidens there was the daughter of a merchant who was truly mischievous. That night she went to heat up the dumplings, and she saw a light from the window while she and her companions were in darkness. Then she turned to the others and said, "Listen to me, girls. I want you to tie the sheet around my waist and lower me out the window, and I'll go and see where the light is coming from."

They lowered her, and she ran toward the light. When she reached the light, she saw an open door and cried out, "Anyone here?"

She didn't see anyone, but she saw a table set for twelve people. Then she entered the kitchen and smelled an odor. Everything was so delicious and beautiful! Therefore, she took all the food and carried it away. Saint Peter, help me, but if this place didn't belong to twelve bandits! Nevertheless, she returned safely to the teacher's house.

"Lower the sheet and pull me up," she said, and when she climbed back into the room, she knelt down and let out all the food so that they could eat and have a good time. Meanwhile the teacher slept. When they became tired, they also went to sleep.

Later the bandits returned, and when they entered their house, they saw that there was nothing there and cried out, "Ahh! My God! Some thieves have come and stolen from us. But tomorrow evening we'll see who's causing all this trouble here."

The next day the teacher saw the maidens talking among themselves and said, "What's going on, girls?"

"My lady," they responded, "we must be quiet, for we want to marry." Then, in the evening, they said, "My lady, we want to spend the night here." And they began to play.

Meanwhile, the bandits prepared their meal, and the chief of the bandits began to eat. At the same time, the youngest maiden had herself lowered down by her companions and ran to the palace.

"Anyone here?" she cried out.

Nobody responded, but the chief of the bandits had hidden himself to see who it was, a man or a woman. Then he saw the maiden enter into the kitchen and take the casserole and all the other things. Just as she was about to leave, the bandit appeared and said, "Ahh! You little rascal! This is the second time, and I've got you now!"

"Who are you?" the maiden said. "I needed some light last night, and I came here before going to sleep. However, what was I to do? Listen, we're twelve maidens, and you're also twelve. Tomorrow evening I'll come with all of them, and we'll amuse ourselves."

As she left, he accompanied her and said, "Give me your word that you'll come back tomorrow evening."

"I give you my word," she said and ran to her companions. After she climbed through the window, she told her friends what had happened.

"But sister, why did you tell them we'd come? They'll be our ruin."

"Not at all, girls. Let me take care of things. Tomorrow evening you'll come with me, and we'll amuse ourselves."

The next day she said to the teacher, "This evening you must come with us, and I'll show you a good time. But each one of us must bring a bottle of drugged wine."

The teacher went about her sewing and did some other things. In the evening she went out with the maidens.

"Anyone here?" the maiden cried out as they entered the palace of the thieves.

"Good evening!"

They found a table for twenty-six people.

"I'm going to take my place next to the bandit chief," the maiden said since she only desired him.

They sat down at the table and began to eat. After a while, they took out the bottles of wine that were drugged, and after the glasses were filled, they began to drink. When the maiden saw they had passed out, she cut off the nose of one bandit, the lip of another, and the finger of another. Then she put them on a dish. She was now content, and she and her companions took everything and left.

Now, let us now turn to the bandits. After they recovered from being drugged, they began to talk.

"How curious! You're missing a nose!"

"And you're missing a lip!"

"And you don't have a finger!"

They broke into a rage, and their chief turned to them and said, "Let me take care of this. That mischief maker will pay for all this with her own blood!"

Now let us return to the maiden, who said to the teacher, "Your lady, you must leave the house."

And the teacher did as she was told. In the meantime, the bandit chief took twelve coal sacks and ordered the twelve bandits get inside them. He placed pieces of coal on top of them. Then he disguised himself and went on the road toward Palermo. When he reached the merchant's shop, he offered the twelve sacks of coal to him. They discussed the price, and after the merchant weighed them, they agreed on the price.

Now this merchant's daughter was none other than the mischievous girl, who had been with the teacher and had cut off the noses of the thieves. When she saw the sacks of coal, she said to her father, "Papa, these sacks are not filled with coal. Let me take care of this."

She called the servant, and they made a good fire and heated up the kitchen spits. As soon as the spits were hot enough, *sisss, sisss, sisss*, the maiden took the spits and stuck them into the twelve sacks, killing all the bandits.

The next day the chief waited for the twelve bandits to return with their prize, but he had to keep waiting. Meanwhile, when the father of the mischievous maiden went to the kitchen, there was a terrible smell, and his daughter said to him, "Father, please be quiet because I'm going to show you something."

Soon after she called the servant who took the sacks and opened them. Both her father and the servant were astounded. In turn, the father called for the police and told them what had happened. The police ordered his men to carry off the dead bandits and then went to arrest the chief at his house. The maiden was toasted and celebrated, and the chief was arrested. Then, after flogging him, he was killed.

———————

Told by a woman from Borgo in Palermo

19

THE SILVERSMITH

Once upon a time there was a mother who had three children, two sons and a daughter. Her husband was dead, and her sons supported her through their work. One time—as we know, young people like to enjoy themselves all the time—the sons went hunting, and in the evening they brought their mother a bird with many different colors and a crown of feathers on its head.

"Mamma," they said, "look at this bird. We want you to look after it, and if the bird dies, you'll pay with your life."

The next day, as she was cleaning the birdcage, she found pearls, diamonds, and precious stones. Indeed, she was astounded and took them to a silversmith.

"How much will you give me for these jewels?"

After the man weighed them in his hand and looked at them, he said, "Let's keep it short. Thirty gold coins."

"All right, they're yours."

The next day, as she was cleaning the birdcage, the same thing happened. She went to the silversmith and sold them to him. The third day, the same thing happened. Then also on the fourth. Meanwhile, the silversmith became curious about where the woman got all the jewels. Consequently, one day he said, "Excuse me, lady, where do all these jewels come from?"

"Sir, I have a bird, and when it shits, it spurts out pearls and diamonds."

"Is that so? And do you have any daughters?"

"I have one."

Then one word led to another, and the silversmith said, "I'm single. Would you like me to wed your daughter?"

"Why not?"

Within a short time, they were married. The mother never confided in her children that the bird produced such valuable things. For some time after the wedding the mother continued to gather pearls, but the silversmith didn't enjoy any of this wealth. One time, tempted by the devil, he grabbed hold of the bird and killed it. The poor mother-in-law didn't know what to do because her sons were bound to kill her.

"Where should I go and hide myself when my sons return?"

"Nothing to worry about," her son-in-law said. "If they come, tell them that the cat killed the bird. Buy another one at the market in Palermo, and stick it into the cage."

The mother-in-law did this, and soon her sons showed up.

"Where's the bird?"

"Oh, my dear sons, the cat caught it and killed it. Then I cooked it and put it into the pot. Afterward I went to the market and bought another bird just the same."

"Ahh, what a fool you are, mother!" her sons exclaimed.

They went into the kitchen, and each one of them took a piece of the bird to eat. The older brother grabbed the head with the crown, the younger, took the liver. After eating, they left the house. When they reached the country, the older brother had to go and relieve himself. He went and shat a pouch of gold coins. When he entered the city gate, the guards stopped him.

"Stop! You're under arrest."

"Why?"

"It's been decreed that the first man to enter this city is to be made king."

Therefore, they took him and anointed him king.

The second brother entered but couldn't find his older brother. So he went to an inn and stayed there without knowing where his brother was. The last thing he suspected was that his brother was king! Well, this young man, too, also relieved himself and spewed forth gold and silver, and by dint of this virtue, he became a cavalier. He had lots of clothes, gold chains, and diamond pins. A marvel to behold! Opposite the inn, there was a young woman with an old maid. The cavalier and the woman began to flirt with words and looks until they became engaged. The cavalier spent a good deal of money, and the maiden became curious to know where all his money came from and would have done anything to find out. The stupid cavalier confided the secret to her, and she called for the old woman and told her everything.

"Pretend to be in pain," the old woman said, "and tell him that you need the water of Montepellegrino.[1] When he brings it to you, pretend to drink it, but don't drink it. Then mix it into his lunch, and you'll see that he'll regurgitate the liver, which you're to take and eat. Afterward you'll shit gold."

Everything went well. To be brief, the maiden soon became rich, and the cavalier began to lose money. One day he threatened to kill her if she didn't vomit up the liver and give it back to him. So, the old woman said to the maiden: "Here's what you have to do. Take him into the country where you'll find some particular herbs I'll tell you about. Gather some of these herbs and make a salad for him. Then invite him to eat it together, but you're not to touch it. As soon as he eats the salad, he'll become an ass."

The next day the maiden said, "Don Giovanni, why are you so cold to me? Is it because you threatened me the day before?

---

1 This is a mountain outside Palermo.

But I haven't lost my love for you! I'm still the same, you know! Do you want to go and have a picnic together?"

When he heard those words, he felt more cheerful and said, "Well, if you'd like, let's go."

After they arrived in the country, she gathered some herbs and made a beautiful salad. As soon as they began eating, Don Giovanni turned into an ass. Then she picked up all the things and departed, abandoning him alone like a dog in the country. Then the ass began to wander all over the fields. At the end of one of them, there was an herb that he ate, and he was turned back into the man he was.

"Ahh! I've got it!" Don Giovanni said.

He picked a bunch of herbs that could turn people into asses, and herbs that turned people back into good human beings. Then he left the field. When he reached the city, he went to the inn. As soon as his fiancée saw him, she felt she might die. However, he resumed flirting with her and gave her compliments, even though she was still full of wiles and stood on ceremony. Then, after three or four days, Don Giovanni cooked some herbs that made people turn into asses. He made a delicious dish and sent it to his fiancée. Foolish as she was, she ate the cooked herbs, and after the first fork full, she became an ass.

"Ahh, things are going well," Don Giovanni said.

Then he went and fetched the water of Montepellegrino and made the ass drink it and throw up the liver. Afterward he washed the liver, swallowed it, and began once more to shit gold. Now he took a good halter, harnessed the ass, and hired her out to a miller to carry wheat every day.

One day the ass passed by her own house and began to bray. The old woman who knew everything was standing by the window.

"The poor maiden!" she said. "It's my mistress. I've got to take care of her."

Then she dressed and went to the palace and told everything to the king, who was astonished. He sent a messenger to summon the miller with the ass and his brother. He pretended not to know that it was his brother.

"Well then," he said, "why did you make this maiden become an ass?"

"Ahh, your majesty, I suspect your Highness doesn't know," and he told him everything.

"And you," the king said, "don't you recognize me?"

"No, your majesty."

"How come? Don't you know that I'm your brother?"

"You're my brother?"

Enough said! They recognized each other and embraced.

"Now," the king said to his brother, "let's think about this poor maiden and put an end to her suffering. What herb do you have for turning her back into a woman?"

"There's a particular herb, but . . ."

"No buts, go and gather it!"

The brother could not do otherwise. He went and gathered the herb, and he gave the herb to the ass in front of the king. The ass ate it, and after the first mouthful, the animal was transformed into a woman just as she was before.

"You see that all this is because you behaved so badly," the king said to the maiden. "Now let's put an end to this. Take my brother for your husband, and be happy."

So, his brother married the maiden, and they sent for their mother. Soon everything from their home was now at the palace. The older brother with the crown and the younger brother fabulously rich. Of course,

they lived happy and in peace,
while we sit here picking our teeth.

———————

Told by Agatuzza Messia in Palermo

20

PEPPI, WHO WANDERED OUT
INTO THE WORLD

There was once a widow, who had three children, two girls and a son, who was called Peppi. This son didn't know the first thing about earning his daily bread, while his mother and sisters made a living by spinning.

One day, Peppi said, "Mother, I want to tell you something. I'm going to wander out into the world."

Soon after he took his leave and departed. He walked and walked until he saw a large farmhouse. When he entered, he said, "Do you need a young man to help out here?"

However, as soon he said this, he heard, "Dogs! Dogs, sic him!"

Suddenly, the dogs attacked Peppi, who ran away and continued his journey. When it was almost night, he saw another farmhouse and entered saying, "Viva Maria!"

"And Viva Maria to you! What do you want?"

"If you need a young man . . ."

"Oh," someone said. "Yes. Sit down, sit down. We could probably use a replacement for the cowherd who may be leaving. Wait here while I go ask the boss."

Then one of the farm workers went to ask the owner of the farm, who responded, "Yes. Give him something to eat, and then I'll come down to talk to him about this."

The farmhand gave Peppi some bread and a plate of ricotta, and he began to eat. Meanwhile, the owner came down just as the cowherd had returned, and the owner said to him, "Tell me, are you leaving?"

"Yes, my lord."

Then the owner said to Peppi, "Tomorrow morning you'll go out into the field with the cattle. However, listen to the way

"Get behind me and don't be afraid!" the ox cried out to Peppi. Then the
bull arrived snorting furiously, and the ox and bull went at each other.

things are, my son. If you want to stay here, I can only give you room and board and nothing more."

"All right," Peppi responded. "May God's will be done."

It turned dark, and they all went to sleep. The next morning, Peppi took some bread and butter and went into the fields with the cattle. Some months passed, and Peppi kept taking the cattle into the field and returning to the farmhouse in the evening. When Carnival season approached, Peppi began to sulk, and the owner of the farm came and said,

"Peppi!"

"Oh!"

"What's wrong?'

"Nothing!"

The next morning he left with the cattle, still very sulky. When the owner noticed this, he said to him, "Peppi!"

"Oh!"

"What's wrong?"

"Nothing!"

"Nothing, Peppi? It's better if you tell me."

"And what should I say? The Carnival festivities are approaching, and you have nothing to give me so that I can go to the parties and amuse myself with my mother and my sisters?"

"Hmm, I can give you some things, Peppi, but not money, just as we agreed. If you want bread, take as much as you want."

"But if I want to buy some meat, how can I do that?"

"I can't give you any money. We made a deal long before this."

The next day when it turned light, Peppi went into the field with the calm and patient cattle and was still as sulky as ever. While he was in his gloomy mood, he heard someone calling him: "Peppi!"

He turned around and looked about, and then he said to himself, "It must be fear that's causing me to hear things."

"Peppi, Peppi!"

"Who's calling me?"

"It's me!" One of the oxen said.

"What! You can talk?"

"Yes, but how come you're so sulky?"

"How else should I be? Carnival's coming, and my boss hasn't given me a thing."

"Listen to what you should say, Peppi. When you return this evening, tell him, 'The least you can give me is that old ox.' He will give me to you because he can't stand the sight of me and because I never wanted to work. You'll see, he'll give me to you as a gift."

That evening Peppi returned to the farmhouse gloomier than ever, and his boss said to him, "Peppi, why are you continuing to sulk?"

"I've got to ask you something: why won't you at least give me the ox that's older than a screech owl. At least, when I go home, I can skin it and slice up its hard meat."

"Take it. Get some rope, and take it away!"

The next day Peppi took the ox, put eight loaves of bread in a knapsack, and began walking toward his village. When he reached a large plain, he saw two men on horseback come riding toward him: "Watch out! Watch out! There's a bull on the loose, and it will kill you!"

However, the ox said, "Peppi, tell them, 'If I catch it, will you give it to me?'"

Peppi asked them, and they responded, "What? You'll never be able to catch it. The bull will kill you and the ox together!"

"Get behind me and don't be afraid!" the ox cried out to Peppi.

Then the bull arrived snorting furiously, and the ox and bull went at each other locking horns until the old ox knocked out the bull.

"Peppi, tie the bull up and attach it to my horns," the ox said.

After Peppi tied up the bull, he said good bye to the horsemen and continued on his way with the bull tied to the ox. When the bull revived, it bucked three or four times and then gave up.

After they arrived in another village along the way, Peppi heard a proclamation: "Whoever manages to plow a piece of land and fertilize it within a day will be allowed to wed the king's daughter. In the event that he is already married, he will receive two barrels of gold coins. If he fails, his head will be cut off."

Peppi took the ox and the bull to a stall and then went to the king. The guard didn't want to let him enter because he was so poorly dressed, but the king was at the window and ordered the guard to admit him. When Peppi arrived, he threw himself at the feet of the king.

"What do we have here?"

"I heard the proclamation, and since I have an ox and a bull, I want to see if I can plow the land."

"But did you hear the proclamation well?"

"I heard it. If I fail, I'll lose my head. Nevertheless, your majesty must provide me with a little hay and a plow because I have nothing. I'm just wandering about."

"Bring your ox and bull to my stables, and take care of them," said the king.

Peppi went and took the ox and the bull, and the old ox said to him, "Give me a half a load of the hay, and the bull a whole load."

That evening Peppi was given something to eat, and the next day he was given a plow and four loads of hay, and he left. They indicated which field he was to plow near the village. He harnessed the ox and bull and went to work. By breakfast time, he had plowed almost half the field. So, he ate and gave half a load of hay to the ox and a whole load to the bull. After they finished eating, they continued to work and plow the field.

Meanwhile the king's councilors stood on the balcony and saw how things were going. Then they ran to the king and said, "Your majesty, what's happening? Does your lordship realize that he's almost finished with the plowing? Do you really want to give your daughter to this ugly peasant?"

"Well, what do you advise?" the king said.

"Send him a roast chicken at noon, a bottle of wine that's been drugged, and some good celery."

Soon thereafter, they sent him all of this food and wine, and the servant said to him, "Eat, Peppi. It will refresh you."

Since there only remained a small piece of land to plow, he began to eat along with the animals: the bull, a load and a half of hay, the old ox, one-half a load of hay, while Peppi enjoyed the chicken and the wine. After he drank all the wine and ate the chicken, he fell asleep.

When the old ox saw that the bull had enough hay, it didn't say anything, but when it saw that the bull had finished eating, it began to shake Peppi with its hoof.

"Ah, ah, ah," Peppi said.

"Get up," said the ox. "Get up, or else they'll chop off your head!"

Consequently, Peppi got up, washed his face, and harnessed the ox and the bull. He finished plowing the small piece of earth and began fertilizing it. It was now eight in the evening, and the councilors were watching from the window and saw that he had already fertilized half the field. "Ah, we didn't use enough opium!"

Meanwhile, Peppi was working with all his might, and he finished by midnight. He put away the plow, and after taking care of the ox and the bull, he returned to the palace and addressed the king,

"May your lordship bless me, dear father!"

"Oh-oh! . . . You've finished? . . . What do you want? Do you want two barrels of gold coins?"

"Your majesty, I'm a bachelor. What would I do with the gold coins? I want to get married right away!"

So they immediately took him, washed him, and dressed him like a prince. Indeed, he seemed fit to be a prince. They even gave him a watch. And so, he was married just as the king had married off his two other daughters to princes.

"Now that you've married, you must slaughter me," the old ox said to Peppi. "Then you are to collect my bones in a basket except for one hoof that you're to put in your mattress. Afterward, take the bones that you've collected in the basket and plant them one by one in the field that you've plowed. As for my flesh, you're to give it to the cook and tell him to prepare it any way he wants as rabbit, hare, chicken, sheep, fish, or whatever he wants."

Enough said. Peppi slaughtered the ox. The king didn't want him to do this, but Peppi said, "Nothing to get upset about. I'm doing it so that you'll have plenty of meat."

He ordered the cook to prepare the meat as though it came from different animals and to put the bones and the hoof aside, and a large banquet was prepared. There was a big table, and the king began to eat the different dishes: "This is hare and that's rabbit. What a large feast! The best meat!"

After they ate, they got up from the table, took a beautiful walk, and returned in the evening to go to bed. As soon as Peppi's wife fell asleep, he slipped the hoof into the mattress. Then he took the basket on his back, went into the garden, and planted the bones in orderly fashion. Afterward he returned to the bed without making a sound so that his wife heard nothing.

When they woke up, his wife said, "Oh! Oh! What a dream I had! It was if many cherries and apples were hanging before my mouth. I saw lots of roses, pink carnations, jasmine, and other flowers . . . Oh, what an aroma! It's as if they were still slightly grazing my face!" She stretched out her hand and picked an apple. "Look, my dream is true!" she cried.

"Let's see," her husband responded, and he stretched his hand and gathered some cherries. As soon as he had them, he cried, "How beautiful!"

Now the king and all the people in his court got up, and when they stood at the window, they smelled an aroma that refreshed their hearts. The king began to eat the rare fruit. Then he drank some coffee. Meanwhile his councilors stood on the balcony and looked at the ground that Peppi had plowed, and they saw that it was filled with all sorts of trees. Then they rubbed their eyes and said, "But it's true. Our eyes are not deceiving us!"

They called the king and said, "Your lordship, look. Doesn't that orchard belong to the land that Peppi had plowed and fertilized?"

The king, too, rubbed his eyes and said, "It really is true. My eyes aren't deceiving me."

They got into carriages to go and see, and when they arrived, they found orange trees, lemon trees, plum trees, cherry trees, vineyards, fig trees, peach trees, and many other kinds, all bearing fruit. The king gathered a little fruit and then returned to the palace.

Soon after, when the other two princes saw all this, they said to their wives, "Go and ask your sister how all this was done."

So, they went to her and asked, "How did your husband manage to do all this?"

"How am I supposed to know?"

"You silly thing! Ask him!"

"I'll ask him tonight."

"All right, and then come and tell us."

That evening, when they went to bed, she began to ask her husband with such insistence that he confided everything in her just to keep her quiet. The next day, his wife went and told her sisters, and in turn, they told their husbands.

One day, when they were all together with the king, the princes said to Peppi, "Let's make a bet, cousin Peppi."

"What kind?" Peppi responded.

"We bet that we can guess how you managed to get all those trees to grow."

"Agreed!"

"All right, if we win, you have to give us all the things that you've acquired here, and if you win, we have to give you all that we possess."

They went to a notary and signed an agreement. Once that was done, the princes guessed rightly, and Peppi had to give them everything he owned and was left with nothing—moreover, now he began to starve. Consequently, one day, the disgraced Peppi took a sack, dressed himself in his old clothes, and departed.

After he had walked for some time, he arrived at a hut and knocked.

"Who is it?" a hermit asked.

"It's me, father."

"And where are you going?"

"Can you tell me where the sun rises?"

"Oh, my son! You can spend the night here. Tomorrow morning, you're to follow the path, and you'll meet a man who's much older than I am."

At dawn, the next day, the hermit gave him a little bread. Peppi took his leave and departed. He began walking and reached another hut where a hermit with a white beard that reached his knees was living.

"My blessings, holy father!"

"What do you want? What do you want?"

"Can you tell me where the sun rises?"

"Ah, my son, keep walking. Up ahead there is a man who's much older than I am."

Peppi took his leave and departed. When he arrived at another hut, he kissed the hands of the hermit and said, "May God bless you, my honorable father!"

"Where are you going?"

"Can you tell me where the sun rises?"

"Ah, my son! . . . Enough . . . Perhaps you'll get there. Take this pin. Walk on, and when you hear a lion roar, you're to say, 'Friend lion, your friend the hermit has sent greetings. I've brought this pin to take out the thorn in your paw, and in exchange I ask that you let me speak with the sun.'"

Peppi departed, and when he reached the lion, he removed the thorn from his paw.

"Ah, you've given me back my life!" the lion said.

"Now you must help me speak with the sun."

"Come!" And the lion took him to a large sea of black water. "Don't move from here. A serpent will emerge before the sun appears, and you're to say, 'Oh friend serpent, your friend the lion sends his greetings, and in exchange I'm asking you to help me speak with the sun.'"

The lion left, and Peppi watched as the water began to stir, and when the serpent appeared, Peppi did as the lion told him to do.

"Peppi," replied the serpent, "quick, jump into the water and get under my wings. Otherwise, the sun's rays will burn you!"

Peppi got under a wing, and when the sun rose, the serpent said to him, "Quick, tell the sun what you want to say before it goes away!"

Then Peppi began: "Oh sun, you traitor! It must have been you who deceived me! Why did you do this, you terrible traitor?"

After hearing this accusation, the sun said, "It wasn't me who deceived you. It was your wife! You revealed your secret to her!"

"Well then, please pardon me, oh sun. However, I would like a favor. Can you set at twelve-thirty tonight so that I can go and regain my things?"

"All right, I'll do this favor for you."

Soon after, Peppi took his leave, thanked everyone along the way, and returned home.

When he arrived, his wife brought him some broth so he felt refreshed. Then he sat down once more with the princes and said to them, "Well now, my cousins, let's make a wager."

"What can you bet if you no longer have anything?"

"I'll bet my head, and you bet all your things that you own as well as the things that you acquired from me."

"Agreed, but what should we bet on?"

"Let's bet when the sun will set," Peppi replied.

"Good!" the princes said among themselves. "He's insane. He doesn't even know when the sun will set." Then they turned to Peppi: "All right, we bet the sun will set at eleven thirty."

"And I say that the sun will set at twelve thirty."

They went to sign the agreement and then began watching the sun that began setting at eleven thirty. At this point Peppi said, "Oh sun, is this the way you keep your word?" Then the sun, instead of setting, slowed down so that it finally set at twelve thirty.

"What did I tell you?" Peppi said.

"You were right!" the princes said, and Peppi took all their things and regained all of his own possessions as well. Then he said to the princes, "All right, now I want to show you what a peasant's heart is truly like!"

Indeed, they had always said that he was a peasant! Meanwhile, he gave them back all their things and said, "Take them. I don't want things that belong to other people. I only want what belongs to me."

Consequently, he kept his own and gave back all their things. Then he withdrew to live with his wife as he had lived with her before. As for the king, he embraced Peppi, took off his crown, and set it on Peppi's head. Imagine how angry the princes were when they saw the crown on Peppi's head! However, they didn't show it. The next day there was a magnificent banquet. All the relatives were invited, and they enjoyed themselves. The dishes came one after another and ended with coffee, ice cream, and also cream cakes—and so Peppi, the cowherd, who had once been starving from hunger, became a king.

Told by Antonio Loria and collected by Leonardo Greco at Salaparuta

21

THE MAGIC PURSE, CLOAK, AND HORN

Once upon a time, so it's been told, there was a father who had three sons, and the only thing he had was a house. One day, he sold the house, and he kept the rights to three round tiles laid in the ground in front of the door. When death approached, he wanted to write a will even though his relatives said to him, "What can you leave behind you? You have nothing."

In fact, his sons did not want to call for the notary. However, some other friends went and did this. When the notary arrived and asked the father what he should write, he responded, "I had a small house and sold it, keeping three tiles for myself. I want to leave the first tile to my oldest son, the second to my middle son, and the third to my youngest."

These three sons were not very content. Moreover, they were also starving. When the father died, the eldest son thought about his situation and said, "I can't manage to make a living in this country. It's better that I take the tile that my father left me, and travel to another country."

When he went to the house to detach the tile from the ground, the new owner asked him to leave it alone, for she had paid for it. However, he became annoyed and said, "No, my father left me the tile, and I'm going to take it with me!"

Indeed, he detached the tile and found a tiny purse beneath it. Then he took the purse along with the tile and departed. When he arrived at a certain place, he decided to rest, stuck his hand into the purse, and said, "Purse, give me two coins so that I can buy a little bread." Well, he immediately found two coins inside, and as soon as he saw them, he said, "Oh purse, give me a hundred gold coins." Then the purse gave them to him and continued to give him as much as he wanted.

Soon he became rich and amassed a great deal of money until he had enough to build a palace in front of the king's palace. He often stood by the window, and whenever he looked out, he saw the king's daughter standing in her window. Consequently, he began to flirt with her, and at the same time, he formed a friendship with the king who invited him into his palace. When the princess saw that he was richer than her father was, she said, "I'll take you for my husband, but only after you reveal to me where all your money comes from."

Simple-minded as he was, he trusted her and showed her the purse. Without arousing his suspicion, she drugged him with opium, and after he fell asleep, she had a similar purse made and exchanged it with the one that always produced money. When the young man awoke, he saw that his purse no longer produced money, and in order to eat, he began to sell all his fine things until he became poor again and didn't have a penny left in his pocket.

In the meantime, he learned that his middle brother had become rich, and he decided to seek him out. When he arrived, they kissed and embraced, and the young man told his brother all about his misfortune. Then he asked, "How did you manage to become so rich?"

Then his brother told him that, at one point, he had nothing and, therefore, decided to go and take the tile that their father had left him. To his surprise, he found a cloak beneath the tile. Then he put it on for a joke and realized that people didn't see him. He tried it another time and mingled among many people. However, they didn't see him. So what did he do? Well, since he was dying of hunger, he went into a tavern, took some bread, food, and other things, and left without being seen. Soon thereafter, he began to rob silversmiths and shopkeepers. He even went and plundered the king and became so rich that he didn't know what to do with all the money.

"If this is the way things are," the poor brother said, "well, if this is really the way things are, dear brother, do me a favor and

lend me the cloak until I set things straight again, and then I'll
return it to you."

Since his brother loved him very much, he gave him the cloak
and said, "Of course. Take it. Make yourself rich and then return
it to me."

"As soon as I've restored things, my brother, I'll return it to you."

Then he took his leave and departed. As soon as he was on his
way, he immediately began robbing even more so than his brother
had done. He stole money, gold, silver, and anything he could
find. When he became wealthy again, he began visiting the king
and flirting with the princess. When she saw that he had become
richer than he was before, she began to treat him kindly.

"Where did you get all this money from?" she asked. "And
how did you become richer than my father? If you tell me, I'll
make you happy, and we can marry right away!"

Since she seemed sincere, he placed his trust in her once again
and showed her the cloak. But what did the princess think of doing? Well, she said, "You know what we'll do? First we'll eat, and
then we'll enjoy ourselves."

So, he ate and drank, and she drugged him with opium one
more time. Then she had a similar cloak made and robbed him
of the one that made him invisible. When he was awake again,
he took his leave and went away. Only some time later did he become aware that he no longer had the real magic cloak. He usually visited a maiden who had six brothers and wore the cloak so
that the brothers never saw him kissing her. When he returned
there, they were all together. Therefore, he entered quietly, as he
usually did, approached her, and began kissing her and embracing her, thinking that nobody saw him. However, this time her
brothers saw him quite clearly and became outraged. They ran
after him and gave him a tremendous beating, leaving him more
dead than alive. In disgrace, he had no other choice but to leave
that country and return to his own, limping all the way. During
his journey, he managed to earn some bread by working. Once he

arrived home, he learned that his youngest brother had become quite rich. He had a beautiful palace with many servants. Therefore, he thought, "Now I'll go to visit my brother. I'm sure he won't kick me out."

In fact, when his brother saw him, he said, "Dear brother, where have you been? I thought you were dead."

And he kissed and embraced him with a happy face. When the older brother saw such a warm reception, he summoned his courage and asked, "How did you become so rich?"

"You know that our father left me the third tile," he said. "Well, one day when I was desperate, I went to detach the tile to sell it, and underneath I found a horn. When I saw it, I began blowing it out of fun. As soon as I did this, many soldiers appeared all at once and declared, 'Your desire is our command!' Then I took a deep breath and blew the horn again, and tons of soldiers appeared. When I was sure that everything worked well, I began marching to different cities and ordered my soldiers to start all kinds of wars and battles to get money. As soon as I had enough money, I returned here and had this palace built. Now you know how I managed to become so rich."

After they finished their conversation, the older brother asked him to do him a favor and lend him the horn because he, too, wanted to become rich, and he would return the horn as soon as he did this. The younger brother agreed, provided that he return the horn. Then they embraced and kissed each other, and the poor brother went out to seek his fortune.

In fact, he headed directly toward a city known for its wealth and blew the magic horn. All at once, many soldiers emerged, and when they had filled an entire plain, he ordered them to sack the city. Within a short time, they returned to him loaded with money, silver, and rich merchandise and deposited everything with him. Those soldiers who didn't bring him anything, he blew back into the horn. Then he went to the city where the king was living with his only daughter. He took some rooms in the finest tavern and had all his money and merchandise put in a safe place.

Afterward, he blew the rest of the soldiers back into the horn and then put the horn away. When he went to visit the princess and her family, he was received as usual with great cordiality and remained for dinner.

However, the princess could think of nothing but how she might find out how he had become so rich once again. Therefore, she began to flatter him in her usual way and to treat him kindly until he confided in her that he had a magic horn, and he could even make millions of soldiers come out of it—and he would show it to her.

The princess pretended not to be interested, but at lunch she gave him a drug that would make him sleep twenty-four hours, the time that she needed to get the magic horn and to make a counterfeit one. When he awoke the next day, the king and his daughter pretended to be mortified and sent him away because he had drunk too much.

Humiliated, he went to another country taking with him all his wealth and money that he still possessed. Along the way, however, twelve robbers appeared, and he thought he still had the horn that would quickly take care of them. When he blew it to summon the soldiers and wipe out the twelve robbers, he blew in vain. The thieves robbed him, and they gave him a good beating because he was so bold to have wanted to fight against twelve armed men. They left him lying on the ground, and it was a miracle that he was more alive than dead with the horn in his mouth that he continued to blow. Finally, he realized that it was not the magic one. Thinking that he had ruined himself and his brothers as well, he decided to make an end of his life and throw himself off a cliff.

After walking a great distance, he came to the top of a cliff where he took a great leap and jumped off. However, before he could hit the ground, he found himself caught in a tree of black figs. Seeing that the tree was loaded with such beautiful fruit, he decided to have a fine meal. "At least I'll die with a full stomach!" he said to himself. However, after he had eaten about thirty, he began to feel horns sprouting all over him, on his head and his nose, and he became a real monster. Now he was even more despondent, and he threw himself once more from another cliff to kill himself. Yet, after he fell a few feet, he found himself stuck on another fig tree, this time loaded with white figs, even more than the other tree had. The poor fellow had bruises all over and decided to rest a bit, but when he saw the beautiful figs, he said to himself, "I can't grow any more horns than I already have, and besides I have to die—I might as well make a good meal out of them!"

Then, no sooner did he taste three of them than he discovered that three of his horns disappeared. Therefore, he continued to eat, and with each fig, one of his horns disappeared. Indeed, he kept eating until all the horns had disappeared—and he was better looking than before.

When he saw that he no longer had any horns, he decided to shake the tree and gathered a good quantity of black figs. Then he returned with them to the city more handsome than he ever was. Later, he put the black figs in a beautiful basket, dressed himself as a peasant, and went to the palace to sell them because they were out of season. The guard called him and brought him to the king, who immediately paid him for the figs. After he was paid, he kissed the knees of the king and went away.

At lunch, the king and his entire family ate the beautiful figs. Since the figs pleased the princess so much, she ate more than the others. Once lunch was finished, they suddenly saw that their bodies and faces were covered with horns, and the princess had more than anyone else did. They were all astounded and had no idea how to get rid of the horns. Consequently, they summoned all the doctors of the city, but the doctors said that there was no remedy. Then the king issued a proclamation announcing that whoever could get rid of the horns would be granted any favor he wanted and all his wishes would be fulfilled.

When the seller of the figs heard this proclamation, he returned to the white figs and gathered a beautiful basket full of them. Then he put them in a kind of purse, dressed himself as a doctor, and went to the king. The guard let him pass, and he mounted the palace stairs and presented himself to the king.

"Your majesty, I can save you and everyone else. I know how to get rid of the horns . . ."

When the princess heard these words, she turned to her father and said, "Your highness, let me be the first to have the horns removed!"

The king consented and sent them to a room for a week. As soon as they were alone, the doctor said, "Do you recognize me? Listen to what I have to say: if you restore the purse that produces money, the cloak that makes you invisible, and the magic horn, I will get rid of your horns. If not, I'll cause even more to grow!"

The princess had suffered a great deal of pain, and she knew that the young man had already possessed many magic things. Therefore, she believed him and said, "Yes, I'll return everything to you on the condition that you get rid of all the horns and become my husband."

He consented, and the princess returned the magic purse, cloak, and horn. Consequently, he had her eat as many white figs as there were horns on her—and all the horns disappeared.

After he removed the horns from the princess, he took care of the king, the queen, and all the others who had eaten the figs. Finally, he asked for the hand of the princess as his reward. The king granted his wish, and they were married.

Now the young man returned the cloak and horn to his brothers, and he kept the purse. He remained the king's son-in-law, and after a year, when the king died, he and his wife became king and queen. Of course,

> they were happy and content,
> But we still can't pay the rent.

———

Collected by Salvatore-Pasquale Vigo and told by Lionardo at Màngano

22

KING ANIMMULU

I have heard tell of a shoemaker who had three daughters, Peppa, Nina, and Nunzia, and they were all terribly poor. One day the father went out and scoured the countryside, but he could find nothing, not even a penny. When he returned empty-handed, his wife said to him, "Good-for-nothing that you are, you haven't brought back a single penny!"

This upset him so much that he turned to his daughter Nunzia and said, "Let's go out and try to find some soup greens."

So, off they went and arrived at the Commune.[1] As they began searching, Nunzia discovered a fat fennel plant and called out, "Oh father, father, look what I found! It's too big for me to pull up." So he went over, and when they pulled together, they saw a doorway with a young man looking out.

"Hey pretty girl, what are you looking for?" he said to Nunzia.

"And what do you think we're searching for? We're starving to death, and we've come to pick some soup greens."

"I can make you rich," the young man said to the shoemaker. "Just leave your daughter with me, and I'll give you a sack of money."

At first, the father was reluctant and said, "What? How can I leave my daughter, poor thing?" However, at last, he let himself be persuaded. Consequently, he left his daughter, took the money, and departed.

The maiden, who was left behind, went beneath the ground and discovered a beautiful house filled with riches, so elegantly furnished that she thought she was in heaven. She and the young man lived there together, but she was always weeping for her father.

1 The former fief of Salaparuta.

Let us leave them for now and turn to the father, who was now able to eat meat all day long. While he was thus enjoying himself, his second daughter Peppa asked him, "Father, please take me to see my sister?"

Soon afterward, they went to the same spot where the fennel was, and the same young man looked out, and the father and daughter entered. Once they were inside, Nunzia showed her sister all around the house, but there was one room she wouldn't let her see, because her husband kept the key to himself. Suddenly poor Nunzia didn't feel very well, and so she asked her sister, "Would you mind combing my hair?"

When her sister began combing her hair and started to undo the braid at the back of her head, she found a key attached there. Well, that sneaky sister said to herself, "How selfish my sister is! She's prevented me from seeing the whole house and kept the key to herself!"

So what did she do? As Nunzia was dozing off, her sister detached the key, went to the secret room, and opened it. Well, she found it filled with pretty young women, all doing embroidery. It turns out that Nunzia was expecting a baby, and they were making clothes for it. However, the moment they saw her, their faces all grew yellow and pale and became exceedingly ugly. Then they vanished, some turning into lizards and some into snakes.

When Nunzia woke up, Peppa said to her, "Sister, you must allow me to leave at once, this very instant."

"Why?"

"I simply need to go."

"But won't you at least tell me why?"

"All right. I found the key in your hair, and I went and opened the door and found all those women."

"Oh sister of mine, you've completely destroyed me!" she said, as Peppa departed.

Just then Nunzia's husband returned, and the women in the room—who were fairies, of course—said to him, "You must send your wife away at once!"

He burst into tears and asked, "Why?"

"Just send her away immediately, we command you! Send her away!"

Oh, that poor unhappy maiden! Her husband was forced to go to her and say, "You must leave here at once, otherwise I am lost!"

Nunzia burst into tears, but he said to her, "Here, take this gray ball of yarn and tie it to this doorknob. When you come to the place where the yarn ends, that's where you must stay."

So, she set out walking and traveled a great distance. Finally, she arrived under the balcony of a very beautiful palace, which belonged to King Animmulu.

"Can you please offer me shelter, just a little hut where I can stay?" she called out.

"At this moment my lord and lady are seriously troubled," a servant woman answered her. "Their son has been stolen from them, and they have no way of finding him."

But Nunzia simply repeated her request: "Just a little hut, even a hen-house, just any place where I can stay?"

The servant took pity on her, went to the queen, and said, "There's a poor unfortunate maiden here. Let us give her some shelter."

So they put her in the woodshed and brought her a bit of bread, seeing how famished she was. Well, the queen took a liking to this girl, and every morning she had coffee sent to her. However, when she asked her, "Whose daughter are you?" her only answer was, "Ah, if only you knew what I've gone through!" and she wouldn't say another word.

Meanwhile, after she had been in that house for some time, she gave birth to a baby boy one fine morning. Just then a maid happened to enter her room, and she immediately ran back to the queen saying, "Come quickly, your Majesty! That girl has given birth to a beautiful baby boy, and he's the very image of your son."

Meanwhile—returning to the young prince—the fairies were telling him, "How little you know! Why just this day your wife has given birth to a son. Would you like to go and visit the baby this evening?"

"By God, yes, please take me there!"

And in a few hours they were at her door. After they knocked, Nunzia asked, "Who's there?"

"It's me, please open!" he answered.

As he entered, together with the fairies, the room became covered by gold tapestry; the bed with its hangings became embroidered in gold; the baby's crib became all gold; and there was a light that made it seem like day. Music was everywhere, and the fairies were singing and dancing. Then the father began rocking his son in the cradle and sang to him:

> King Animmulu should now know
> His son has produced an heir to the throne!
> Swaddling of gold enfolds you,
> A golden cradle rocks you.
> Ah! I would keep you all night long!
> Now sleep, my love, to my cradle song.

In the meantime, the fairies danced, and as they looked out the window, they sang this song:

> No roosters are crowing,
> No clock is striking.
> Dawn has yet to ring—not yet!

Now let us leave them there and return to the queen. A maid came to her and shouted, "Oh my queen, you must come and see what is going on in the stranger's room! It's no longer a hen house—it's all illuminated and looks like paradise! I hear singing that sounds like your son's voice. Just come and listen!"

So, the queen went to listen. However, they couldn't hear anything, and so they returned to the palace. The next morning, the fairies departed, and the queen herself went down to the hen house to bring the maiden's coffee. "Are you willing to tell me who was here last night?"

"I really can't tell you," Nunzia replied. "But if you only knew who had been here!"

"Ah then," replied the queen, "could it have been my son?" When she carried on so much, the maiden finally had to tell her the whole story, starting from where she went looking for soup greens and up to the present. When she finished, the queen said to her, "And so you are my son's wife," and began giving her hugs and kisses. Then she said, "Ask him how he can be freed from the spell."

"I'll ask him tonight."

When nighttime arrived, the fairies came again at the same hour with the king's son. Once again, they all danced while he rocked his son in the cradle and sang to him: "King Animmulu should now know . . ."

While the fairies were dancing, the maiden said to her husband, "Ask the fairies how you can be freed from the spell."

"I know what can set me free," he answered. "You must prevent the roosters from crowing, the clock from striking, and the morning bells from ringing. Moreover, you have to cover the whole street with a great dark canvas that looks like the sky, with the moon and stars in it, so that no one can see when dawn arrives. Then, just at the moment when the sun reaches mid-heaven, snatch away the canvas! The fairies will all turn into snakes and lizards and disappear."

In the morning, the queen came to her and asked, "What did my son tell you?"

Then the maiden told her all that they had to do. Consequently, the king issued an edict: "Let no bells or clocks ring! Let all roosters be killed!"

Everything was prepared as it had to be. When evening came, the fairies again began to sing and make music, and the prince began his song: "King Animmulu should now know . . ."

The fairies looked out the window and sang their song:

No rooster is crowing,
No clock is striking.
Dawn has yet to ring—not yet!

They spent the whole night dancing and frequently looked out the window, but seeing that it was still nighttime, they continued their song: "No rooster is crowing . . ." The moment finally came when the sun had reached mid-heaven. At that moment, the king's servants pulled away the canvas, and all at once, the fairies turned into snakes and lizards and disappeared. Now the king's son and his wife could go to the royal palace and take their rightful place. They had a wedding with a beautiful banquet, and all enjoyed a lovely feast.

So they remained, happy and content,
While we here cannot even pay our rent.

————————

Told by Rosa Cascio La Giucca and collected by Leonardo Greco in Salaparuta

23

TRIDICINU

Here's a story they tell over and over again. Once there was a father with thirteen sons, and the smallest was called Tridicinu.[1] The father was unable to support his sons, but he did whatever he could to get soup on the family table. Their mother would call them to the table crying out, "First come, first served for hot soup." Tridicinu always arrived there first, and received

1 From the word for thirteen, *tridici* (Ital. *tredici*). An English equivalent might be "Thirteeny."

the first portion of minestrone. For that reason, his brothers began to hate him and were ready to use any means to get rid of him.

Now, it so happened that the king issued a proclamation to the whole city that whoever was brave enough to go and steal the Papa-ogre's winter blanket would receive a bushel of gold coins. Upon hearing this, the brothers went to the king and said, "Your Majesty, we have a brother called Tridicinu, who is brave enough to do this and more besides."

"Bring him to me at once!" replied the king.

Soon thereafter, they brought Tridicinu to the king.

"Your Majesty," he asked, "how could I possibly steal the ogre's blanket? When he sees me, he'll eat me."

"Don't worry, just go!" said the king. "I know that you are brave, and you'll be able to perform this courageous act."

When Tridicinu arrived at the Papa-ogre's house, he found that the ogre had gone out, but the Mamma-ogre was in the kitchen. Tridicinu sneaked in quietly and hid under the bed. In the evening, the Papa-ogre returned, ate dinner, and went to bed. As he lay down, he growled:

I smell the scent of human meat!
Whoever I see, I'm ready to eat.

The Mamma-ogre answered, "Calm yourself and go to sleep. No one has come into this house."

When the ogre began to snore, Tridicinu gave a little tug on his blanket. The ogre woke up.

"Who's there?"

"Meow! Meow!" answered Tridicinu, pretending it was the cat. The Mamma-ogre clapped her hands with a "Scat! Scat!" and then went back to sleep beside her ogre husband.

At this point Tridicinu gave a huge tug, snatched the blanket, and ran off. The ogre heard him running, recognized him in the dark, and said, "I know who you are—you're Tridicinu! No doubt about it!"

Some time went by, and the king issued another proclamation announcing that whoever could capture the ogre's horse and bring it to him would receive a bushel of gold coins. Tridicinu offered himself again, and this time he asked the king for a silken ladder and a sack of honey-cakes. Once he received these items, Tridicinu set out and arrived at the ogre's house at night. He entered without being heard and went to the stable. The horse whinnied when he saw him, but Tridicinu gave him a honey-cake and said, "See how sweet this is? If you come with me, my master will supply you with these forever." Then he gave him another and said, "Just let me mount you, and I'll show you how to get there." And so, he mounted the horse, feeding him honey-cakes as they went, and delivered him to the king's stable.

Now the king issued still another proclamation that he would give *two* bushels of gold coins to whoever brought him the bolster from the ogre's bed. Tridicinu said, "Your Majesty, who would ever be able to do this? That bolster is full of little bells, and the ogre sleeps so lightly that even a breath of air will wake him up."

"That's not my concern," said the king. "I must have it at all costs."

Therefore, once again, Tridicinu went off and managed to hide himself under the ogre's bed. When it was midnight, he stretched out his hand, gently . . . gently . . . but the little bells all started ringing.

"Who's there?" asked the ogre.

"It's nothing," answered his wife. "Maybe it's the wind that's making the bells ring."

However, now the ogre's suspicions were aroused. He only pretended to sleep, but kept his ears open. Tridicinu stretched out his hand again, and *bam!* The ogre grabbed hold of him.

"Caught you this time!" he said. "Now just watch how I'll make you cry for all you're worth!"

Then he threw Tridicinu into a barrel and began feeding him with figs and raisins. After some time went by, the ogre said, "Stick out your finger, Tridicinu, so I can see how fatter you are."

However, Tridicinu had found a mouse's tail, and he stuck that out instead of his finger.

"Oh, how skinny you are," said the ogre, "and also a bit smelly! Eat, my son, take more figs and raisins so you'll fatten up quickly."

More days passed, and the ogre again asked him to show his finger. This time Tridicinu stuck out the tip of a spindle. "Poor boy, still thin as a rail, are you? Well, eat some more so you'll soon get fat."

By the end of a month, Tridicinu had run out of things to substitute and had no choice but to show his own finger. The ogre began shouting for joy: "Hooray! He's finally nice and fat!" The ogress came running, and he said to her, "Quick, my dear wife, start up the oven and keep it hot for three days while I go and round up all our relatives. This Tridicinu will make for a glorious feast!"

The ogress spent three days heating up the oven, and at the end of this time she took Tridicinu out of the barrel and said, "Come here, Tridicinu, and look, we're about to roast the lamb."

But he read her thoughts, and when he was close to the oven, he said, "Oh ogress, what's that nasty black thing I see deep in the corner?"

The ogress bent down a little but saw nothing.

"Bend a little closer," said Tridicinu, "so you can see it."

When she bent a little further, Tridicinu grabbed her by the feet, threw her into the oven, and covered it with a heavy slab. When she was fully cooked, he took her out all neat and clean, divided her at the waist, cut up her legs into small portions and set them out on the table. Then he set her torso with her arms and head on her bed under the sheets and tied one string to her chin and another behind her brow.

When the ogre arrived with his guests, they found the plates all set out on the table. Then they went to the bed and asked, "Madam ogress, would you like to eat?"

Tridicinu tugged the string and the ogress raised her head to say "no."

"What's the matter, are you tired?"

Tridicinu from under the bed tugged the other string, making her nod down for "yes." One of the guests, however, went up close, moved away the sheets, and discovered that the ogress was dead and only half a body.

"We've been tricked! We've been tricked!" he shouted, and everybody came running to the bed. In all this hubbub and confusion, Tridicinu managed to escape and make his way back to the king, taking with him the bed-bolster and the best of the ogre's possessions.

When all this was accomplished, the king said to Tridicinu, "Listen, Tridicinu, to complete all your acts of bravery, I want you to bring me the Papa-ogre himself, in person, alive and well."

Tridicinu's first reply was, "Your Majesty, really!" However, immediately he recovered himself and said, "I'll manage it."

So he had a very strong chest made, dressed himself like a monk with a long fake beard down to his knees, went up the hill where the ogre lived, and stood in front of his house. Then he began to shout, calling the ogre and saying, "You know that rascal Tridicinu? He just killed our chief monk. If you manage to catch him, shut him up in this chest."

At these words, the ogre came out and said, "Yes, I want to help you catch that murderer! You have no idea what he has done to me, that criminal!" Then he told him the whole story.

"But how will we manage it?" said the false monk. "I don't know what Tridicinu looks like. Do you know?"

"Of course I do."

"Well then, tell me, how tall is he?"

"About my height."

"Since that's the case," said Tridicinu the false monk, "let's try out whether you fit inside this chest. Because if you can fit in here, then so can he."

"Fine," said the ogre, and he got inside the chest.

"Take a good look, ogre, to see if there are any openings," Tridicinu said.

"No, there aren't any."

"Wait a minute, while I see that it closes properly, and that it's not too heavy to carry."

Tridicinu closed the chest and nailed it shut. Then he loaded it on his back and began running toward the city. The ogre called out, "That's enough!"

However, Tridicinu just ran faster, laughing, and to mock the ogre he sang a little song:

Tridicinu is my name,
And I'm carrying you on my back.
You're in my power now.
Soon the king will tie you to his rack.

When they reached the king, he had the ogre put in chains with iron bonds on his hands and feet that chafed his bones for the rest of his miserable life. As for Tridicinu, he gave him all the riches and treasures he could possibly give, and wanted him forever at his side as a brave fellow of the very first rank.

So Tridicinu lived on, in contentment and peace,
While we just sit here, picking our teeth.

Told by Francesca Leto to Salvatore Salomone-Marino in Borgetto

24

THE STORY *of a* QUEEN

Once upon a time there was a king with seven daughters, who always stood on the balcony. It seemed to their father that the people might disapprove of this, and he scolded them.

"What's the matter, Papa?" one of his daughters responded. "Can't we even stand on the balcony?"

"No, daughter. That's not proper. Stay inside. If you don't, I'll lock you up behind bars and give you only bread and water."

Since his daughters wouldn't listen to a thing he said, their father had them locked up behind bars. After they passed some time in isolation, the sisters had a discussion among themselves.

"What are we going to do? We've got to think of something because we won't be able to live off pieces of bread and drops of water for very long!"

"You're right," another sister said. "Let's discard our women's garments and put on men's clothes. We'll get a tailor to come here and make clothes for us, and at three thirty we'll mount our horses and ride into the city."

"Wonderful! Wonderful!" the others agreed.

They called for a tailor, and once they gave him their measurements, he made men's clothes for them. Then they dug an underground tunnel, and after dressing themselves in men's clothes, they went through the tunnel, mounted their horses, and fled. At exactly four o'clock, their father arrived with bread and water and couldn't find his daughters.

"Guards! Guards! Guards! I've been tricked!" he cried out.

But what were the guards and servants to do? In the meantime, when night came, the sisters dismounted and walked along a road. Soon they saw a light, got back on their horses, and rode toward a large farm. Once they arrived, they knocked at the door.

"Oh, cavalier!" they called out to the owner of the farm.

A sorcerer appeared at the window, and they mistook him for a cavalier.

"Why have you come to my house?" he asked.

"Ahh! Please be so kind as to let us stay here tonight. We're tired from our journey."

"All right. Tristana, open the door for them, and let these poor unfortunates enter. But first help them get off their horses and give the beasts some barley. Then I want you to provide these poor maidens with something to eat so they can refresh themselves."

(I forgot to mention that they had already taken off their men's clothes and had put on women's clothes.)

Then the sorcerer turned to the princesses and said, "I'll put you with my daughters. There are seven of them like you, and you can stay together."

After they had gotten off their horses, the princesses went upstairs where they found things to eat, and they washed themselves. Toward midnight Tristana, the sorcerer's wife, turned to him and said, "You know, husband, I've been thinking about eating them?"

Meanwhile, one of the sisters, who was very cunning and knew how to use her head, overheard her.

"Sisters," she alerted them, "we must escape. If not, we are lost. I just heard that the sorcerer's wife wants to eat us."

The sisters began to discuss the situation among themselves, and when Tristana heard them, she said, "Why are you talking?"

"We're wiped out from the journey," they said. "We can't manage to sleep."

"Well, before we go to sleep, we must switch places with the sorcerer's daughters."

Right before midnight, the sorcerer and his wife returned to them. However, they approached the bed of their own daughters, and thinking that it was the bed of the seven strangers, they ate their own daughters. Meanwhile, one of the princesses turned to the others and said, "Ignazia, let's get out of here. If not, we'll soon be dead!"

Therefore, they dressed themselves as men again. Then they went down the stairs very slowly, mounted their horses, and slipped away. They rode until daylight, and they continued riding until they arrived at a city called Vienna. Soon after their arrival, they entered an inn.

"What's there to eat?"

"There's everything here. Whatever your lords command. But, first you must tell me, who you are. Are you sons of kings or sons of cavaliers?"

However, they said nothing. They ate, mounted their horses, and rode off in a flash to Genova, where they once again became young ladies. What did they do in Genova? They rented a palace, for they had plenty of money, and they remained there. Since they were all beautiful daughters of a king, they had a true royal bearing and thus many cavaliers came and proposed to them. As each one of the princesses found the husband she wanted, she got married. The eldest took a count, the second a British nobleman, the third a cavalier, the fourth a gentleman, the fifth a wealthy farmer, the sixth, I'm not sure (let's say a good artisan), and the last, Agatuzza, who was the most clever of all, took a king. Soon they were all settled and looking after their affairs, and one of the brothers-in-law said to the king:

"Your majesty, it's true that you're a king, but you don't know the talents that your wife has, and there's nobody in the world who knows them."

"Why are you saying this?"

"Because I know that she's confident and could go and get the ring of the sorcerer's wife."

After hearing this, the king ordered his wife to go and get the ring of the sorcerer's wife.

"Well, if you want to send me to my death, so be it," she responded. "I'll fetch the ring of the sorcerer's wife. Just give me a horse and barley, and something to eat, and I'll go. However, listen carefully to what I say to you. If I have not returned in a year, a month, and a day, you can be sure that I'm dead!"

Poor Agatuzza began her journey, and soon after she arrived at the sorcerer's farmhouse, she put the horse in the stable and went up into the palace.

"Oh, Donna Tristana, will you let me stay here tonight?"

"Yes, my daughter," Tristana responded. "But I've just experienced some terrible treachery. I was tricked into eating my own daughters. So who in her right mind would want to come now and stay in my house?"

"What does all this have to do with me? I regard you as my own mother and father," Agatuzza said, turning to the sorcerer.

It seemed all right to the sorcerer and his wife to let her stay there, especially because they had nobody. They gave her some pigeons and chickens to eat in order to fatten her up. Five months passed, and Tristana said, "Agatuzza! Agatuzza! Just look at how large you've grown!"

When his wife uttered these words, the sorcerer said, "You know what I'm thinking, Tristana? Heat up the oven for seven nights and seven days, and then cook the girl for me and put her on a plate, and when I arrive, I'll eat her."

And he meant poor Agatuzza.

When the time came, the sorcerer's wife said, "Come here, Agatuzza, and watch how I heat up the oven."

"Ahh, mamma mia!" responded the maiden as she approached. "I've never watched you at work and how you do such things. So why don't you look into the oven first?"

The sorcerer's wife went over to the oven, and all at once, Agatuzza grabbed her from behind, and as she pushed her into the oven, she quickly took off the ring from her finger. Later, she pulled the sorcerer's wife from the oven and put her on top of the table. Then she put a long wooden beam on the bed and covered it with a blanket to make it seem the sorcerer's wife was sick. Immediately after doing this, she mounted her horse and returned to the king.

When the sorcerer returned and saw that the table was set, he cried out, "Oh! Tristana, what's the matter? Are you sick? Don't you want any? Look how nice and fat she is! Why don't you want to eat any?"

Without waiting for a reply, he sat down and ate. Then he went to the bed and discovered the wooden beam.

"I've been tricked! I've eaten my own wife!"

A good deal of time passed before Agatuzza reached the royal palace.

"Oh, my wife, how long has it been since I've seen you! It's been one year, one month, and a day!"

"Oh, you nasty dog!" Agatuzza responded. "You wanted to send me to the guillotine! You wanted my death!"

The brothers-in-law were more jealous than ever and didn't know how to get rid of this queen whom they couldn't stand. Therefore, they went to the king and said, "Now, brother-in-law, you're the king. You have the ring from your wife, but you're missing the sorcerer's horse. There's no one in all of Sicily and in the entire world who has a horse like this one."

After Agatuzza heard this, she said to her husband, "Do you really want me to go there? Well then, I'll gladly ride to my death. Give me something to eat and something for the horse, and I'll go and get it."

They embraced, and she kissed her husband.

"If I'm not back in a year, a month, and a day, you can be sure that I'm dead."

Off she ran, and at the end of a year, Agatuzza arrived at the sorcerer's palace. Now it was impossible to capture the sorcerer's horse unless you first mounted it, but when she tried to do this, the horse cried out, "Master, help! Master, help me!"

"Be quiet!" she responded.

However, the horse neighed.

"Watch out!" Agatuzza said. "I've got a stick, and I'll give you a good beating if you're not quiet!"

In short, Agatuzza kept talking and doing things until she had the bridle on the horse, and then she was able to mount it. As Agatuzza was leaving the stable, however, the sorcerer rushed to the window and saw what was happening.

"Oh! You wicked, godless thing! What are you doing to me?" the sorcerer cried out, and then he said, "If you give me back the horse, I'll give you everything I own."

"Hey, sorcerer, I'm the one who made you kill your daughters, and I'm the one who stole the ring from your wife's finger!"

"Please, give me back my horse!"

"No, the horse must come with me to my palace."

As soon as Agatuzza arrived at the palace, she immediately sent news to the king. Then an escort of soldiers arrived to take charge of the magnificent horse. When the king saw his wife, he embraced and kissed her. Soon all the brothers-in-law came to the palace.

"Long live the queen! Long live the queen! This is the best horse in all of Sicily!" they cried out. "But do you know what you're missing? The instrument that speaks by itself."

The capricious king told this to his wife, and Agatuzza, who had the courage for two, left on her horse and with food, saying, "If I'm not back in a year, a month, and a day, you can be sure that I'm dead."

Meanwhile, the instrument said to the sorcerer, "Pay attention because the maiden who had you eat your daughters, took the ring, and robbed your horse, is now coming to take me. Be on your guard!"

As Agatuzza rode toward the sorcerer's house, the instrument spied on her for the sorcerer:

"Where is she now?"

"She's halfway here."

"Where is she now?"

"At the end of the road."

"Where is she now?"

"At the gate."

"Where is she now?"

"On the stairs."

"Where is she now?"

"On the last step."

As Agatuzza mounted the last step, the sorcerer grabbed her by the hair and lifted her up.

"Ahh, you've walked into your death!" he cried.

"All right, I know that I'm dead," she said. "Give me something to eat so I can become fat. Right now I'm like a skinny chicken, like a wretched dog."

"All right. I'll fatten you up for two months, and then we'll see to it," the sorcerer said and turned to his new wife. "Give her something to eat because I have to go. I'll return later."

After he left, Agatuzza said to the wife, "I'd like a favor. I want to sleep in this bed for a while."

So, she was allowed to go to the bed and pretended to sleep. Instead, Agatuzza seized the instrument, mounted her horse, and departed. Just at that moment the sorcerer returned.

"Ahh! She's even taken the instrument. I told you, bumbling wife, to keep an eye on that maiden!"

Meanwhile, as Agatuzza approached the king's palace, he was glad to send for soldiers to escort her with the instrument. Afterward, there were celebrations and parties, and once again, the brothers-in-law came.

"King, it's true that you have the ring, the horse, and the instrument. However, to be really happy, you should send your wife to fetch the sorcerer alive. That would be something spectacular."

"All right, you nasty dog," Agatuzza responded when he told her what he wanted. "You let yourself be persuaded by anyone's words. You yield to my sisters, but I hope I can avoid death and even overcome this obstacle."

"No, wife, I'm not a nasty dog, and I don't want you to die."

"Stop all the chattering and give me a pair of trousers from Calabria, a board, a hatchet, four tables, and some penny nails."

Then Agatuzza mounted her horse and went to the sorcerer's castle. As she approached it, she took out the hatchet from her belt and began to dig a hole in front of the castle. Right at that moment the sorcerer appeared at the window.

"What are you doing?" he asked Agatuzza, who was dressed as a man.

"There's supposed to be a pool of water here. I want to make a water geyser to amuse the sorcerer."

After she reached a depth of a yard and a half, the sorcerer came down from the palace to look at the hole. As he was approaching, his feet slipped, and he fell down into the hole.

"Oww! Oww!" he cried out. "I've broken something. How am I going to get out of here?"

"Try to get on these tables," Agatuzza said. "I'll pull you up on them. Let me put four nails there. Otherwise you'll fall backwards."

After she nailed the tables into the form of a box, she said, "Get up into it and tell me if there are rays of light."

"There's some light."

Then Agatuzza hit another nail into the box.

"Is there still light?"

"No!"

"Now," she said, "let's see how we're going to get you on the horse."

Agatuzza took the box and pulled it with a rope onto the back of the horse. Then she traveled a long time, brought the box to the royal palace, and presented it to the king. Imagine how happy he was! The instrument sounded the signal when the queen arrived. After the box was unloaded, they put the sorcerer in chains and released four lions from their cages. Soon he was torn to pieces.

Agatuzza was very happy about her victory. Her sisters and brothers-in-law had sour faces because they had tried to get rid of her in so many wicked ways. All in vain. In the end, the king remained with his clever wife, the ring, the horse, and the instrument, and we are still here without a cent.

Told by Vincenzo Graffagnino, a peasant, in the house of
Professor Vincenzo Di Giovanni, in Salaparuta

25

THE HERB-GATHERER'S DAUGHTERS;
or, THE SECRET *of the* TALKING BIRD

There was once an herb-gatherer called Uncle Peppi, who had three daughters, and they earned their living by spinning. One day their father died and left them all alone in the world. Now, the king often went through the streets at night, listening at the doors to hear what the people said about him. One evening, he stopped at the door of the house where the three sisters lived and listened to them having an argument.

"If I were to become the wife of the royal butler," the eldest said, "I would give the whole court some water to drink out of a single glass, and there would be some water left over."

"If I were to become the wife of the keeper of the royal wardrobe," the second sister said, "I would make clothes for all the servants with one piece of cloth and still have some cloth left over."

"If I were to become the king's wife," the youngest asserted, "I would bear him three children—two sons with apples in their hands and a daughter with a star on her forehead."

After hearing this, the king went back to his palace, and the next morning he sent for the sisters. When they appeared before the king, they were bewildered.

"Don't be frightened," the king said. "I just want you to tell me what you were discussing last night."

The oldest turned to him and said, "Your majesty, I said if I were to become the wife of the royal butler, I would give the whole court some water to drink out of a single glass, and there would be some water left over."

"Prove it to me!" the king commanded and called for a glass of water. "I want the proof!"

Well, she took the glass and first gave the servants some water to drink and then everyone at court, and there was some left over.

There was nothing left for her to do but to dress like a page and set out on a journey. When she approached the first hermit, he asked, "Where are you going, my fine lad?"

"Bravo! You've passed the test!" cried the king, and then he summoned the butler. "This man is your husband. Now it's your turn," the king said to the next sister.

"Your majesty, I said that if I were to become the wife of the keeper of the royal wardrobe, I would make clothes for all the servants with one piece of cloth and still have some cloth left over."

"Prove it to me!" the king exclaimed and ordered his servants to bring a piece of cloth. Then, the young girl immediately cut out garments for all the servants and had some cloth left over.

"Bravo! You've passed the test!" cried the king, and then he called the royal wardrobe keeper and said, "This man is now your husband."

Finally, he turned to the youngest sister and said, "Now it's your turn."

"Your majesty," she responded. "I said that if I were the king's wife, I would bear him three children—two sons with apples in their hands, and a daughter with a star on her forehead."

"If what you say is true," the king stated, "you will be queen. But if it isn't, you will die," and he married her right away.

In very little time, the two older sisters became envious of the youngest.

"Look," they said, "she's the queen, and we must be her servants!"

Soon the envy turned to hate.

Meanwhile the queen became pregnant, and two months before she was to give birth, the king declared war against another kingdom and had to depart. However, first he placed one of his men in charge of everything and said, "My wife is about to give birth. If she has three children—two sons with apples in their hands and a daughter with a star on her forehead—she is to be respected as queen. If not, you're to write to me, and I'll tell you what to do."

Then he set out for the war.

Well, who were the people the queen trusted most? They were her sisters, and when she had great labor pains, she called them, and they came to her. However, the sisters had arranged with the midwife that, when the queen gave birth, she was to cart the babies away and replace them with puppies. Indeed, the queen gave birth to three children—two boys with apples in their hands and one girl with a star on her forehead. After she recovered from the labor pains of giving birth, the queen turned to the midwife and said, "Old woman, what are my babies like?"

"They're three puppies, your majesty."

"Three puppies! But I heard three babies crying!"

"It was your imagination, your majesty."

The midwife had taken away the three innocent babes. So, the man who had been placed in charge of everything wrote to the king: "Your majesty, the queen gave birth to three puppies. Please write and tell me what I'm to do."

When the king received the news, he wrote back: "Take care of her for two weeks. Then send her to the treadmill."

Now let us leave the king and return to the midwife who had carried the babies outside.

"I'll let the dogs eat them up," she said and left them alone.

While they lay out in the open, three fairies passed by and cried out, "Oh, how beautiful these children are!"

They bent over them, and while they were kneeling, one of the fairies said, "What gift shall we give these children? I shall give them a deer that will nurse all three."

"And I shall grant them a purse, and whenever they reach inside, it will always be full of money."

"And I," said the third fairy, "shall give them a ring that will change its color whenever misfortune should strike one of them."

After saying these words, they departed, and the deer began to nurse the children who grew by leaps and bounds while their father was at war. A year passed, two, then three, until they were fully-grown. Then the fairy who had given them the deer came and said, "Now that you're all grown up, why should you stay here any longer?"

"Very well," said one of the brothers, "I shall go to the city and rent a house."

"Make sure," the deer remarked, "that you rent a house opposite the royal palace."

So they all went to the city and rented a palace. Since they had plenty of money, they bought chairs, beds, and sofas. Indeed, they furnished the palace as if they had been royalty and had coaches, horses, and everything they needed. When their aunts saw these young people, you can imagine their fright!

"They're alive!" they said. It was impossible to mistake them, for there were the apples in the boys' hands, and a star on the girl's forehead. Consequently, they summoned the midwife and said to her, "Old woman, what does this mean? Are our nephews and niece alive?"

The midwife went to the window and watched until she saw the two brothers depart. Then, when she knew the maiden was alone, she went over as if to make a visit to the new house. As she entered, she said, "How are things going for you, my daughter? You're happy here, aren't you? You seem to have everything, but do you know what would make you truly happy? It is the Dancing Water. If your brothers love you, they will fetch it for you!"

The midwife remained a while longer and then departed. When one of the brothers returned, the maiden said to him, "Ah! My brother, if you really love me, you'll fetch the Dancing Water for me."

"Of course, I'll go, my sister."

The next morning he mounted a splendid horse and departed. On his way, he met a hermit, who asked him, "Where are you going, cavalier?"

"I'm going to fetch the Dancing Water."

"You're going to your death, my son. But keep on traveling until you meet a hermit older than I am."

He continued his journey until he met another hermit, who asked, "Where are you going, cavalier?"

"I'm going to fetch the Dancing Water."

"You're going to your death, my son, but keep on traveling until you meet a hermit much older than I am."

So, he continued his journey until he met another hermit, older than the other two. He had a white beard that came down to his feet, and he told the young man: "You're going to your death, but I have some instructions for you. Do you see that mountain over there? You must climb to the top where you will find a great plain and a house with a beautiful gate. In front of the gate, you will see four giants with swords in their hands. Pay attention. Don't make a mistake. If you do, it will be the end of you! When the giants have their eyes closed, do not enter. When their eyes are open, feel free to enter. Then you will come to a door. If you find it open, don't enter. If you find it shut, push it open and enter. Then you will find four lions. If they have their eyes shut, don't enter. When their eyes are open, enter, and you will find the Dancing Water."

The young man took leave of the hermit, mounted his horse, and rode off. Meanwhile, his sister kept looking at the ring constantly to see whether the stone had changed color. Since it remained the same, she was relieved.

A few days after leaving the hermit, the young man arrived at the top of the mountain and saw the palace with the four giants standing before it. They had their eyes shut, and the door was open.

"No," said the young man. "That won't do."

Therefore, he waited and kept on the lookout. When the giants opened their eyes, and the door closed, he entered and waited for the lions to open their eyes and entered the next room, where he found the Dancing Water and filled his bottles with it. Then he escaped when the lions again opened their eyes.

Now let us leave him on his journey home and turn to the aunts, who were delighted because their nephew did not return.

However, within a few days he reappeared and embraced his sister. Then they had two golden basins made and put the Dancing Water into them and watched the water leap from one basin to the other. When the aunts saw it, they exclaimed, "Ah! How did he manage to get that water?"

Enraged, they called the midwife, who again waited until the sister was alone and then visited her.

"You see," she said, "how beautiful the Dancing Water is! But do you know what you want now? The Singing Apple."

After she departed, the brother, who had brought the Dancing Water, returned, and his sister said to him, "My brother, do you know what you must fetch for me if you love me? You must fetch the Singing Apple."

"I understand, sister, and I'll go and get it."

The next morning he mounted his horse and went straight to the first hermit, who said to him, "Where are you going, cavalier?"

"I'm going to fetch the Singing Apple."

"You're heading for trouble, my son. But keep on traveling until you meet a hermit older than I am."

So he continued his journey until he encountered the second hermit who said, "Where are you going, cavalier?"

"I'm going to fetch the Singing Apple."

"It's quite a task to get the Singing Apple. So listen to what you must do. First, you must climb the mountain. Beware of the giants, the door, and the lions. Then you will find a little door and a pair of scissors in it. If the scissors are open, enter. If they are closed, do not risk it. Now get out of here!"

The young man continued on his way, and after he climbed the mountain, he entered the palace and found the situation favorable. When he saw the scissors open, he went into a room and saw a wonderful tree on top of which was an apple. He climbed up and tried to pick the apple, but the top of the tree swayed back and forth. He waited until it was still for a moment, grabbed hold of the branch, and picked the apple. Everything was again favorable. Therefore, he mounted his horse and rode home. All along the way, the apple kept making sounds!

His aunts had again been very glad because their nephew had been absent so long. However, when they saw him return, they felt as though the house had fallen on them. Once again, they summoned the midwife, and again she visited the young woman when her brothers were not there.

"See how beautiful they are, the Dancing Water and the Singing Apple!" she remarked. "But you should see the Talking Bird, and then you will have seen all there is to see!"

"Very well," said the young girl. "We'll see whether my brother will get it for me."

When her brother came, she asked, "My brother, if you really love me, you'll go and fetch the Talking Bird for me?"

"Of course, sister," and he mounted his horse and departed. When he met the first hermit, the old man asked, "Where are you going, cavalier?"

"I'm going to fetch the Talking Bird."

"You're heading for trouble, my son. But keep on traveling until you meet a hermit older than I am."

He traveled onward until he came to the second hermit who asked him where he was going and sent him on to a third one, who said to him, "Now I'll tell you what you have to do. You're to climb the mountain and enter the palace. You will find many statues. Then you will come to a garden where you will find a basin in the middle, and on the basin is the Talking Bird. If it should say anything to you, do not respond. Pick a feather from the bird's wing, dip it into the basin, and touch all the statues with it. Keep your eyes open, and everything will go well."

Since the young man was already very familiar with the way, he was soon in the palace. He found the garden and the bird, which immediately exclaimed, "What's the matter, cavalier? Have you come for me? Have you come to pick my feather? You won't get it. Your aunts have sent you to your death, and you must remain here. Your mother has been sent to the treadmill."

"My mother is in the treadmill?" cried the young man, and no sooner did he utter these words than he became a statue like all the others.

When the sister looked at her ring, she saw that it had become misty.

"Ah!" she exclaimed.

So now her other brother departed, and when he came to the first hermit, the old man asked, "Where are you going, cavalier?"

"I'm going to fetch the Talking Bird."

"You're heading for your death, my son. But keep on traveling until you meet a hermit older than I am."

So, he continued traveling until he came to the second hermit, who said the same thing. Finally, he reached the oldest hermit, who told him what to do. Soon he began climbing the mountain where he encountered the giants with their eyes open. Then he entered and found the door closed. He opened it and went past the lion and the scissors. Finally, he continued through the room until he saw the entrance to the garden in which he found the statues and the Talking Bird on top of the basin.

Meanwhile, the aunts, who saw that both their nephews were missing, were very glad. At the same time, the sister took out the ring and noticed that it had become clear once again. Yet, when the Talking Bird saw her second brother appear in the garden, it said to him, "Do you see what has happened to your brother? And your mother has been sent to the treadmill."

"Alas, my mother is in the treadmill?"

As soon as he uttered these words, he became a statue. The sister looked at her ring, and it had become black. Poor girl! There was nothing left for her to do but to dress like a page and set out on a journey. When she approached the first hermit, he asked, "Where are you going, my fine lad?"

"I'm going to fetch the Talking Bird."

"You're heading for trouble, my son. But keep on traveling until you'll meet a hermit older than I am."

Therefore, she went to the second hermit, who told her the same thing. Finally, she came to the third hermit who told her everything she had to do.

"Keep your eyes open," he added. "If you respond when the bird talks, you will lose your life! Be on your guard, my daughter!"

Upon listening to his words, she took her leave and traveled until she reached the garden. When the bird saw her, it cried out, "Ah! You're here, too? Now you'll become just like your brothers! Do you see them? One, two, and you will make three . . . Your father is at war . . . Your mother is in the treadmill . . . Your aunts are rejoicing."

However, she didn't reply. Instead, she let the bird sing on. When it had said all it had to say, it flew down, and the young girl ran and caught it. Then she pulled a feather from its wing, dipped it into the basin, and brushed the nostrils of her brothers with it. All at once, they came to life again. Then she did the same with all the other statues, with the lions and the giants, until they all became alive once more. Afterward she departed with her brothers, while all the noblemen, dukes, barons, and princes, who had been statues, celebrated their freedom.

As they turned their backs on the palace, it disappeared, and the hermits vanished, for they had been the three fairies. When the brothers and their sister returned to the city, the servants came, and there was a party that evening. The following day they summoned a goldsmith and told him to make a gold chain and to attach it to the bird. When their aunts looked out their window, they saw the Dancing Water, the Singing Apple, and the Talking Bird in the palace opposite them.

"Well," they said, "now we're in real trouble!"

Indeed, let me tell you what happened.

The bird cried out, "Mistress!"

"What do you want?" she asked.

"Call your brothers."

"What do you want?" they asked.

"I want you to provide us with a grand coach, more elegant than the king's."

And they did this right away.

"I want you to provide twenty-four attendants and cooks and servants more splendid than the king's."

And they also did this right away.

When the aunts saw all this, they were ready to explode with rage. However, just at this time, the king returned from the war, and his subjects told him all the news of the kingdom, but they didn't tell him about his wife and children.

Now, one day, the king went out on his balcony and saw that there was a palace across from his that was furnished in a magnificent manner.

"Who lives there?" he asked, but no one could answer him. He looked again and saw the brothers and sister. The brothers had apples in their hands, and the sister, a star on her forehead.

"Jesus!" he cried out. "If I didn't know that my wife had given birth to three puppies, I would say that those were my children!"

On another day, he stood by the window and enjoyed the Dancing Water and the Singing Apple, but the bird was silent. After the king had heard all the music, the bird spoke to him across the way: "What does your majesty think about this?"

The king was astonished at hearing the Talking Bird and said: "What should I think? It's marvelous."

"There is something more marvelous," the bird said. "Just wait!"

Then the bird turned away from the king and cried out, "Mistress, call your brothers."

When they were all together, the bird spoke, "The king has returned. Let us invite him to dinner on Sunday. Is this all right with you?"

"Yes, yes," they all said.

Consequently, the bird turned back to the king and invited him, and he accepted.

On Sunday, the bird had a grand dinner prepared. When the king came and saw the young people, he clapped his hands and said, "I don't understand all this, but they seem to be my children."

He went through the palace and was astonished by all its wealth. Then they went to dinner, and while they were eating, the king said, "Bird, everyone is talking, but you alone are silent."

"Ah! Your majesty, I am sick, but next Sunday, I shall be well and be able to talk. Indeed, I shall come and dine at your palace with this young lady and these gentlemen, if it pleases you."

"Yes, bird," the king replied.

The following Sunday the bird called his mistress and her brothers and told them to put on their finest clothes. When they were fully dressed, they looked like royalty. Then they departed with the bird. The king showed them around his palace and treated them with great courtesy, while the aunts, who had been invited, felt they were about to die. When they had all seated themselves at the table, the king said, "Come, bird, you promised me you would talk. Have you nothing to say?"

Then the bird began to talk and related all that had happened from the time that the king had listened at the door until his poor wife had been sent to the treadmill. At the very end, the bird added, "These are your children, and your wife was sent to the mill and is dying."

As soon as the king heard all this, he rushed to embrace his children and then went to find his poor wife, who had been reduced to skin and bones and was on the verge of death. He knelt before her and begged her pardon. Then he summoned her sisters and the midwife, and when they were in his presence, he said to the bird, "Bird, you who have told me everything may now pronounce their sentence."

"Well, if you want me to sentence them, your majesty, I say that the midwife is to be thrown head-first from the window, and your sisters-in-law are to be cast into a kettle of boiling oil."

The king had the bird's sentence carried out. The midwife was immediately thrown out of the window, and the aunts were cast into a kettle. Afterward, the king never tired of embracing his wife. Meanwhile, the bird departed, and the king and his wife and children lived together in blessed peace.

Well, they remained happy and content,
While we can't even pay the rent.

Told by Rosalia Varrica in Palermo

26

ROSEMARY

Once upon a time there was a king and a queen who did not have any children. One day the queen descended into the garden, saw a rose bush that had many buds, and said, "Just look at that! A mere rosebush has many children, while I who am queen have none!"

After a few days, she became pregnant. It didn't take long, and within nine months, she gave birth to a rosemary bush. Afterward, she watered this plant with milk and kept it in a pot on the table. One of her nephews, the son of the King of Spain, happened to see the bush and asked, "Your majesty, why is this rosemary plant sitting there?"

"I gave birth to this rosemary bush," his aunt told him what had happened, "and I water it four times every day."

Meanwhile, the young man said to himself, "I want this rosemary bush!"

He prepared a beautiful pot on his ship, bought a goat to provide milk, took the rosemary bush, and disappeared. Four times a day he gave the plant milk. When he arrived at his city, he had the rosemary bush planted in his garden.

This King of Spain had three sisters, and he amused himself by playing a flute. One day, while he was playing in the garden, he saw a maiden appear and said to her, "Where did you come from?"

"I came from the rosemary bush."

You should have seen the king! From that moment on, he didn't leave the palace. As soon as he finished his affairs as king, he went down into the garden, played the flute, and enjoyed himself by conversing with the maiden.

In the meantime, war was declared against the king, and he said to the maiden, "Listen, my Rosemary, I must be off, but when I return, I'll play the flute three times, and you can come out again."

Then he called the gardener and told him to water the rosemary bush four times a day with milk, and if, upon his return, he found the rosemary had wilted, he would cut off his head. Thereupon, he left the flute in his room, took his leave from his sisters, and departed.

His sisters had become curious about their brother's behavior and said, "What did our brother do with that flute?"

The first sister found it and played it, then the second, and finally the third. At the third time, the maiden appeared.

"Ah, this explains why our brother no longer left the palace," they said, "and why he spent all his days in the garden!"

They grabbed her and beat her until she was more dead than alive. Somehow, the poor maiden managed to crawl to the rosemary plant, and she disappeared. When the gardener came and found that the rosemary had wilted, he said, "Poor me, what will the king do to me when he returns?" So, he ran to his wife and said, "I must leave, and I want you to continue watering the rosemary bush."

After he departed, he walked through the countryside until night overtook him in the forest. Since he didn't want to be eaten by ferocious beasts, he climbed a tree. At midnight the ogre Mamma-drago and the ogress Mamma-draga arrived and threw themselves down against the tree, snorting in a frightful way.

"What's new?" the Mamma-draga asked.

"What's there new to tell?" responded the Mamma-drago with a shrug.

"You don't have anything new to tell me?"

"One thing I can tell you. The life of the king's gardener is in danger."

"Why's that?"

"Don't you know that the king returned with a rosemary bush that he took from his aunt, and that there was a maiden enchanted inside the bush? Then he took the bush into his garden and had it watered four times a day with milk. One day, when he was playing the flute, the maiden came out of the rosemary bush. All this you know, but you don't know that the king had to go off to war and placed the gardener in charge of the plant, and he left the flute in his room. However, his sisters took it and played it, causing the maiden to come out of the rosemary bush. They gave her a good beating and left her more dead than alive. So the rosemary wilted, and the gardener fled in fear of his life."

"But isn't there a remedy?"

"Of course, there's a remedy, but I don't want to tell you because there are ears everywhere in the woods, and the walls have ears."

"Come on! Who can hear us in this place?"

"All right. Listen. The blood from my veins and the flesh of the nape of your neck have to be boiled together. Then all this has to be spread like an ointment on the rosemary bush, and the maiden will emerge."

"Ah," said the gardener, "please help me, my fate!"

As soon as the ogres went to sleep, he climbed down the tree, took a large club and killed them. Then he took the blood from the ogre and the flesh from the nape from the ogress, ran back home, and spread it all over the rosemary bush. Immediately the maiden emerged, and the rosemary bush wilted. He took the maiden by the hand, led her to his house, and put her to bed where he nursed her with broth and medicine. About the time that her health was beginning to improve, the king returned from the war and ran immediately into the garden where he played the flute. However, no matter how much he played, the maiden did not appear. Then, when he went to the rosemary bush, he found it dried up.

The poor gardener had not been able to summon the courage to tell the king what had happened because Rosemary was still somewhat sick. However, the king bellowed, "Either you tell me what has happened to Rosemary, or I'll have your head cut off!"

So the gardener said, "Your majesty, come into my house, and I'll show you something beautiful."

"What am I supposed to do in your house, you scoundrel! I want Rosemary!"

"But your majesty! Just come inside, and then you can do what you want with me."

When the king heard this, he went inside. As soon as he entered, he saw Rosemary in the bed with tears in her eyes.

"What happened?" he asked.

The maiden responded, "I got these wounds from your sisters who beat me, and when the poor gardener saw that I was dying, he spread a certain ointment over me, and now I'm recovering."

Just think how much the king detested his sisters! Just think how grateful he was to the gardener who brought Rosemary back to life!

When she was fully recovered, the king told her that he wanted to marry her. He wrote to his uncle, the king, and told him that the rosemary plant had become a beautiful young lady and that they had set the day of the wedding, and he invited him and his wife, the queen. The ambassadors departed with the invitation, and as soon as the king received this news that he had a daughter, you can imagine his joy.

The king and queen set out on the journey to attend the wedding, and when they arrived, they were greeted with canons— "*Boom! Boom!*"

"Who's arrived?"

"The king has arrived!"

When the king and queen saw their daughter, they embraced and kissed her, and the maiden became acquainted with her father and mother. Then the wedding was celebrated, and there was a grand party thrown for all of Spain.

> They remained content and in peace,
> While we're still sitting and picking our teeth.

Told by a woman in the house of Professor Carmelo Pardi in Palermo

27

THE MAGIC BALLS

Once upon a time there was a king who believed he was handsome. He had a mirror and used to say all the time:

> Beautiful mirror, tell me sweetly, or I shall cry:
> Who in the world is more handsome than I?

His wife tolerated this for one, two, three, four times, but finally she said:

> Keep quiet, my king, there's nothing to do,
> There's someone I know more handsome than you.

Infuriated, he responded, "If you don't tell me within three days who's more handsome than I am, you'll be killed!"

The poor queen became bewildered and retired to her rooms where she stayed the entire time. As she was trying to think of some-one on the last day, she went out onto the balcony. An old woman passed by and said, "Your majesty, I beg you for some alms."

"Let me be, good woman," the queen responded. "I've got my own troubles."

"I know everything," the old woman said, "and I also know how to make your trouble go away."

"Then come up here!" said the queen.

The old woman mounted the stairs, and the queen asked, "What do you know?"

"Everything that the king said," she replied.

"And so there's some way for me to get out of this?"

"Yes, my lady."

"I'll give you whatever you want," said the queen.

"I don't want anything," the old woman declared. "At noon, you are to have lunch with the king. Then you are to ask him a favor, and he will say, 'What favor? To grant you your life?' You are to respond, 'No.' Then he will say, 'So, you concede?' And you will tell him: 'No, the son of the Emperor of France, covered with seven veils, is more handsome than you.'"

The old woman departed, and the queen did as she said. Then the king responded, "If this prince is truly better looking than I am, you can do with me as you wish."

Three days later, the king left with his retinue to seek out the Emperor of France. When he presented himself, he said, "I would like to see your son."

"All right," the emperor replied, "but he is sleeping just now."

After some time had passed, the emperor brought the king into the room where his son was sleeping. When he lifted the first veil, there was a glow. When he took off the second veil, the glow in-creased. Then the third and fourth veils were lifted, and when he came to the last, the flames of the son's beauty grew even more radiant until the prince appeared with a scepter in his hand and a sword at his side. Dazzled by such beauty, the king fainted and collapsed on the ground, and they had to give him smelling salts and essence to revive him.

The emperor had him carried to his rooms and kept him there for three days.

"Before this king departs," the prince said to his father, "I would like to talk to him."

Soon thereafter he went to the king, and they began conversing until the prince said, "Would you like to see me when you are at your home?"

"How is that possible?"

"Take these three gold balls, and when you would like to see me, throw them into a golden basin filled with three quarts of clean and pure milk, and I shall appear just as I am now."

Therefore, the king took the three gold balls and bid him farewell. When he returned home, he said to his wife, "Here I am. Do with me what you like."

And the queen responded, "May you be blessed."

The king told her what had happened and showed her the three gold balls. However, the king had suffered so much from the stress of his journey that he died at the end of three days. The queen was most distressed, but after four days, she called for a faithful chambermaid and said, "Go and fetch three quarts of clean, pure milk!"

Then she prepared the basin, and after filling it with milk, she threw the three balls into the basin, and gradually the sword appeared, then the scepter, and finally the prince in person. They talked and conversed together, and then he left. The queen put the milk aside, and the next day she filled the basin with fresh milk, and the prince appeared again. She did the same thing for many days until the chambermaid became tired of this and said to herself, "There's got to be something extraordinary beneath all this!"

So what did the chambermaid do? She broke a glass bottle, ground it into powder, and hid the powder in her bosom. The next day, when the queen sent her to fetch the milk as she usually did, the chambermaid poured the powder into the milk while she was on the stairs. Then, as soon as the queen threw the three balls into the basin, she saw the sword and scepter appear covered with blood and then the prince in a bath of blood from wounds caused by the splinters of glass.

When he saw her, he said, "Ah, you've betrayed me!"

The queen begged his pardon a thousand times, but the prince's time was up, and he vanished and went back to his country. When his father saw his condition, he issued a proclamation that said he would give anything if a doctor could be found capable of healing his son. Meanwhile, the city was draped in mourning, and the bells tolled for the prince.

After having seen the prince in such a terrible condition, the queen couldn't take her mind off him. Consequently, after she dressed herself as a shepherd, she set out for his city in France. When it turned dark the first night, she entered a forest, where she took refuge in a tree in an open space and began saying her prayers. At midnight, all the devils of hell arrived at the open space, and they sat down in a circle around their chief, who began to ask each one what they had done until he came to the last one who was the Lame Devil called Zoppo.

"And you, you ugly thing, who never knows anything good to report!"

"My lord," he replied. "It's true that I've worked many years without much success, but this time I've something good to report . . ."

And he told the story about the king and the queen and the prince and how he had caused the chambermaid to deceive the queen. "But now," he added, "the prince has only three days to live, and since there's no hope for him, we'll be able to cart him away."

"But tell me," the chief devil asked, "isn't it possible that some-one will be able to cure this prince?"

"There's a remedy, but I won't tell it," Zoppo responded.

"And why won't you tell us?"

"Because somebody might be listening."

"What are you saying, you fool?" they all said. "Who can hear you here? If there were someone here, he'd already be dead from fright!"

Nevertheless, he continued to say no while the chief devil argued with him. Finally, they all forced him to tell them the remedy, and he said, "One day's walk from here there is a certain woods with a monastery that has glass herbs growing nearby. It's necessary to carry a couple of bags to gather the herbs. Once you have them, you've got to ground the herbs with a mortar and gather the juice into a glass. Then the juice has to be smeared on the prince from head to toe, and he'll be just as good as he was before."

Upon hearing the remedy, the queen decided that it was time now to go to the monastery and find the glass herbs. Well, she walked and walked, and finally she reached the monastery, where she called out to the hermits. However, they exorcised her and barred her from entering.

"Don't exorcise me," she cried out. "I've been baptized!"

Upon hearing this, they opened the door, and she asked for some glass herbs, and they gave them to her that very same eve-ning. The next day she departed for the prince's city, which she found, draped in mourning. Dressed as a shepherd, she presented herself to a guard who would not allow her to enter. However, when the emperor heard her, he ordered the guard to let her pass. Then she mounted the palace stairs, asked the emperor to dismiss all the doctors, and assured him that in two days she would cure the prince. The emperor, who didn't know what more could be done for his son, granted the request and ordered the servants to give the shepherd all that he demanded. Therefore, they brought him a mortar, and he crushed the herbs. Then he collected the juice and began to spread it on the prince from head to toe. Wherever he smeared the juice, the wounds were cleaned. The shepherd did this for two days until the prince was completely cured.

Then the shepherd called the emperor and returned his son to him, healthier and more handsome than ever before. The emperor wanted to give him many treasures, but the shepherd didn't want anything and was already about to leave when the prince said to him, "Here, at least accept this ring as a souvenir."

"This is the only thing I'll take," the shepherd replied and then said farewell.

The poor queen returned to her home as soon as she could. Upon her return, she stopped the chambermaid from fetching the milk as she usually did. Instead, she went and fetched it by herself, clean and pure. Then she shut herself in her room, poured the milk into the basin, and threw in the three magic balls. All of a sudden, the prince appeared, but as soon as he saw her, he wanted to kill her. However, the queen threw herself at his feet and said, "No, it wasn't me who betrayed you! I was the one who saved you." Then she showed him his ring.

Upon seeing the ring, the prince calmed himself, and the queen told him about her hardships and the story of the devil Zoppo. Then they decided to get married, and the prince set out for his own country. When he arrived at his father's palace, he told him all that had happened and that he wanted to marry the queen. The emperor was very pleased, and they departed together to fetch the queen. When they arrived at the palace, they killed the chambermaid and took the queen with them. Once they returned to their realm, the wedding was celebrated.

So they enjoyed life with all its fruits,
While we sit here like a bunch of dried-out roots.

Told by Pasquale-Salvatore Vigo in Acireale

28

THE BEAUTY *of the* SEVEN MOUNTAINS OF GOLD

Once upon a time there was a merchant without any children, and he prayed to the Lord to send him a son. Soon after—to everyone's delight—his wife became pregnant and gave birth to a handsome baby boy. Imagine the happiness of the father whose wish had been fulfilled!

Well, our story moves quickly. As soon as the boy grew up, his father sent him to school. However, at school, he was a devil and very restless. He hit one student on the head. He tipped over someone else's inkstand. He pushed another student. He made promises that he didn't keep. The poor teacher couldn't control him and said to his father: "We must put an end to this! Take your son home. I don't want him at school anymore."

Yet, when he was home, the boy caused more mischief. Consequently, his father and mother decided to send him to board at a monastery. Then, as soon as he entered, he began to pick a quarrel with this person and that person until the teacher kicked him out.

The poor father didn't know what to do anymore. Whenever he saw his son touch something, it broke.

"Let's put him in a seminary!"

Once he arrived at the seminary, he did more damage: he fractured someone's head and scratched someone else's face. He hurt another boy so much that he howled. One day he did something so bad that he knew the prefect would beat him. As a result, he became scared and made a rope out of some sheets, let himself down through a window, and ran away.

When he arrived home, his father said to him, "You're here again? Get out of here! I don't want to see you anymore."

Consequently, his father drove him away.

Now the boy went off and became a soldier. He had a little money, and whenever he was supposed to do guard duty, he greased the hand of one of his superior officers so that he didn't have to do guard duty. However, his money ran out, and one day, it was his turn to guard the castle at night. After a half an hour, he saw that nobody was in sight. Therefore, he took off his gun and put his coat on top of it and his hat on top of the bayonet. Then he left.

Now let us leave him and turn to the other soldiers. When they saw that the guard was no longer moving or saying, "Halt, who goes there!" they went to him and found the hat, the coat, and the gun but no guard.

So, let us now return to Don Giuseppe. Actually, I think I said that the boy had been called Peppino, but now that he was grown up, he was called Don Giuseppe. Well anyway, Don Giuseppe set out for the countryside. He walked and walked until he found himself in a forest. Dying of hunger, he looked around to see what he could do. While he was looking, he saw a palace made entirely of gold. As he approached it, he saw a goat tied up before the gate. All at once, his heart jumped for joy at the thought of killing the goat and cooking it.

However, as soon as the goat realized it was about to be grabbed, it said, "Don't kill me. I've been baptized and confirmed just like you!"

When he heard the goat talk, he was stunned and became frightened.

"How did you get in this condition?" he said.

"How did I get into this condition? Well, I can't tell you right now. But let me tell you what you must do. You're to go inside, where you'll find a table already set. Eat to your heart's content, and when you return, we can talk."

He went up into the palace, found a beautiful table already set, sat down, and ate like a prince. When he was full, he went back outside to the goat, who said to him, "I've been enchanted, and I can't leave here. I was the daughter of a king, and everyone called me 'Beauty of the Seven Mountains of Gold.'"

"What has to be done to free you?" Don Giuseppe asked.

"What has to be done? I need a courageous man."

"Well, if you want a courageous man, you want Don Giuseppe. Tell me what to do!"

"You've got to go back up into the palace, and in one of the rooms you'll find a magnificent bed, already made up. Then all you have to do is get undressed and get into bed. When you are about to fall asleep, three kings dressed in gold will appear and say to you: 'How dare you come up into the palace and get into this bed?' However, you're not to make a peep. 'Speak up! Listen!' one of them will say, 'Who's sent you? What's your name?' Again, you're not to respond to them, otherwise you'll be cast under a spell, just like I was. When they see that you won't talk, they will threaten you and pretend that they want to kill you. But it's all bluff. Don't be frightened. Then they will treat you gently and take you to a room filled with gold, just to make you talk. But you must remain firm! And no matter whether they do this or that to you, don't be scared. Even if they put you into a kettle of boiling oil, it won't harm you because at the end they'll spread an ointment on you, and you'll return better looking and better fit than ever before."

That night everything happened as the goat said it would. As soon as the three kings saw that Don Giuseppe didn't want to talk, they threw him into a kettle of boiling oil. But Don Giuseppe, who knew everything in advance, let them do it. He was killed; he was thrown into the oil, but then he became more handsome than ever before. When he woke up, he found himself in the bed fresh as a rose.

Incidentally, I forgot to say that the goat had three beautiful veils that covered her face.

When Don Giuseppe awoke, he couldn't find his clothes. Instead, there was a suit adorned with gold and silver. Immediately thereafter, he stood up, and his first thought was to go down and see the goat. Well, he found her, minus one of the veils, and she had the face of a lady, but her arms and the rest of her body were that of a goat. When she saw him, she celebrated and said, "I'm so blessed that you were sent to me! Tell me, who sent you to free me, dear Don Giuseppe?" Then she added: "Go and eat, and later we can talk."

After Don Giuseppe went to eat, he returned from the palace.

"Listen to me carefully," the goat said. "Tonight you'll have to go and sleep in the same bed as yesterday. Once again, they'll make many threats and do other things. However, you are to keep your eyes open and not say a word. They will torture you and tear you to pieces, but don't be afraid because they can't do anything to you."

That night Don Giuseppe got undressed and went to bed. Immediately thereafter, the three kings arrived.

"What's your name?... Who sent you here?... He's certainly stubborn!... Talk... This one deserves to die!"

All three kept saying things, but Don Giuseppe kept looking at them with his eyes open and without speaking. When they saw how firm he was, they ordered him to be torn to pieces—and they made a pickled tuna fish out of him. Then they spread an ointment on him, and he became more handsome than ever before.

When he awoke, Don Giuseppe said, "Gentlemen, I thank you!" and he felt himself reinvigorated. When he got out of bed, he couldn't find his suit from the day before. Instead, there was a blue suit adorned with gold. He got dressed, and his first thought was to go and see the goat. When he found her, she was now a lady from her head to the waist. However, her legs and feet were those of a goat. There was only one veil over her face. Just think of how happy the goat was to see him in his clothes and herself almost a lady!

I forgot to mention this, but there was a handkerchief lined with silver in the first suit, and Don Giuseppe had given it to the goat and had said, "I want you to keep this!" And she kept it. The second night there was another handkerchief lined with gold, and this, too, he gave to her, and she saved it.

It's impossible to say how happy she was or to tell how she felt. She never tired of saying: "The Lord sent you to free me!" Then she added: "Tonight will be worse than all the others so you've got to pay attention because the three kings will bring servants with them carrying kitchen spits, and they'll stick them into you as if you were a sausage to roast on a grill. However, don't be afraid because they will use a certain ointment to make you become more handsome than ever before. But stay alert and don't talk!"

Don Giuseppe went up into the palace. He ate in peace, got undressed, and went to sleep. While he was sleeping, the three kings, who were marvelously dressed, appeared and tried to intimidate him. "Now you're finished!" they said. "Your life is no longer yours!"

Then one of them turned to him and said, "Just wait! But, before we kill you, you must get up and come with us!"

He got up, and they took him to the room where there was a lot of dirt.

"Take a fistful!" one of the kings said.

Don Giuseppe took a fistful in his hand, and it became a bunch of gold.

"You see," the king said, "this entire room is yours. You only have to tell me your name and who sent you here."

However, Don Giuseppe remained firm and looked him in the eyes without speaking. Therefore, when the kings saw this, they had a furnace lit and ordered four men to slice him like a sausage and throw him into the fire. Finally, they took a bottle and spread ointment on him, and he became more handsome and vigorous than ever before. Afterward, they put him back into the bed, and he fell into a deep sleep.

When it turned day, he saw that he was more handsome than ever before. Then he went to get dressed and found a white suit lined with gold and decorated with precious stones and a white handkerchief. After he descended, he went to the goat and found a young lady as beautiful as the sun. As soon as she saw him appear, she said, "Oh, Don Giuseppe, you are the one who has freed me from this evil spell!"

In turn, he took the white handkerchief and gave it to her. Now the maiden was dressed in the regal clothes that she had on when she had been carried off by the fairies from the royal palace. "Don Giuseppe," she said to him, "There's no time to lose. Let's be off!"

So, they went to the stable, gathered provisions of food and money, and took two handsome horses. Then they jumped onto the saddles, and as they were leaving, they heard a huge roar: "Boom!" The palace crumbled. The ground opened, and everything disappeared. The only thing that remained was clean open space.

They set out, and once they reached a forest they couldn't decide which path to take. They rode and rode and became separated from another. Don Giuseppe found his way to an inn, and nearby there was a church. He took lodgings at the inn where he told an old witch, who was serving the food, what had happened. She pretended not to understand anything. The next day Don Giuseppe went into the church. While he was hearing the mass, the old witch arrived and stuck a hairpin into his head. Immediately, Don Giuseppe fell asleep. And who do you suppose entered at that very moment? The Beauty of the Seven Mountains! She approached and found him asleep. "Don Giuseppe, Don Giuseppe!" She tugged at him, but she couldn't wake him from his deep sleep. Then she left behind one of her handkerchiefs as a sign.

When Don Giuseppe woke up and saw the handkerchief, he said, "Poor me! What am I to do? Where can I find her?"

The next day, as if the princess had said to him, "go into the church," he went into the church. The old witch returned with the hairpin, and she stuck him a second time. Beauty returned and was not able to wake him. Therefore, she left another handkerchief. In short, this happened three consecutive times. The third day the princess departed and left a letter with these exact words: "Dear Don Giuseppe, since I haven't been able to wake you, I'm leaving for my father's kingdom. I shall expect you in a year, a month, and a day. I'm leaving one more handkerchief for you that you should find useful."

After a long journey, the princess reached her father's kingdom. As soon as her ship entered the port, she was greeted by a salvo of guns just as it was done for royal ships. The king asked who had arrived, and as soon as he heard that it was his daughter, he and the queen ran to meet her. Just think of the great celebration that was held after the princess had been missing for so long! She told them all that had happened, how the fairies had carried her off, how she had become a goat, how the courageous Don Giuseppe had helped her become a lady again, and all the rest.

Once her story spread throughout the world, many princes arrived to ask for her hand in marriage. However, she always responded with no, because she was engaged to Don Giuseppe.

"But, my daughter," her mother said, "you must understand that we cannot live forever. 'If the young can die, the old cannot live,' as they say. One day or another we shall die, and who will take over the kingdom?"

The maiden asked for some more time and said, "I'll only get married after a year, a month, and a day have passed since my return."

Now let us turn to Don Giuseppe, who was unable to find peace of mind ever since he had become separated from his Beauty of the Seven Mountains of Gold. He wandered here and there, and after one year and twenty-nine days he arrived at the coast near the city of his beloved and saw a fisherman with a small boat. He was going fishing, and Don Giuseppe approached him and asked, "Good man, what are you doing?"

"What am I doing? I'm going fishing."

"Wait a moment!"

"I can't wait because the king's daughter is getting married tomorrow, and the king has ordered that all the fish that are caught are to be brought to the royal palace."

"Could you tell me how I can get to the royal palace?"

"Yes, my lord, come with me."

After the fisherman showed him the way to the royal palace, Don Giuseppe went for a walk in the esplanade but didn't see anyone. The next day he did this again, and let me tell you, he walked back and forth a thousand times, and that's not an exaggeration!

But let us now turn to the princess. She, too, had been unable to find any peace of mind and constantly looked out at the esplanade to see whether anyone had arrived. Indeed, he was there, but she didn't realize that it was Don Giuseppe. Then, at a certain moment, it dawned on him that she was looking at him, and so what did he do? He took out the black handkerchief and displayed it. As soon as she saw it, she said, "Oh, that's Don Giuseppe!"

He answered by putting away the black handkerchief and taking out the blue one. She took a closer look and said, "Oh! That's Don Giuseppe!"

Finally, he took out the white handkerchief adorned with gold and precious stones. She saw it and said, "There's no time to lose!" She called to one of the ladies of the court, who went and asked him to come up to the princess, and his heart jumped with joy. He mounted the stairs, and the Beauty of the Seven Mountains of Gold went toward him. They recognized each other and embraced. Just imagine the scene!

At this point, her mother arrived and said, "Who is this? What's going on here?"

"Ah, mother, this is the man who freed me from the evil spell!"

Then she took Don Giuseppe into the throne room and told her mother everything. The prince who was supposed to marry the Beauty of the Seven Mountains of Gold was also there, and he renounced his claim. He understood that Don Giuseppe had the right to marry Beauty because he had saved her.

All the preparations that had been made for this prince were now changed to serve Don Giuseppe. The priest was present, and to the delight and pleasure of the king, queen, and their entire court, Don Giuseppe wed the Beauty of the Seven Mountains of Gold.

They remained happy, content, and in peace,
While we're still here picking our teeth.

Told by Rosa Brusca in Palermo

29

THE FIG-AND-RAISIN FOOL

Once upon a time there was a foolish son who would eat nothing but figs and raisins. His friends said to him, "Do you want to come with us to collect wood?" and he answered, "Will there be figs and raisins there?"

"If you want them," they replied, "we'll certainly get you some."

"All right, then, I'm coming," was his answer.

So, he went with them to collect wood, and after much effort he amassed a huge bunch of branches.

"You dolt!" his friends exclaimed. "How do you expect to carry all of that back? Why don't you go find even more to pile on?"

Then they went off to another spot.

Now, in his search for more wood, the young fool came upon a fountain, and there he saw three nymphs sleeping nearby in the shade with their faces exposed to the sun. Consequently, the youth took some leaves and covered their faces. When the nymphs woke up, they realized that someone had passed by and had kindly shaded their faces to keep the sun from burning them. Consequently, they said, "May the person who was so kind to us be granted whatever wish his heart desires as long as he lives."

Right at this moment the foolish youth had tied up his entire bundle of wood, and when he looked at its size, he exclaimed, "Now that you're all tied up, who's going to carry you? You should be carrying me!"

All at once, the bundle of wood swept beneath him and carried him all the way back to Palermo and right to his own front door. On the way, however, he passed through the street where the king's daughter happened to be looking out the window, and she burst out laughing at him.

"I wish I could make that maiden pregnant!" was the youth's response when he saw her.

And that's exactly what happened. Then, as soon as the king became aware of his daughter's condition, he gave her a great scolding, while she insisted on her innocence. When she finally gave birth, the king proclaimed that, once they found the man who was responsible, both he and the princess would be placed in a bronze barrel and thrown into the sea.

Soon the king devised a scheme for discovering who the man was. He ordered a three-day banquet to be held, the first day for the nobility, the second day for the merchant class, and the third day for the common people. At each banquet, he told his daughter's child to walk around and find his father. At the banquet for the nobility, the child made the rounds without identifying anyone. At the banquet for the merchants, the same thing happened. At the banquet for the common folk, the fool's friends all said, "Look, today all the commoners are invited to dine at the royal palace. Aren't you going to come?"

"Will there be figs and raisins there?" asked the young man.

"Oh, good grief! Always figs and raisins, raisins and figs! Of course they'll have that to eat as well, so why don't you come along with us?"

Once they were inside the palace, the young fool began to feel uncomfortable. He twisted this way and that, he stretched and he yawned, until finally it was time for the banquet, and the king said to the child, "Go and find your father."

The innocent young creature walked this way and that way and ended up directly in front of the fool. "This is my father," he declared.

"Oh, you stupid creature!" said the king to his daughter. "Were your eyes screwed in backwards? You've managed to fall in love with a total fool! Oh, what a disaster! But just wait—I have a remedy for this."

Consequently, he ordered a bronze barrel to be built. Once it was finished, he had the fool and his daughter packed inside with their son and tossed into the sea. Now the fool was able to recount his whole story to the princess, beginning with his going to collect wood and his encounter with the nymphs.

"Do you recall," he asked, "when you saw me go by riding on the bundle of wood and you laughed at me? Well, that's when I said, 'I wish I could make that maiden pregnant.'"

"Oh," replied the princess, "so those were the words I saw you muttering under your breath! Well, if you have such powers, why don't you bring this barrel back to dry land?"

Well, all at once, they were back on land.

"Now make the barrel open and release us."

"If I do, will you give me figs and raisins?"

"Yes, my husband. Of course I will."

In an instant, they were all outside the barrel.

Now that they were free, they purchased a large palace and surrounded it with a magnificent garden filled with every kind of delectable plant. Then they hired a guard to stand at the entrance and direct every passerby to read what was written above the portal:

You may look, but you must not touch! Take a pear or a bunch of grapes,
and you lose your life!

Well, various people visited the garden, and among them was
the king himself. The fool recognized him and said, "Could the
king's pocket be hiding a bunch of grapes?"

In fact, this was true because the fool had ordered a guard to
slip the grapes into the king's pocket.

"Seize that thief!" he shouted to his guard. "Hold him right
there!"

The king was at a loss for what to do, and when they searched
his pockets, they found the grapes. The fool now declared that
the king must be put to death. The king begged for mercy, asking the fool to take pity on him and spare his life. Finally, the fool
consented, revealing his true identity to the king.

And so they all lived on, happy and content,
While we cannot even pay our rent.

———————

Collected by Giuseppe-Vincenzo Marotta in Cerda

30

THE HAUGHTY KING

Once upon a time there was a merchant, and this merchant
had three daughters. One day he called the three of them
to him and said, "My girls, I must depart because of some business
affairs. What do you want me to bring back to you?"

One daughter, the eldest, said to him, "I want a rose-colored
dress."

The next one said, "I want an aqua-colored dress."

"And I want you to go to the king and tell him that I am weeping for him," said the youngest.

The father had to travel to Portugal, and so he said farewell to his daughters and departed.

No sooner did the merchant arrive in Portugal than he took care of his business and then bought a rose-colored dress for his eldest daughter and an aqua-colored dress for the middle daughter. Then he decided to go to the king. Consequently, he sent a message to the palace, and soon thereafter, he appeared before the king and said, "Your majesty, I have a daughter who is weeping for you."

Upon hearing this, the king took a handkerchief and said, "Take it and give it to her to dry her tears."

Just imagine how the father felt! Well, he returned home with this weight wrenching in his stomach and said to his daughters, "Here, take this rose-colored dress. Take this aqua-colored dress. And you, here's a handkerchief that the King of Portugal has sent so that you can dry your tears when you weep."

Consequently, the maiden began to weep like a baby.

Some time later, the father had to depart again to take care of his business affairs. The older daughters submitted their requests for gifts, and the youngest said to him, "I'd appreciate it if you would go to the King of Portugal and tell him that I'm going to drown myself for him."

"Oh, my daughter, do you think that I want to go back to the king after what he said to me?"

"That really doesn't matter, father. You must do me this favor!"

In short, he had to do it. Therefore, the father departed for Portugal, and soon after he had taken care of his affairs, he went to the palace.

"Your Majesty, my daughter is going to drown herself for you."

"Oh, is that right? Well then, take this rope for her," he replied and gave him a piece of rope.

Meanwhile, the father felt like dying. Then, as soon as he returned home, he called for his youngest daughter and said, "Do you know what happened? You've got me into another mess with the king. He's sent you this piece of rope."

Consequently, his daughter burst into tears.

Several more months passed. The father had to depart another time.

"Papa," the youngest daughter said. "Will you do me a favor? Go to the king and tell him that I am going to kill myself for him."

"My daughter," her father replied, "you're crazy if you think that I am going to return to the king's palace!"

"But you must do this favor for me!"

"No, my daughter."

"Yes, you must do this favor for me."

"No, I'm not going to do it."

In short, in the end, her father agreed to do what she requested. Indeed, once he arrived in Portugal and finished taking care of his affairs, he went up to the royal palace and asked for an audience with the king. No sooner did the king learn that the daughter wanted to kill herself, he took a knife and gave it to the merchant. The poor father felt as if he were going to die . . . but then he returned home, and soon thereafter, his daughter appeared before him.

"Take this," the father said. "The king sent you this knife!"

After this occurred, the poor maiden no longer had any peace of mind and decided to depart for Portugal herself. Her father did all he possibly could to prevent her from leaving, but once he realized that he it was impossible to convince her, he had a horse saddled for her, gave her a large purse of gold coins, and wished her farewell.

Well, she rode and rode and rode until she arrived in Portugal, where one of her cousins, the son of his father's sister, was living. As soon as she went to his house, she told him right away all that had happened, and she ended by saying that she wanted to be sold to the king as a slave. Well, once the king saw this beautiful maiden, he immediately bought her.

After they returned to the palace, the king could think of nothing else but this maiden. When the time arrived for him to take a stroll around the grounds, he suddenly turned around to look for her and speak with her. In short, he fell in love with her.

One beautiful day, he said to her, "Rosina (that was the way she was called), do you see this? I'm always weeping for you."

Well, she took the handkerchief that the king had sent to her and said, "Take this, and dry your tears."

The king opened the handkerchief and recognized it. Then he said to himself, "What am I seeing? Could she be the merchant's daughter?"

After some days passed, he said, "Rosina, if you don't love me very much, I'm going to drown myself."

"Well then, drown yourself," she said and gave him the rope.

Of course, he recognized it and said to himself, "It's certain that she's the merchant's daughter!"

So he returned to her and said, "Rosina, don't you really love me? Look, if you don't love me, I'm going to kill myself!"

"Well then, go and kill yourself!" she said and handed him the knife.

At this point, the king was firmly convinced that she was the merchant's daughter. Therefore, he said, "Look, I've recognized you. Either you love me, or I'll kill myself!"

Upon hearing this, she turned and replied again, "Well then, kill yourself!"

As a result, the king pretended to kill himself, and she left him and went down to her room (for she had a room in the palace with a balcony that overlooked the court).

The next day the king had himself put into a coffin and had it carried below the slave's balcony. Then she appeared on the balcony, and no sooner than she saw him (indeed, she knew it was all a fiction), she spit on him, "Phooey! Think of how much you could have done for a lady!" Then she closed the balcony in his face.

In short, he constantly pleaded with her for some days, and finally, she said, yes, she would marry the king. Once she agreed to his proposal, they sent for her father and her sisters and celebrated their marriage in great pomp.

They all remained happy and at ease,
While we sit here grinding our teeth.

———————

Told by Rosa Brusca, blind woman, in Palermo

31

THE HAUGHTY QUEEN

Once upon a time, so they say, there was a king and queen. Now, the queen was haughty and rude. If the king said a word to her, she responded badly. In the morning, when the damsels of the court brought her coffee, she would throw the coffee at them if she became irritated. Consequently, the damsels decided to go to the king.

"Your Majesty," they said to him, "we can no longer serve the queen. Whatever we bring to her, she throws at our faces. If we say the wrong word, she suddenly loses her patience. What kind of manners are these?"

The king became concerned, and consequently, one day he called his councilors together, and they advised him to send for a sorcerer. Well, no sooner did the sorcerer arrive than the king told him everything—about the wife he had, the fact that she was unbearable, and everything else. Then the sorcerer said to him, "Your Majesty, I'd like to get to know this queen."

"That's not so easy," the king said to him. "You have to disguise yourself as a general, and then you must leave here and come back on a ship in your disguise as a general and pretend to be a stranger when you go to the palace."

Well, the sorcerer did just this. He embarked and then returned, let us say, in Naples. He fired a salute from his ship and called for celebrations

"A general's arrived!" the people cried. "It's an English ship!"

There was great pandemonium and excitement. Then the general got off the ship, and the king went toward him to greet him. When they arrived at the palace, the king took him to the grand courtroom and sent a servant to bring his wife.

"What do you want?" the queen asked as usual.

"An English general has arrived. It's only proper that you show him some respect and come to two ceremonies."

"Get out of here! I'll arrive at the proper hour."

Eventually, the queen was persuaded to come and present herself to the general. She remained there a while and then retired to her chamber. After she had gone, the king turned and said, "Sorcerer, what do you think of the queen?"

"Majesty, give me a month's time, and I'll take care of the queen."

So, the sorcerer began to stroll about all of Naples and arrived at the Basso Porto where he saw a fish shop that he thought would serve well as the retreat for the queen. He used his magic to have the fish dealer's wife take the place of the queen at the palace and for the queen to take the place of the fish dealer's wife.

The next morning the fish dealer called his wife and told her to start the fire to cook some tripe.

"Get up and light the fire. It's late!"

The queen, now the fish dealer's wife, turned and said, "What fire? I'm the queen."

"Get up! If you don't, I'll give you a good beating, and I'll make you see whether you're the queen."

"You must be joking!" she responded. "Fire? What fire?"

However, seeing that her husband was serious, she began thinking perhaps all this was the Lord's punishment for the haughtiness that she had always shown. In the meantime, the fish dealer, her husband, saw that she wasn't going to get up. So, he got up and lit the fire, grumbling as he finished the discussion. Right after doing this, he left the room to call his mother-in-law, who went to her daughter (convinced that she was her real daughter) and said to her, "My daughter, what's come into your head to think that you are the queen? That queen who's in the palace is queen! You're just the poor wife of a fish dealer."

"I'm queen!"

"Queen? You must be joking! Don't you see that you'll wind up going crazy?"

When it came time to eat breakfast, the mother-in-law gave her a little piece of the fish's entrails.

"What's this?" the queen asked. "I don't eat things like this. I'm queen."

Then, at noon, it was the same, and she remained on a hunger strike. In short, she led this life for some days and eventually convinced herself that she was no longer queen because she was guilty of being haughty. That's why she began to take her place at the caldron to sell the broth and the tripe.

But let us leave her selling the fish and turn to the fish dealer's wife who found herself at the royal palace.

The next day the damsels of the court came to her to bring her coffee, and they found her and everything else completely dirty and smeared—just imagine how strange everything seemed to them! Then they turned and said to her, "Majesty, would you like some coffee?"

The fish dealer's wife didn't know what to respond. She was stunned and looked at all the ladies. Then she took the coffee and thanked them. Right after this the damsels took her into the bathroom, and after bathing her, the fisher dealer's wife came out looking beautiful and clean. Finally, they went to the king.

"Your Majesty," they said. "Perhaps the queen has desired to transform herself?... She took the coffee without throwing it at us."

As soon as the king heard this, he went to the queen: "Your Highness, how did you spend the night?"

And the stunned fish dealer's wife replied, "Very well. And you?"

"Very well," said the king, who was surprised that, for one time, the queen responded to him without haughtiness.

After three days passed, the sorcerer went to the king and asked him, "Majesty, how has the queen been behaving?"

"The queen is some other person," the king told him. "She's no longer haughty, and she responds without being sour. I'd say that she's changed her attitude and habits."

Then the king paid the sorcerer a good deal of money. Of course, the sorcerer took the money and went away.

Now, let us turn to the real queen who received a good drubbing day and night because she didn't want to get up in the morning and didn't want to eat the fish. Whenever the real queen became fussy, the fish dealer (who was convinced that she was his real wife) struck her badly, and she always screamed: "This is not my house! I'm queen, and my house is the royal palace!"

As a result of the constant beating, the queen fell ill, and so they called for someone to cure her. Well, you can imagine whom they called. The sorcerer, of course. Then, as soon as he saw her, he became convinced that she had now regretted her haughty behavior and had changed her attitude and habits. Consequently, he gave her some medicine that cured her right away, and that night, he decided to turn her back into the queen and to return the fish dealer's wife to the fish dealer's shop.

The next day, the damsels went to bring the coffee to the queen and once again found her dirty and smeared. They could barely look at her. (Of course! She had just stopped selling fish and living in the fish dealer's house.) However, even if she was smeared and filthy, her manners were good because her haughtiness had now passed away, and she had stopped putting on airs. The first thing the queen did was to call the king, and no sooner did she see him, she embraced him and told him about everything that had happened: that she had been in a very poor house of a fish dealer without eating and received a good drubbing. When the king heard this, he turned to her and said, "Well, are you now aware of your haughtiness?"

"Certainly I am aware of it. From now on, I'll be humble and good with everyone because I'm convinced that all that I experienced was a warning from the Lord."

And so, they turned to each other, embraced, and kissed, and the king became the love of her life. From that day onward, they no longer argued.

> They remained husband and wife,
> While we asses are reined without a life.

Collected by Professor Carlo Siriani in Ragusa Inferiore

32

THE LITTLE BIRD

Once upon a time, so they say, there was a husband and wife, who had two young children. They were actually his children, while the wife was their stepmother. The girl and boy loved each other very much and were each the apple of each other's eyes.

One day, the stepmother became fed up with the boy because she really couldn't stand him. Secretly, she took the boy away from his sister, cut him into pieces, and cooked him.

When the husband returned home, he asked, "Where's the boy?"

"What do I know?" the wife said. "I didn't see him the entire day."

When the little sister heard this, she burst into tears.

Then lunchtime arrived, and they sat down at the table and began eating. When the meat was served, each one ate his or her food, but the little girl refused because her heart told her that it was the flesh of her brother. So, what did she do? She gathered all the little bones of the flesh and kept them in a chest.

One day, she went and opened the chest, and all at once a little bird flew out. She wanted to catch it, but the little bird escaped.

Now a few days passed, and the little bird came to her window and began singing:

"Peep, peep, peep!
My stepmother, she has murdered me.
My father he has eaten me.
My sister refused to touch me.
She's gathered my bones for all to see."

Upon hearing this, the sister asked, "What are you saying? What are you saying, little bird?"

Then the bird responded: "Hold on, and take this," and he threw a little piece of paper that his sister kept.

The next day the little bird flew to the mattress maker and sang:

"Peep, peep, peep!
My stepmother, she has murdered me.
My father he has eaten me.
My sister refused to touch me.
She's gathered my bones for all to see."

Upon hearing this, the mattress maker responded quickly: "What are you saying, what are you saying, little bird?"

"What am I saying? Can you give me two mattresses? If you do, I'll tell you what I've said."

The mattress maker immediately prepared two mattresses and brought them out to the bird. Then the little bird sang:

"Peep, peep, peep!
My stepmother, she has murdered me.
My father he has eaten me.
My sister refused to touch me.
She's gathered my bones for all to see."

No sooner did the bird finish singing than it took the mattresses in its beak (which was enchanted) and carried them away. I won't tell you how surprised the mattress maker was! He couldn't believe that the little bird would succeed in carrying the mattresses in its beak and yelled, "Catch it! Catch the bird!"

However, who could possibly hope to catch the bird even if that person had been able to see it fly! Therefore, the little bird returned to his sister and sang the same song. His sister opened her window, and the bird threw the mattresses to her so that she could set them aside for her dowry.

The next day the little bird went to the chair maker and sang the same song, and the carpenter responded, "What are you saying, what are you saying, little bird?"

Then the bird responded, "If I tell you, you must set out twelve chairs for me."

Therefore, the carpenter prepared twelve chairs for the bird, and the little bird sang the same song. No sooner had the bird finished than it grabbed the chairs in its beak, and flew away.

The carpenter remained standing and watched it fly away badly disappointed. Meanwhile, the little bird went to his sister and left the chairs there.

"Hold on, and set these chairs aside for your dowry."

Then the bird flew to the silversmith and sang the same song, convincing the silversmith to prepare a diamond ring. As soon as the ring was finished and ready, the little bird sang, then grabbed the ring, and brought it through the air to his sister. In short, the little bird brought a dowry for his little sister, one piece at a time, including the nightgowns, combs, and shoes.

In the meantime, the stepmother, who had seen all these beautiful things arrive, became jealous. Consequently, she turned to the bird and said, "Little bird, little bird, haven't you brought me anything?"

"Indeed," the little bird replied, "tomorrow I'll bring you something beautiful."

And what did he do? The little bird flew to a woman who sold nails and had her give him a sack, and as usual, he sang the same song:

"Peep, peep, peep!
My stepmother, she has murdered me.
My father he has eaten me.
My sister refused to touch me.
She's gathered my bones for all to see."

Then the little bird flew with the sack of nails to the stepmother and sang his song:

"Peep, peep, peep!
My stepmother, she has murdered me.
My father he has eaten me.
My sister refused to touch me.
She's gathered my bones for all to see."

No sooner did the stepmother see the bird arrive, she said, "Little bird, what have you brought me?"

"Lie down flat on your back showing me your stomach, and I'll give you what I've brought you."

The stepmother laid down flat on her back showing her stomach, and *pow!* The bird threw the little sack of nails straight down on her stomach. Then the stepmother breathed her last breath and died.

His sister was frightened and began to weep when she thought about her father. However, the little bird turned neither green nor yellow, and said, "It doesn't matter. Don't be afraid. When your father comes, you're to give him the little piece of paper that I threw at you so that he will understand who it was who killed his wife."

Then the bird disappeared.

When the father returned home, he was troubled by the disaster. His daughter was crying and told him everything, but her father wouldn't believe her because he was convinced that it was she who killed his wife. When his daughter saw that her father was so obstinate, she took the little letter and gave it to him. And what was written in this letter? Everything that the stepmother had done to the little boy recorded in exhaustive detail. Then the little girl told him about the entire dowry that the little bird had brought to her, and her father finally realized that the wicked person was really his wife.

> They remained happy and content,
> While we sit here without a cent.

––––––––––

Told by Giovannina of Monreale in Palermo

❖

GIUFÀ THE FOOL
TALES

THE NAME OF GIUFÀ WAS ALWAYS MODIFIED
and changed depending on the village, city, and country. In Sicily,
for example, the name is Giucà in Trapani and Giuzà in Piana de'
Greci and Palazzo Adriano as well as in some regions of Albania. In
Calabria the name is Giurali; in Tuscany, Rome, and The Marches,
the name is Giucca. The name Giufà stems from an Arab tribe, and
there are similar figures in Sdirrameddu and in Maju longu (Polizzi),
Loccu di li passuli e ficu (Cerda), and Martinu (Palermo)—all are
fantastic characters whose foolish acts are also attributed to Giufà. Oth-
ers can be found in Trianniscia (Terra d'Otranto), Mato (Venezia),
Simonëtt, Bertoldino, and Cacasenno (Piemonte).

33

GIUFÀ *and the* PLASTER STATUE

There's a tale I heard about a mother who had a son named Giufà. This mother lived in poverty, and her son Giufà was a simple-minded and lazy rogue. His mother had a piece of cloth and said to Giufà, "Take this piece of cloth, and go sell it in the village. Make sure you sell it to a person who doesn't talk too much."

So, Giufà departed with the cloth with the intention of selling it. When he arrived in the village, he began shouting, "Who wants to buy some cloth!"

He cried out to the people and began to speak to some who talked a great deal and to some who refused to buy his cloth because he demanded too much. Giufà made certain not to sell the cloth to people who talked a great deal. He walked here and there until he entered a courtyard. Nobody was there except a plaster statue, and Giufà spoke to it: "Do you want to buy this cloth?"

The statute didn't say a word, and seeing that it spoke very little, Giufà said, "Since you don't speak much, I've got to sell the cloth to you."

Therefore, he took the cloth and hung it over the statue.

"Tomorrow, I'll return for the money." And he went away.

The next day he came for the money and found that the cloth had been taken.

"Give me the money for the cloth," he demanded, but the statue said nothing.

"Well, if you won't give me the money, I'll show you who I am!" And he ran to borrow a hammer, and when he returned, he smashed the statue until it fell to pieces, and he found a jar of money inside it. He put the money into a sack and went to his mother. When he arrived home, he said to his mother, "I sold the cloth to someone who didn't talk much, but he didn't give me any money last night. So, I went back this morning with a hammer to kill him. When he fell to the ground, he gave me this money."

His mother, who was smart, replied, "Don't tell anyone about this. We'll spend this money little by little."

———

Told by Giuseppe La Duca and collected by Gaetano Di Giovani in Casteltermini.

34

GIUFÀ *and the* PIECE OF CLOTH

Another time his mother said to him, "Giufà, I have this piece of cloth that's got to be dyed. Go to the dyer who dyes the cloth green or black and leave it at his shop."

Giufà put the cloth over his shoulder and left. As he was walking he saw a large beautiful snake, and seeing that it was green, he said, "My mother has sent me, and she wants this cloth dyed green. Tomorrow I'll come and get it." And he left it there.

When he returned home, and his mother heard what he had done, she began to tear out her hair. "Ah, you fool! You'll be the end of me! . . . Run back and seen if it's still there!"

Giufà went back, but the cloth was gone.

———

Told by Rosa Brusca in Palermo

35

GIUFÀ *and the* JUDGE

One morning Giufà went out to gather wild herbs to eat, and before he returned to his village, it became dark. While he was walking, the moon appeared, but it was cloudy, and the moon kept disappearing and reappearing. He sat down on top of a rock, and began to watch the moon that disappeared and reappeared, and each time it appeared and disappeared, he cried out, "It's coming! It's coming! It's hiding! It's hiding!"

Meanwhile there were some thieves nearby, and they happened to be skinning a calf that they had stolen. When they heard, "It's coming! It's hiding!" they were frightened that the law officers were coming, and they ran away and left the meat behind them. When Giufà saw them running away, he went to see what was there and found the skinned calf. He took his knife, began to cut off some of the meat, and filled his sack with it. Then he left, and when he arrived home, he said to his mother, "Here I am."

"How come you're so late?" his mother asked.

"I'm late because I've brought you some meat, and tomorrow you're to sell all of it because I need the money."

"Tomorrow I want you to go into the countryside, and I'll sell the meat," his mother said.

The next day Giufà went into the countryside, and his mother sold the meat. At night, Giufà returned and said, "Did you sell the meat, mother?"

"Yes, I gave it to the flies on credit."

"And when will they give you the money?"

"When they have it."

A week passed, and the flies didn't bring the money. So Giufà went to the judge and said, "Your honor, I want justice. I gave the meat to the flies on credit, and they haven't come to pay me."

"Well, then I'll sentence them to be killed by you," the judge said.

Just at that moment a fly landed right on the head of the judge, and Giufà gave him such as blow with his fist that he broke the judge's head.

Told by Giuseppe La Duca and collected by Gaetano Di Giovani in Casteltermini

36

"EAT, MY FINE CLOTHING"

S ince Giufà was half a fool, nobody treated him very kindly. He was never invited anywhere, and nobody ever gave him a gift. One time Giufà went to a large farm and asked for something to eat, but as soon as the farmers saw him—dirty and poorly dressed as he was—it didn't take much for them to set the dogs on him. Therefore, he left much worse off than before. His mother understood the reason for the treatment he received and bought him a beautiful jacket, a pair of pants, and a velvet waistcoat.

Now, Giufà, dressed in an impressive way, went back to the farm, and you should have seen the great honors they bestowed on him! They even invited him to dine at the table. And they did this in a very ceremonious way. Giufà didn't know how to read or write, and when the meal arrived, he stuffed food into his belly with one hand, and with the other, he stuffed food into the pockets of his jacket and pants. In addition, with each thing he saved in his jacket, he said "Eat, my fine clothing. After all, you're the ones who were invited."

Told by Francesca Amato in Palermo

37

"GIUFÀ, PULL THE DOOR!"

One day, before Giufà's mother went to church, she said to her son, "Giufà, I'm going to mass. Take care, and after I close the door, make sure you pull it."

As soon she left, Giufà went to the door and began to pull it. He pulled and pulled so hard that it came off the hinges. He carried the door on his back and went to the church to bring it to his mother.

"Here's the door you told me to pull."

Now tell me what you think about this.

Told by Rosa Brusca in Palermo

38

GIUFÀ *and the* HEN

Once upon a time, so it's been told, there was Giufà, and before his mother went out, she said to him, "I'm going to mass. Look after the hen that's about to hatch her eggs. Take it and give it some bread and wine in a soup to eat, then put it back on the nest immediately so that the eggs don't get cold."

Giufà took the hen, prepared a soup of bread and wine, and stuck it in its throat with such force that the hen choked and died. When Giufà saw that the hen was dead, he said, "What am I going to do now? The eggs will get cold. I'd better get on top of them to hatch them."

Therefore, he took off his pants and sat down on the eggs. When his mother returned, she began looking for him.

"Giufà! Giufà!" she cried.

"Cluck, cluck, cluck!" he responded. "I can't come. I'm a hen, and I'm hatching my eggs. If you take me away from the nest, the eggs will get cold."

"You stupid fool, you! You've crushed all the eggs."

Giufà got off the nest, and all the eggs were a mess.

———

Told by the teacher Vincenzo Aricò and collected by Gaetano Di Giovanni in Casteltermini

FIRRAZZANU
TALES

ACCORDING TO PITRÈ, FIRRAZZANU IS THE *personification of Sicilian caprice, cunning, pleasantry, and jest, like the sly characters who personify cunning, jest, and caprice in other regions and countries of Europe and the Middle East. They are known as the clever fools.*

In general, almost all of Firrazzanu's caprices can be found in a little book, Le Buffonerie del Gonnella, Cosa Piacevole et da Ridere ecc. *Pitrè never read this book, but he recommended G. B. Passano,* I Novellieri Italiani in Verso Indicati e Descritti *(Bologna: Romagnoli, 1868).*

39

FIRRAZZANU'S WIFE *and the* QUEEN

Gentlemen, let me tell you about Firrazzanu, who was quite unique. Indeed, his antics could make even a mute laugh.

Firrazzanu was, let's say, a valet . . . to be more precise . . . a man who served the Prince of Palermo. He even played his tricks on this prince, but since Firrazzanu was well known and delighted everyone, the prince overlooked them, and Firrazzanu often got away with them.

One time the queen was in Palermo and wanted to get to know Firrazzanu. So, she invited him to amuse her a while.

"Are your married or single?" she asked.

"Married, your majesty."

"May I become acquainted with your wife?"

"I'm afraid it's impossible, your majesty. My wife's somewhat deaf."

(This was something Firrazzanu made up off the top of his head because it wasn't true.)

"That doesn't matter," the queen replied. "When I speak with her, I'll shout. Go and bring your wife here."

Firrazzanu went home and said to his wife, "Cicca, the queen wants to make your acquaintance. But you must know that she's hard of hearing, and when you talk to her, you must speak in a loud voice."

"Very well," his wife said. "Let's go."

So, they departed for the palace. When they arrived, she said to the queen in a loud voice, "I'm at your majesty's service!"

The queen said to herself, "Oh, now I see! She's shouting because she believes everyone else is deaf." Then she turned and spoke in a loud voice to Firrazzanu's wife, "Good day, my friend, how are you?"

"I'm fine, your majesty!" she responded in a voice even louder.

To make herself heard better, the queen raised her voice and began to scream, while Cicca also screamed louder and louder so that it seemed as if they were quarreling. All this was too much for Firrazzanu to take, and he burst out laughing because he couldn't hold himself back. Now the queen realized the joke, and if Firrazzanu had not run away, perhaps, perhaps she would have had him arrested, and who knows how it might have ended?

Collected in Palermo

40

FIRRAZZANU *and the* SWINEHERD

One time Firrazzanu was as desperate as a bee in winter and racked his brains to try to find a way to stir things up. So he left Palermo, and when he saw a nice herd of pigs, he was struck by the large number of huge and fat pigs. Along the way, he met the swineherd, and he pretended to be a rich and grand person. When the swineherd saw him dressed so well and with a top hat, he said, "I kiss your hand, my lord! Would you like something?"

"Nothing," said Firrazzanu, "I was just admiring these pigs as they eat."

And this was the way Firrazzanu got to know the swineherd, and they began having long talks. Slowly Firrazzanu discovered who owned the pigs, when the pigs went out to pasture, when they ate, and many other things. Finally, he wished to see the pigs eat the beans.

"Oh!" he cried out. "How graciously they eat, my little pigs! I love them very much because they cheer me up."

Afterward, Firrazzanu took out six gold coins and gave them to the swineherd as a gift.

"This is for you," he said, "and from now on you would do me a great favor by waiting for me to come every day before you feed the pigs because it delights me so much to watch them eat."

For the swineherd this request seemed strange, but he said to himself, "Just look at the kinds of taste rich people have nowadays! But what's it to me? These are how the times are."

The next day Firrazzanu did the same thing, and after he saw the pigs eat, he said just what he said before: "How graciously they eat, my little pigs!" and then he gave six coins to the swineherd. To be brief, Firrazzanu began to lead this life for a few days, and the swineherd was pleased because it was as if God's providence had descended on him without his even searching for it.

Now, one day Firrazzanu went to the meat market and began negotiating with two butchers.

"Do you want to buy my herd of pigs?"

"Why not?"

"There are two hundred."

"How much do you want?"

"A lot. Let's say, two thousand gold coins."

"We'll give you a thousand eight hundred."

"No, sir. Give me a thousand nine hundred, and they're yours."

"No, sir."

"Yes, it's a gift."

"All right," they said, "but when can we see the pigs?"

"Come with me now."

And they departed to go and see the pigs.

By the way, I forgot to mention that Firrazzanu had told the swineherd that his name was Baron Patruni . . . So, now when they arrived at the pigpen, the swineherd came running and took off his cap to greet Firrazzanu, for he had become accustomed to receiving the six coins.

"Oh, Baron Patruni!" he cried out. "What is your command, my lord?"

"Have you given my pigs their beans?"

"No, my lord," he replied. "I was waiting for you, my lord. I'll do it right away."

While the swineherd went to fetch the beans, Firrazzanu said to the butchers, "Do me a favor and don't say anything to the swineherd about the sale of the pigs. The poor man loves them so much so that if he hears that they are to be sold, he'll die on the spot. So, now, tell me, what do you think? Are you satisfied?—Is it a deal?"

"Yes, my lord."

"Well then, let's return to Palermo."

At this point Firrazzanu called the swineherd and said, "You, Peppi, tomorrow these gentlemen are going to come. I want you to treat them as if they were me, and whatever they tell you, you're to do."

"Tomorrow, I'll treat them as if they were you, my lord."

"Good bye."

"I kiss your hand, my lord."

The next morning, after the butchers had paid Firrazzanu, they went to fetch the pigs. However, the swineherd began to make a fuss.

"What, are you crazy? You want the pigs? Get out of here! Scram!"

"They're ours!"

"Yours? They belong to my master!"

"He sold them to us."

"You're crazy. The Prince of Messina (let's just say that this was his name) didn't sell you a thing!"

"What Prince of Messina?" they cried out. "It was your master, the baron, who sold us the pigs. Just yesterday we settled on the price, and he sold them to us."

"That's not my master," the swineherd said. "My master is the Prince of Messina. The man you're talking about, the man you met yesterday, is the one who comes and gives me six coins a day to see the pigs eat and I respect him. But he's not my master!"

"Is it true what you say?"

"I swear upon my heart!"

"Ah, he's tricked us, that crook! Quick, let's go search for him!"

The two of them ran off to hunt for the Baron Patruni. But who was the baron! Firrazzanu had taken off the clothes of the baron that he had used, and he put on a beard. Moreover, he left the country to enjoy the good sum of money that he had taken from the two butchers.

————————

Collected in Borgetto

41

THE TWENTY PERCENT

Once a very rich prince, let us call him, Prince Partanna, had many rents to collect, and he couldn't manage to get them all. So he thought of making Firrazzanu the procurer.

"I'm making you my procurer," he said, "and you're to collect my rents. If you do your job, I'll give you twenty percent of what you collect."

Firrazzanu went off to a village where he was to collect the rents, and he summoned all the peasants who owed money. Then, what do you think her did? Well, he had them pay only his part, the twenty percent, and nothing more than that.

"You can pay the rent to the prince another year," he said. "Now get out of here!"

Then Firrazzanu returned to the prince, who asked, "What did you do, Firrazzanu? Did you collect all the rents?"

"What rent was there to collect? I was barely able to collect my own twenty percent."

"What do you mean by this?"

"They had trouble just paying me the twenty percent that belonged to me. I told them that they could pay you your rent next year."

Imagine how the prince reacted! At first, he kept quiet, and then he burst into laughter. Consequently, Firrazzanu went away cheerful and content.

Collected in Borgetto

42

THE HUNDRED BEATINGS

Just listen to what Firrazzanu did another time:

His master wanted to teach him a good lesson and give him a taste of a wood stick on his back. So, what do you think he did? He spoke with the commander of the castle and said, "In the next few days I'm going to send you my servant with a letter, and you're to do whatever I say in that letter."

Well, after a few days, let us say a week, the prince summoned Firrazzanu and said, "Firrazzanu, I want you to go to the commander of the castle, and you're to tell him that he's to do what I've written in this letter."

Firrazzanu left, and he read the letter from top to bottom and was not pleased by its contents. Just at that moment, he encountered another servant and said, "Listen, I want you to do me a favor and carry this letter to the commander of the castle and tell him that he's to do what the letter says. When you return, we'll have a nice glass of wine together."

The servant went to the commander, who opened the letter, and this is what it said: "I order the commander to beat my servant with a stick a hundred times because he is truly impertinent. Then you are to send him back to me."

"Wait here," said the commander, who called the executioner, and he, in turn, put the servant on top of a trestle. Then the commander ordered him to give him 100 beatings with a stick. The poor innocent servant moaned and groaned and screamed that he hadn't done a thing, but the executioner told him that he had to follow orders.

Enough said. The poor servant left there more dead than alive, and when he returned to the palace, Firrazzanu burst out laughing and said, "My brother, between you and me, it's better you than me."

Collected in Palermo

❖

COLA PESCE
LEGENDS

THE LEGEND OF COLA PESCE OR PESCECOLA IS
practically the "national" legend of Sicily, and there are numerous versions that have been collected and recorded since the twelfth century.
The "standard" plot concerns a young man named Nicola (Cola of
Messina), the son of a fisherman, who is called Colapesce because he
can swim like a fish and has the ability to spend hours beneath the sea.
When the King of Sicily, Emperor Frederick II of Sweden, hears about
his ability, he decides to test him and embarks for Messina, where he
throws a gold cup into the sea, which Colapesce retrieves. Then the
king throws his gold crown, which Colapesce retrieves. Finally, the
king throws his gold ring into the deepest part of the sea. This time
Colapesce does not retrieve it and is not seen again. In another widespread version the King of Sicily is curious to know what lies beneath
Mount Etna, the gigantic volcano, and he sends Colapesce to discover
what is supporting the island and the volcano. Colapesce reports first
that there are three columns holding up Sicily, two of which are broken. He also reports that there is a dangerous fire beneath the volcano.
The king wants proof and sends Colapesce back down under. Colapesce
does not re-surface but a piece of wood that he had been carrying with
him returns to the surface. It is thought that Colapesce has replaced
the broken columns and is supporting all of Sicily.

43

COLA PESCE

Cola Pesce was from Torre Faro[1] and knew how to swim better than a fish. Suffice to say, he swam from Messina to Catania and from Catania to Messina always under water.

One time the king came to Messina and learned that there was this marvelous man living in the city who was the best of all swimmers. Upon hearing this, the king wanted to meet him. Therefore, he sent a message and had Cola Pesce appear before him.

"Tell me," the king said to him, "is it true that you swim so well?"

"Yes, your majesty!"

All at once, the king threw a sword into the sea, and Cola plunged after it to bring it back to the king. After viewing this, the queen threw a ring into the sea, for she was convinced that Cola wouldn't succeed in retrieving it. However, Cola Pesce did retrieve it.

"Well, now you must tell me what is below at the foot of Salvatore,[2]" the king said to him.

So, Cola dove into the sea, observed everything there was to see, and returned to the surface.

"Your majesty, do you know what's there? I saw a cavern with a large fire inside."

But the king was not satisfied with this answer and said: "That's nothing, You really haven't told me anything. But if it's true that there is a cavern below, you must bring me the ashes of this fire, and I'll give you a very good reward."

Cola went back down, and when he arrived below, he burned his hands and returned to the surface once again.

---

1 A town six kilometers from Messina.

2 The reference is to the sixteenth-century fort of Santissimo Salvatore that is at the extreme point of San Ranieri, near the port of Messina.

In ancient times, people told tales about an animal that appeared on the beach of Messina. It was half man and half fish and was known as Pescecola.

"There you have it, Majesty," Cola said and showed the king his burned hands.

"I'm still not satisfied," responded the king. "You must enter that cavern and tell me what connection this fire has to anything."

"Your Majesty," Cola said, "if I dive into the sea again, I won't return. I am sure of this." (He told the king all this from his heart.) However, the king wanted to goad him into doing this and told him that a valiant man is never afraid of anything.

"Well, if you want this," Cola responded, "I'll do it, but it will be the end of my life." Upon saying this, he picked up a rod and said, "If this rod returns afloat and shows that it's been burned, it will mean that I am dead. If it returns unburned, then I'm alive."

Then Cola plunged into the sea and entered the cave with the rod in his hand. The rod was burned and returned to the surface. Cola Pesce remained below, burned to death and never surfaced again.

The king had made him do this to see if it was true that the subterranean cavern was connected to Sicily and was one of the supports that held up the island.

––––––––

Told at Santa Barbiera by a non-literate girl and collected in October 1882

44

PESCECOLA

In ancient times, people told tales about an animal that appeared on the beach of Messina. It was half man and half fish and was known as Pescecola. Now this creature called together all the people living in Messina and spoke like this,

"People of Messina, listen

Your country is called Messina

But the day will come when it will be called paltry and petty."[1]

Upon hearing these words, the people of Messina beat their breasts, and with tears in their eyes, they asked Pescecola why this would happen. Then he replied: "Messina is supported by three columns: one is broken, another is split, and the third is whole. Therefore, there's nothing but one column at the base of Messina, and it will not last much longer. Consequently, the day will come when Messina will collapse."

Immediately, the people of Messina began weeping, and a group of them pleaded with Pescecola to dive to the bottom again to see if he could find another column that could support the city. However, Pescecola said that it was impossible because the sea was sunk deep at this point, and if he were to try to dive toward the bottom, he'd never be able to resurface, and this is why he was unable to please them.

However, the people of Messina pleaded with tears in their eyes and eventually convinced him.

They waited and waited. The people of Messina waited in vain because Pesceola never resurfaced.

The sailors say that when they lower the anchor at Faro, their eyes catch fire from the chains.

———————

Told by Antonina Fiorello, ninety-years-old, and collected by Professor Salvatore Salomone-Marino

---

1 There is a play of words here.

Messinesi, sentite:

La vostra patria si chiama Messina,

Ma verrà il giorno che si ciamerà meschina.

Messina is a city at the strait between Sicily and the tip of Italy. Meschino can mean narrow, paltry, putrid, scurvy.

45

PESCECOLA

In Messina there was a young man, son of a washerwoman, who always lived near the sea. One day he fell into the sea and realized that he knew how to swim like a fish. The people who saw him spread the word that he really knew how to swim very well. One day, an educated gentleman summoned him and said: "Tell me a bit whether you're able to go to the bottom and see what's supporting Messina?"

And the boy responded, yes.

Upon hearing this, the gentleman asked, "Aren't you afraid of the red fish?"

"If the fish arrive," the young man responded, "I'll cut them up with this knife"—he carried a knife in his pocket—"and if I die, you'll see my blood rise to the surface as a sign."

Then he plunged into the sea.

The next day he returned to the surface and told the people of Messina what he had done:

"When I arrived at the bottom, I began to search about and saw a large bronze door suspended between two arches attached to a dock. I rang the doorbell, and nobody responded. Therefore, I tried to open the door but didn't succeed. Then I decided to try with all my might, and while I was making every effort to open the door, it opened suddenly, and a red fish swallowed me. Well, I had a knife in my pocket and cut the fish in two. Then, when I climbed out of the fish, I saw a large clearing in the sea where there were three columns that supported Messina: one was broken, the next one split, and the last was whole. This is why Messina is in danger of collapsing."

Ever since then the young man was called Pescecola.

Told by a fisherman to Alberto Lauria, alumnus of the Nautical Institute of Trapani, and forwarded to me by Professor Carlo Siriani

❖

ANIMAL STORIES

46

BRANCALIUNI!

Once upon a time there was a peasant from the hills who had an ass and earned his living by collecting firewood. One day, as he was returning from gathering wood, the ass fell and couldn't get up. The peasant took off the saddle and left the ass on the ground for dead and went away. That night the ass came back to life and went to some field where it began to eat and gradually became nice and fat. One day a wolf appeared, began to look around, and approached the ass slowly but surely. When the ass saw the wolf, it said, "Oh what a bitter fate! The wolf's going to eat me!"

Therefore, the ass assumed a haughty posture with ears stiff, the tail up high, and the back arched, and it looked at the wolf straight in the eyes. When the wolf saw this ferocious-looking ass, it asked, "What's your name?"

"I'm called Bran . . . ca . . . liuni."[1]

"What a terrible name you have!" the wolf responded, and it approached slowly. When the ass saw it coming so close, it became scared and let off four great farts.

"Brancaliuni, what have you shot off?" the wolf asked.

"Those were shots from my cannon," the ass responded. "I've got a cannon, and when I shoot it, I can kill wolves and all sorts of things."

When the wolf heard this, it said, "I'd like to eat a little chicken meat. So, I want you to kill some chickens for me tomorrow with your cannon. I'll come back here, and you'll give me something to eat."

"All right, come back tomorrow," said the ass.

When the wolf departed, the ass became worried.

---

1 Brancaliuni literally means the claw of the lion.

"How am I going to do this?" he said and went to lie down in small spot and pretended to be dead. All at once, some crows and vultures swooped down, thinking the ass was dead, and they approached his head to eat him. When the ass, however, saw the right time, it began kicking and biting and killed a few of the birds. Then the ass got up and left the dead birds there. Sometime later, the wolf arrived.

"Brancaliuni, where are the birds?"

Then the ass brought out the birds from the spot where he had killed them.

"Here they are. Eat them."

The wolf ate the birds and said, "Oh how good they are! I've never eaten birds as delicious as these!"

"Now, my friend," the ass said, "it's your turn to do what I did."

"Well, then," replied the wolf, "I'll get some rabbits, and you'll eat them."

"No, my friend, I suffer from acids, and I can't eat rabbit. You've got to get me some green things to eat."

"My friend, Brancaliuni," said the wolf, "I know a garden filled with cabbages that are marvelous. I'll bring you there."

Immediately, they went to the garden, and the ass began to eat and filled his stomach so much that he couldn't walk any more.

"We had better go," the wolf said. "The owner's coming."

There was a high fence, and the wolf jumped over, but the ass couldn't make it, and his feet became caught in the fence. The wolf grabbed his feet to help him and pull him over. Then the ass began to fart so much that pellets of turd went flying, and many hit the wolf. When the wolf felt the pellets of turd—some of them hit his legs—he cried out, "Oh friend Brancaliuni, what are you doing?"

"I'm just amusing myself, my friend," the ass responded.

In the meantime, the wolf began to run because he was afraid of the pellets, and he limped away.

The ass laughed and said, "All the better now that I'm rid of you thanks to this strategy."

While the wolf was running, he came across the lion, who asked him, "Why are you running so fast?"

"I've got to run because Brancaliuni shot me in the leg with some pellets from his cannon. He's made me lame!"

"My friend," responded the lion, "I want to go and see this Brancaliuni."

"Oh, brother lion, he's more powerful than you are."

"Well then, here's what we'll do. We'll attack him from the rear with a rope. If you can't walk because you're lame, I'll drag you along."

Consequently, they began walking back to the ass, and when they approached and were near, the ass saw them, and as usual he raised his ears straight, arched his back, and raised his tail. "Now," he said to himself, "the time has come."

When the lion saw that the ass was prepared for them, he said, "Let's approach him slowly but surely."

As they advanced, the ass was totally frightened and began to discharge pellets of turd. When the wolf heard the pellets, he cried out, "Oh, brother lion, let's run. If we're hit with one of the pellets, we'll be killed."

The wolf couldn't run because he was lame. So the lion had to drag the wolf away. This was how the ass liberated himself and managed not to be devoured by the lion and the wolf. Then the ass said to himself, "I'd better leave this region. If I don't, the wolf will return and eat me."

So, the ass began to walk and eventually returned to his owner. When his owner saw that the ass had become nice and fat, he gladly took the animal back. He put a saddle on the the ass and led him off. Then the ass began to carry wood once again just as he had done before.

Told by Vincenzo Midulla, a miner, and collected
by Gaetano Di Giovani at Casteltermini

47

THE MAN, THE WOLF, *and the* FOX

People say that there was once a poor woodcutter who made his living by carrying wood on his shoulders from the forest to sell in the city. One morning, while he was on his way to the city, he heard some cries and moans. So he went toward the place where he heard the cries, and when he arrived, he saw a deep hole. A wolf had fallen into it, and on top of him, there was a large rock so that he couldn't get out. When the wolf saw the woodcutter, he said, "Do me a favor, and get me out of here, and I'll return the favor."

However, the woodcutter thought about this and then responded, "I'd gladly do this, but after I save your life, I'm sure you'll repay me by eating me."

"No, I'd never do such a thing!" the wolf replied. "Instead, if you are ever in the forest when some other wolf comes and wants to eat you, I'll defend you with my life."

After saying this, he made a thousand other pledges. Then the poor woodcutter said to him, "All right, I'm going to look for a ladder, and I'll return soon to get you out of the hole."

Indeed, he quickly fetched a ladder, returned to the wolf, and set the ladder down into the hole. Then he pulled as hard as he could to get the rock off the wolf and saved the poor beast from death.

When the wolf was able to get out of the hole totally worn out and flayed, the woodcutter took the ladder and said goodbye to the wolf. But then the wolf said, "Not so fast, my friend. Where are you going? I haven't eaten in three days, my good sir, and I'm dying of hunger. So, what better thing to eat than you?"

"What?" said the woodcutter. "You want to eat me?"

And he stood there trembling with fright. Then he summoned his courage and said, "Let's remember our deal. What has happened to everything that you promised? How good is your word? Is this the reward I get for saving your life? Now you want to eat me! Oh no, this isn't fair! How can you be such a bully?"

"Stop all your chattering!" the wolf cried. "I'm dying of hunger. So let's just walk further on toward the shade where I can eat you."

The wolf pushed him with his tail, and finally the woodcutter said, "Let's walk along the path until we meet three people. We'll explain what happened, and that you want to eat me, and if they say, yes, then you should eat me, and if they say no, you've got to let me go free."

When the wolf saw how clever he was, he said, "All right, we'll do as you say," and they began to walk along the path.

They walked and walked until they encountered a man, and the woodcutter told him all that had happened. Then the wolf added, "Well, I'm hungry, and I don't know what to do. So you decide what I should do."

The man was frightened that the wolf would grab him and eat him, and therefore, he said, "I don't have anything to say against what you want because hunger is a terrible thing."

Upon hearing this, the wolf turned to the woodcutter and said, "You see, this first man agrees, and I have one in favor of me."

They continued to walk a while until they encountered a fox. Now the wolf and the man called the fox to them, and each explained his side of the story. Then the fox replied, "Whenever I'm hungry, I'd even eat the dirt on the ground, because I'd rather eat rotten bread than die."

Then the wolf turned to the woodcutter and said, "You only have one more turn. My hunger's growing, and I think it was a bad idea to let you live."

However, the woodcutter made him walk on for a while to meet someone else, and indeed, when they went on a bit, they met a lion, and the woodcutter said to himself, "I'm dead for sure! The lion will certainly say the wolf is right, and both of them will eat me." The wolf, on the other hand, was pleased and said this was the perfect time to tell the story. So both of them approached the lion, and the poor woodcutter, completely frightened, recounted all that had happened and how he had saved the wolf from certain death and that the wolf had made many promises, and afterward, the wolf wouldn't listen to reason and wanted to eat him. Therefore, everything depended on the lion's judgment whether the wolf should eat him or not, according to the pact made between the man and the wolf. When the lion heard all the facts, he said, "I can't say who is right or who is wrong if I don't see the hole, the rock, and how the wolf was lying there and how the woodcutter managed to save the wolf's life. After I see this, I'll give you my decision."

Consequently, this is what they did. They returned to the hole once more, and the wolf climbed down into it. Then the lion said to him, "Put yourself in the same position you were, and we'll slowly place the rock on top of you."

Indeed, the wolf lay down, and they went to get the rock. After they returned with the rock, the lion said, "Now wait until we both climb back up, and I'll determine what the woodcutter did to you."

So now, they climbed back up and pulled up the ladder. Then the lion looked down at wolf from above and said, "Listen, you notorious and cunning wolf, you may always change your skin, but you can't change your vice. Stay there, and may you die of hunger until those who dug this hole come back and kill you. If you had been an honorable and courteous creature, you would have thanked and kissed the person who saved your life instead of wanting to eat him. And you, my good man," (turning to the woodcutter), "go about your business. May you toil and provide food for your children, and teach them that they must learn the right way to do a good deed and must know something about the person they're doing it for."

After saying this, the lion took his leave and went away. The poor woodcutter returned to his home and told everyone the story, more wasted and more dead than alive.

———————

Collected by Salvatore-Pasquale Vigo at Etna

48

THE KING *of the* ANIMALS, THE WOLF, *and the* FOX

During the time when the animals could speak, the lion was king and assigned the wolf to be his guard and the ass to be his secretary at the palace. When the king became sick one day, all the animals came to visit him except the fox. Since the poor king was so sick, he didn't notice the fox's absence, and none of the other animals said anything to the king about this, out of either love or fear.

However, because the vile wolf could not stand the fox, he went and slyly spied on the fox so he could do him some harm. When he returned to the royal palace, he said, "Your Majesty, I've observed with wonder how all your people have come to visit your highness, but I don't know why the fox hasn't appeared one single time."

When the king heard this, he became upset by the fox and said to the wolf, "Are you telling me the truth? Well then, what a rogue! What a miserable creature! He shall be dealt with the way he deserves!"

Therefore, he ordered the wolf to go and fetch the fox right away. After he seized him, he was to take his reward and bring him to the palace.

The wolf went at once to search for the fox in the countryside. In the meantime, the secretary, who had overheard this discussion and was ashamed of the wolf, went straight to the hare, who was his messenger and said, "I want you to do me a favor. You're to go and find the fox quickly and tell him what I'm about to tell you."

The hare ran as fast as he could and brought the message to the fox before the wolf got there. When the fox heard the story, he said to himself, "You spying cop of a wolf, you may be right, but I'll secretly denounce you to the king and repay you! No doubt about it!"

Without losing any time, he appeared before the king and said, "I'm at your service, your Majesty. I know that your highness has criticized me for not coming to visit you while you've been sick. But I want you to know, your Majesty, that I haven't neglected my duty because I had practically broken my bones traveling from country to country for your sake, that is, to look for a good medicine for your Majesty. Finally, I found the medicine, and a great doctor prescribed the cure. As soon as your majesty takes the medicine, you will be healed. If you don't take it, you'll die."

The king was appeased by these words and asked, "What is this medicine?"

"The boiled intestines of a wolf," the fox responded.

What was so important about the health of one of his subjects, thought the king, when it came to his own health? Therefore, he ordered his guard to kill the wolf. As a result, the wolf was seized, his intestines taken out, boiled, and brought to the king. The king ate them and was soon as good as ever.

Told by the fisherman I. Cumella and collected by
G. Patiri at Termini-Imerese

49

THE FOX

Once there was a fisherman who found a dead fox on the ground. He picked up the animal and threw him over his back. However, the fox was alive, and with his paw, he began to take the sardines that the fisherman had caught from a basket and threw them on the ground. When they were all gone, *zoom!* He jumped to the ground and escaped. All the fisherman could do was to remark, "He's smart, and I fell for it!"

Consequently, he continued on his way, while the fox began collecting all the sardines he had thrown on the ground so that he could take them home and fry them. However, he had a wolf for a neighbor who annoyed him, and he didn't know how to get rid of him. What was he to do?

"How did you manage to get these fish?" the wolf asked him.

"How?" the fox responded. "I had to use a jug. I tied it to my back, and then I jumped into the middle of the seaway. Once I was far out, I pulled out the cork and went deep down to catch the fish."

"Give me one of the fish," the wolf said. "Later I want to go fishing, and I'll give you part of what I catch."

The fox said to himself, "Let's hope this will be the last time," and he gave him some fish.

That night the fox attached the jug to the wolf's back and took him to a reef.

"Now," he said to the wolf, "if you want to catch a lot of sardines, you have to swim far out into the sea, and when I give you the signal, you're to pull out the cork, and you'll see how much you'll catch."

The wolf believed him and began to swim out into the sea. Each time he turned, the fox indicated that he should keep swimming further out until he was very far. Then the fox yelled, "Now you can do it!"

The wolf popped the cork, and soon he sunk and drowned. And this is how the malicious fox got rid of that rogue of a wolf.

Told by a peasant named Giovanni Cordova at Ficarazzi

50

THE WOLF *and the* CARDINAL

Once upon a time there was a cock, and he usually scraped about in a garbage heap. He scratched and scraped and found a little book, which he opened, and there, on the very first page that he read, stood the name *King Cock*. As soon as he saw it, he began beating his wings in content. "Cockle-doodle-do! Cockle-doodle-do!"

All at once the hen came running and said, "Why such a commotion! What's making you so happy?"

"What's making me so happy?" replied the cock. "I found this little book, and as I began reading it, the first thing I came across was *King Cock!*"

"Oh how beautiful!" exclaimed the hen. "Oh how beautiful! Can I look on with you?"

The cock turned another page and read, *Queen Hen*.

"Oh how happy I am!" the hen cried out. "Cackle, cackle, cackle!"

And she began to beat her wings.

Just then, a viper passed by and said, "What's going on here that's making you all so cheerful?"

"We've found a little book, and there's something about us printed in it."

"No fooling! Let me look at it with you."

The cock turned another page of the little book and read, *Chambermaid Viper*.

"Really! Oh how happy I am! *Tirr! Tirr!*" and the viper began to twist her body and dance happily to celebrate the appearance of her name.

At this point a wolf passed by and asked, "What's happened that's making you celebrate this way?"

"What's making me celebrate? We've found a little book here, and there's something about all of us printed here."

"Oh, what a curious thing! Would you mind seeing if there's anything about me?"

The cock turned the page and read, *Father Wolf the Pope!*

"Oh how fortunate, my friend! I feel very pleased. *Hoooo! Hoooo!*" And he began to jump and turn about cheerfully because he was a father priest.

Just then a cardinal came flying by and saw all four dancing with joy.

"What's making you all so joyful?" the bird asked.

"What's making us so joyful? We found a little book about animals in this garbage heap, and the cock read what was printed there: King Cock, then after, Queen Hen, and next, chambermaid viper, and finally, Father Wolf the Pope. This is why we're all so happy!"

"And there's nothing about me? Look and see! Look and see!"

The cock turned another page and read what was printed: *Cardinal, soldier and guardian of the castle.* Upon hearing this, the cardinal beat its wings and began singing the best song it knew with all its heart.

"What are we going to do now?" the wolf asked. "We're all here, and there's a well-bred king. You know what I say? I say that since I'm the Pope and we all want to begin a good reign, I can start by confessing all of you."

"Good idea! Good idea!" they all cried.

"You'll come into the confession booth one by one."

So, they went to the confession booth, and the first one to enter was the cock (for the wolf was already seated in the confessional booth). As soon as the cock entered, the wolf fell upon him, opened his mouth and . . . *Gulp!* He swallowed the King Cock. The next one to enter was the Queen Hen, and the same thing happened. He devoured her with great pleasure. Then the viper entered, and *gulp!* She made a nice bite full! The last one to enter was the cardinal who was very uneasy. He looked about him, and when he saw the feathers, he realized what they meant. "Ahh," he thought, "that's why nobody has returned from confession! Maybe the Pope has swallowed each one of them, bones and all. Just wait and see how I'll accommodate you!"

Therefore, the cardinal sat down in the confessional booth and said, "All right Father Pope, raise your head and open your mouth, and I'll tell you my sins."

The wolf who was hoping to swallow the cardinal, raised his head and opened his mouth, but the cardinal stuck its tail in the wolf's mouth and shat. Then it flew off singing,

> You ate the poor king and the queen,
> Then you swallowed the viper clean.
> And you thought the cardinal would be sweet,
> But he gave you nothing but shit to eat.

The wolf stood there, feeling like a fool and wondering what had happened to the cardinal that he had wanted to catch.

> May the tale be long, may the tale be fine,
> It's time to tell yours, for I'm done with mine.

———————

Told by Margherita Martorana, a washerwoman, to Salvatore Salomone-Marino in Partinico

Notes

These notes, including some variants of the tales, are based on material that Joseph Russo and I gathered from the following works:

Aarne, Antti, and Stith Thompson. *The Types of the Folktale: A Classification and a Bibliography*. 2nd rev. ed. FF Communications No. 3. Helsinki: Suomalainen Tiedeakatemia, 1961.

Pitrè, Giuseppe. *Fiabe, novelle e racconti populari siciliani*. 4 vols. Palermo: L. Pedone Lauriel, 1875.

Uther, Hans-Jörg. *The Types of International Folktales: A Classification and a Bibliography*. 3 vols. Helsinki: Suomalainen Tiedeakatemia, 2004.

Zipes, Jack, ed. *The Great Fairy Tale Tradition: From Straparola and Basile to the Brothers Grimm*. New York: Norton, 2001.

———, ed. *Beautiful Angiola: The Great Treasury of Sicilian Folk and Fairy Tales Collected by Laura Gonzenbach*. New York: Routledge, 2004.

———, ed. *The Robber with a Witch's Head: More Stories from The Great Treasury of Sicilian Folk and Fairy Tales Collected by Laura Gonzenbach*. New York: Routledge, 2005.

Most of the comments are based on Pitrè's own notes and different versions of the tales. The references to various tales and collections have been kept in the original language with some exceptions. I have added important information and deleted some of the original sources and variants.

Each tale title in English is accompanied with the Sicilian title. The titles are followed by the tale-type classification in Uther's revision and expansion of Aarne/Thompson *The Types of International Folktales* as a helpful reference. In some cases, there is no tale-type classification because many of the tales are particular to Sicily.

The following list contains names of authors and books cited in the notes:

Apuleius, Lucius. *The Golden Ass*. Translated and edited by Jack Lindsay. Bloomington: Indiana University Press, 1962.

Aulnoy, Marie-Catherine Le Jumel de Barneville, Baronne de. *Les Contes de fées.* 4 vols. Paris: Claude Barbin, 1697.

———. *Contes Nouveaux ou les Fées à la mode.* 2 vols. Paris: Veuve de Théodore Girard, 1698.

Bandello, Matteo. *La prima parte de le novelle del Bandello.* Lucca: Il Bustrago, 1554.

———. *Delle novelle del Bandello.* Venice: Francheschini, 1566.

Basile, Giambattista. *Lo cunto de li cunti overo Lo trattenemiento de peccerille. De Gian Alessio Abbattutis.* 5 vols. Naples: Ottavio Beltrano, 1634–36.

———. *The Pentamerone of Giambattista Basile.* Translated and edited by N. M. Penzer. 2 vols. London: John Lane and the Bodley Head, 1932.

———. *The Tale of Tales, or Entertainment for Little Ones.* Translated by Nancy Canepa. Illustrated by Carmelo Lettere. Detroit: Wayne State University Press, 2007.

Bechstein, Ludwig. *Deutsches Märchenbuch.* Leipzig: Wigand, 1845.

Bernoni, Domenico Giuseppe. *Leggende fantastiche popolari veneziane.* Venice: Fontana-Ottolini, 1873.

———. *Indovinelli popolari veneziani.* Venice: Antonelli, 1874.

———. *Fiabe popolari veneziane.* Venice: Fontana-Ottolini, 1875.

Besozzi, Antonio. *Brancaleone, historia piacevole et morale dalla quale può ciascuno havere utilissimi documenti per governo se stesso & d'altri.* Milan: Alzato, 1610.

Boccaccio, Giovanni. *Decameron.* Edited by Vittore Branca. Turin: Einaudi, 1984.

Busk, Rachel Henriette. *The Folk-Lore of Rome Collected by Word of Mouth from the People.* London: Longmans, Green and Co., 1874.

Calvino, Italo, ed. *Fiabe.* Torino: Einaudi, 1956.

———. *Italian Folktales.* Translated by George Martin. New York: Harcourt Brace Jovanovich, 1980.

Comparetti, Domenico. *Virgilio nel medio-evo.* 2 vols. Livorno: F. Vigo, 1872.

———. *Novelline popolari italiene.* Turin: Loescher, 1875.

Coronedi-Berti, Carolina. *Novelle popolari bolognesi.* Bologna: Fava and Garagnai, 1874.

———. *Favole bolognesi.* Bologna: Forni, 1883.

Corrao, Francesa Maria, ed. *Le storie di Giufà.* Palermo: Sellerio, 2001.

Crane, Thomas Frederick. *Italian Popular Tales.* Boston: Houghton, Mifflin, 1889.

De Gubernatis, Angelo. *Le Novelline di Santo Stefano.* Turin: Negro, 1869.

———. *Storia delle novellini popolari.* Milan: Hoepli, 1883.

France, Marie de. *The Lais of Marie de France*. Edited by Glyn Burgess and Keith Busby. Harmondsworth, England: Penguin, 1986.

Galland, Antoine. *Les Milles et une nuit*. 12 vols. Vols. 1–4, Paris: Florentin Delaulne, 1704; Vols. 5–7, Paris: Florentin Delaulne, 1706; Vol. 8, Paris: Florentin Delaulne, 1709; Vols. 9–10, Florentin Delaulne, 1712; Vols. 11–12, Lyon: Briasson, 1717.

Gesta Romanorum, or Entertaining Moral Stories. Translated with notes by Rev. Charles Swan. Revised and corrected by Wynnard Hooper. New York: Dover, 1959. (Reprint of the Bohn Library Edition 1876.)

Gonzenbach, Laura. *Sicilianische Märchen*. 2 vols. Leipzig: W. Engelmann, 1870.

———. *Beautiful Angiola: The Lost Sicilian Folk and Fairy Tales of Laura Gonzenbach*. Translated by Jack Zipes. New York: Routledge, 2006.

Gozzi, Carlo. *Opere ed inedite*. Venice: Zanardi, 1801–2.

———. *Five Tales for the Theatre*. Translated and edited by Albert Bermel and Ted Emery. Chicago: University of Chicago Press, 1989.

Grimm, Jacob, and Wilhelm Grimm. *Kinder- und Hausmärchen. Gesammelt durch die Brüder Grimm*. Vol. 1. Berlin: Realschulbuchhandlung, 1812.

———. *Kinder- und Hausmärchen. Gesammelt durch die Brüder Grimm*. Vol. 2. Berlin: Realschulbuchhandlung, 1815.

———. *Kinder- und Hausmärchen. Gesammelt durch die Brüder Grimm*. 7th revised and expanded edition. 2 vols. Göttingen: Dieterich, 1857.

———. *The Complete Fairy Tales of the Brothers Grimm*. Ed. Jack Zipes. 3rd revised and enlarged edition. New York: Bantam, 2003.

Histoire de la belle Hélène de Constantinople. Troyes: Garnier, 1700.

Imbriani, Vittorio. *La Novellaja fiorentina*. Livorno: F. Vigo, 1871.

Knust, Hermann. *Italienische Märchen in Jahrbuch für romanische und englische Literatur* VII (1866): 381–401.

La Force, Charlotte-Rose Caumont de. *Les contes des contes par Mlle ***. Paris: S. Bernard, 1698.

Le Noble, Eustache. *Le Gage touché, hisoires galantes*. Amsterdam: Jaques Desbordes, 1700.

Le Prince de Beaumont, Marie. *Magasin des enfans, ou Dialogue d'une sage gouvernante avec ses élèves de la première distinction*. Lyon: Reguilliat, 1756.

Lhéritier de Villandon, Marie-Jeanne. *Oeuvres meslées*. Paris: J. Guignard, 1696.

Mailly, Jean de. *Les Illustres fées, contes galans. Dédié aux dames*. Paris: M-M. Brunet, 1698.

Murat, Henriette Julie de Castelnau, Comtesse de. *Contes de fées*. Paris: Claude Barbin, 1698.

Nerucci, Gherardo. *Sessanta novelle popolari montalesi*. Florence: Le Monnier, 1880.

Perrault, Charles. *Griseldis, nouvelle. Avec le conte de Peau d'Ane, et celui des Souhaits ridicules*. Paris: Jean Baptiste Coignard, 1694.

———. *Histoires ou contes du temps passè*. Paris: Claude Barbin, 1697.

Pitrè, Giuseppe. *Fiabe e Leggende Populari Siciliani*. Palermo: Lauriel, 1870.

———. *Fiabe, novelle e racconti populari siciliani*. 4 vols. Palermo: Lauriel, 1875.

———. *Fiabe e Leggende popolari siciliane*. Palermo: Lauriel, 1888.

Ryder, Arthur W., trans. *The Panchatantra*. Chicago: University of Chicago Press, 1956.

Schneller, Christian. *Märchen und Sagen aus Wälschtirol*. Innsbruck: Wagner, 1867.

Schulz, Friedrich. *Kleine Romane*. 5 vols. Leipzig: Göschen, 1788–90.

Somadeva. *The Ocean of Story*. Edited by N. M. Penzer. Translated by Charles H. Tawney. 10 vols. Indian Edition. Delhi: Motilal Banarsidass, 1968.

Straparola, Giovan Francesco. *Le piacevoli notti*. 2 vols. Venice: Comin da Trino, 1550/1553.

———. *Le piacevoli notti*. Edited by Donato Pirovano. 2 vols. Rome: Salerno, 2000.

———. *The Facetious Nights of Straparola*. Translated by William G. Waters. Illustrated by Jules Garnier and E. R. Hughes. 4 vols. London: Lawrence and Bullen, 1894.

———. *The Pleasant Nights*. Edited by Donald Beecher. 2 vols. Toronto: University of Toronto Press, 2012.

Testa, Francesco. *De vita et rebus gestis Guilelmi II*. Monregali: Bentivenga, 1769.

Widter-Wolf, Georg, and Adam Wolf. "Volksmärchen aus Venetien." *Jahrbuch für romantische und englische Literatur* VII (1866): 1–36; 121–54; 249–90.

1. CATARINA THE WISE (*CATARINA LA SAPIENTI*)

Tale Type ATU 891: The Man Who Deserted His Wife. The closest variant is Laura Gonzenbach's, "Sorfarina," *Sicilianische Märchen*. Earlier parallels are Boccaccio, "Giletta di Nerbona," *Decameron*; Straparola's "Ortodosio Simeoni," *Le Piacevoli Notti*; Basile, "La Sapia Liccarda," *Lo Cunto de li Cunti*; and Marie-Jeanne Lhéritier, "The Discreet Princess, or the Adventures of Finette," *Oeuvres meslées*. The tale type was first recorded in India in the eleventh century. Pitrè also provided the following variant.

Beautiful-and-Wise (*Bella-e-sapiente*)

Beautiful-and-Wise was the name of a princess who attended a school for boys and girls, where the husband taught the boys and his wife, the girls.

One day the two teachers had to be absent to attend a wedding party. The male teacher assigned his classes to a boy who was the king's son, and the female teacher gave hers to Beautiful-and-Wise, who was the best of her students. The male and female students began to enjoy themselves, and the prince declared that one day he would marry Beautiful-and-Wise. She gave him a slap and complained to the female teacher, who gave her an enchanted wand. Soon the prince and Beautiful-and-Wise were married. When they were alone on their wedding night, the prince asked her if she recalled the slap and was sorry for it, and she answered no. Thereupon her husband bound her, placed her in an underground chamber, and departed for Rome. She used her magic to get free and arrive in Rome before him, setting herself up in a palace facing his. Soon they got together, but he didn't recognize her. When she became pregnant by him, she gave birth to a son whom she called Romano. Then he went to the city of Lucia, and she again preceded him there and had a second child of his, called Luciano. Finally, he made a third trip to Alexandria, and there she bore him a girl called Alessandrina. Between each trip he returned home to repeat the question to his wife, but she remained obstinate and refused to repent. He then decided to marry the King of France's daughter. But Beautiful-and-Wise came to the wedding with the three children and had them confront their father.

Collected from Giuseppa Furia in Ficarazzi

2. SNOW WHITE, BLAZING RED (*BIANCA-COMU-NIVI-RUSSA-COMU-FOCU*)

Tale Type ATU 310: The Maiden in the Tower. Here is a short summary of a convoluted Sicilian variant published by Pitrè.

Beautiful Maiurana (*La bella Maiurana*)

A king has three daughters and a son. The daughters marry three sons of a magician. The king's son, who has broken the egg in a basket of an old woman, is cursed and cannot be happy until he finds the beautiful Maiurana. Therefore, he leaves, and after a week's journey, he asks for something to drink at a house. He is treated horribly there, but then he is recognized as the brother-in-law and brother of the owners of the house. As a result, he is given better care and good advice. After he resumes his journey, the same thing happens with the other brothers-in-law and sisters in two other houses. Finally, he finds the beautiful Maiurana, kept prisoner through an enchantment by an ogre and a sorceress, parents of his brothers-in-law. The prince kills the ogre and sorceress on top of a mountain, and he frees himself, the beautiful Maiurana, his sisters, and his brothers-in-law from a magic spell.

Collected in Cianciana

For more thorough information about the background of this tale, see the following note.

3. THE OLD HAG'S GARDEN (*LA VECCHIA DI L'ORTU*)

Tale Type ATU 310: The Maiden in the Tower. Extremely popular throughout Europe, this tale has an illustrious literary history with the following key works: Giambattista Basile, "Petrosinella," *Lo Cunto de li Cunti*; Charlotte-Rose de Caumont de la Force, "Persinette," *Les Contes des contes*; Schulz, "Rapunzel," *Kleine Romane*; Jacob and Wilhelm Grimm, "Rapunzel," *Kinder-und Hausmärchen*; Ludwig Bechstein, "Rapunzel," *Deutsches Märchenbuch*; and Imbriani, "Prezzemolina," *Novellaja Fiorentina*. The incarceration of a young woman in a tower (often to protect her chastity during puberty) was a common motif in various European and Oriental myths and became part of the standard repertoire of medieval tales, lais, and romances throughout Europe and the Orient. In addition, the motif of a pregnant woman who has a strong craving for an extravagant dish or extraordinary food is very important. In many peasant societies people believed that it was necessary to fulfill the longings of a pregnant woman, otherwise something terrible, like a miscarriage or bad luck, might occur. Therefore, it was incumbent on the husband and other friends and relatives to use spells or charms or other means to fulfill the cravings.

In Sicily there is a variant from Polizzi with the title "Li Cummari," in which the old woman is an ogress. Otherwise, some other important versions are: Laura Gonzenbach, "Beautiful Angiola," *Sicilianische Märchen*; Bernoni, "La Parzemolina," *Fiabe e Novelle Popolari Veneziane*; Coronedi-Berti, "La Fola di Zuannein," *Novelle Popolari Bolognesi*; and Widter-Wolf and Wolf, "Die Prinzessin im Sarg und die Schildwache," *Volksmärchen aus Venetien*.

4. THE MAGICAL LITTLE DATE TREE (*GRÀTTULA-BEDDÀTULA*)

Tale Type ATU 510A: Cinderella and ATU 480: The Kind and Unkind Girls. There are thousands of oral and literary versions of "Cinderella," one of the most popular fairy tales in the world. Early versions may have originated in ancient China or Egypt. The shoe or slipper test may have been connected to a marriage custom in which the bridegroom takes off the bride's old shoes and replaces them with new ones. However, this thesis has never been completely verified, and depending on the society and customs, shoes are used in many different ways in marriage celebrations. For the most part, Cinderella must prove that she is the rightful successor in a house in which she has been deprived of her rights. She receives help from her dead mother in the guise of doves, fairies, and godmothers. Belief in the regeneration of the dead who can help the living in the form of plants or animals underlies one of the key motifs of the fairy tale. The best known versions are Charles Perrault's "Cinderella" (1697) and the Brothers Grimm's "Cinderella" (1812). Clearly, many different literary and oral tales fostered a huge Cinderella cycle in the East and the West. Alan Dundes's *Cinderella: A Folklore Casebook* (1982) provides valuable background information and discussions about the cycle and different interpretations. In Pitrè's Sicilian tale, it is obvious that the youngest sister, Ninetta, is a type of Cinderella and is an active protagonist, who determines her own destiny with the help of fairies and a magical fruit.

5. PILUSEDDA (*PILUSEDDA*)

Tale Type ATU 510: Cinderella and Peau d'Âne and Tale Type ATU 510B: Peau d'Asne. In the Western world, the theme of incest took on significance in literature during the eleventh century. Stories dealing with this topic that may have influenced Straparola, Basile, Perrault, and the Grimms appeared in Ser Giovanni Fiorentino's *Il Pecorone* (1385) as "Dionigia and the King of England" and in the fifteenth-century verse romance of *Belle Hélène de Constantinople*, of which there are also prose manuscripts. It became a very popular story and was published in chapbooks and folk collections up to the nineteenth century. Many of the motifs in these narratives stem from byzantine and Greek tales and medieval legends. The father's incestuous desire has always been depicted as sinful, and for the most part, the heroine is a princess. Her purity and integrity are tested, and she proves through a ring or shoe test that she is worthy of her rank. Depending on the attitude of the storyteller or writer, the incestuous father is punished or forgiven. Sometimes he is just forgotten. Some of the key versions are: Straparola, "Tebaldo," *Le Piacevoli Notti*; Basile, "The Bear," *Lo Cunto de li Cunti*; Perrault, "Donkey-Skin" *Griseldis, nouvelle. Avec le conte de Peau d'Ane, et celui des Souhaits ridicules*; Grimm, "All Fur," *Kinder-und Hausmärchen*. See also Gonzenbach's "Betta Pilusa," *Sicilianische Märchen*; Imbriani, "La Scindirouera," *Novellaja Milanese*, and "Verdea" and "Cenerentola" in *Novellaja Fiorentina*; Calvino's "Wooden

Maria," *Italian Folk Tales*, is a composite of a tale collected by Giggi Zanazzo, *Novelle, Favole e Leggende Romanesche* and several other versions.

6. THE EMPRESS ROSINA (*RUSINA 'MPERATRICI*)

Tale Type ATU 425: The Search for the Lost Husband, ATU 425A: The Animal as Bridegroom, and ATU 884: A Forsaken Fiancée: Service as Menial. This tale is similar to "The Pig King" in Gonzenbach's *Sicilianische Märchen* and forms part of the well-known Beast-Bridegroom cycle that has its literary antecedent in the Roman writer Apuleius's "Cupid and Psyche," *The Golden Ass*, which appeared in the middle of the second century. The most important literary versions of this tale, which was widespread in Europe and the Orient, are: Straparola, "Galeotto" *Le Piacevoli Notti*; Basile, "Lo serpe," *Lo Cunto de li Cunti*; Mme d'Aulnoy, "Le Mouton," *Les Contes de fées*; Mme de Murat, "Le Roy Porc," *Histoires Sublimes et Allégoriques*; Mme Leprince de Beaumont, "La Belle et la Bête," *Magasin des enfans*; Lamb, *Beauty and the Beast: or a Rough Outside with a Gentle Heart*; Grimm, "The Singing, Springing Lark" and "Hans My Hedgehog," *Kinder-und Hausmärchen*; Gonzenbach, "Zafarana," "King Cardiddu," and "Prince Scursini," *Sicilianische Märchen*.

7. THE LITTLE MOUSE WITH THE STINKY TAIL (*LU SURCITEDDU CU LA CUDA FITUSA*)

Tale Type ATU 425: The Search for Lost Husband and ATU 425A: The Animal as Bridegroom. Although Pitrè offered no parallels, it is clear that this tale is close to the Grimms' "The Frog Prince." Moreover, the theme of the "animal groom" (a suitor who comes in frightening or repulsive bestial form but is finally released from enchantment, revealed as royal, and marries the heroine) is known throughout the world. Pitrè's version is distinctive for its use of pitiful lamentation sung by the heroine as she wanders in search of her lost mouse, whom she initially despises, but after a traumatic incident (in a surprisingly instant conversion) she desperately desires him. Her long penance—comprising wandering, isolation, physical hardship, persistence, and willingness to follow orders she cannot fathom—earns her the reunion with her enchanted groom.

8. SUN, PEARL, AND ANNA (*SULI, PERNA E ANNA*)

Tale Type ATU 510: Cinderella. See the note 4 to "The Magical Little Date Tree." Pitrè included another Sicilian version:

The Son of a King (Lu Figghiu d'un Regnanti)

A royal prince goes hunting with his entourage and finds a beautiful maiden in an uninhabited palace. Shortly thereafter, he marries her and offers her a wedding dress that resembles the dress his mother, the queen, had used for her wedding. At the court, nobody knows about the prince's wedding. In the meantime, two children, Sun and Moon, are born to the prince. When his mother the queen discovers this, she fetches the two children. Then she has them put into the oven and gives them to the prince to eat. When the queen sends for the princess, she is dressed in the similar wedding dress and cries out for her husband who arrives and saves her. Then he has his mother, the queen, baked in the oven.

Collected in Polizzi-Generosa.

There are two similar versions in Gonzenbach, "Maruzzedda" and "Beautiful Anna," *Sicilianische Märchen*; Imbriani, "Il Re che andava a caccia," *Novellaja Fiorentina*.

9. COUNT JOSEPH PEAR (*DON GIUSEPPI PIRU*)

Tale Type ATU 545 B: Puss in Boots. This tale type is one of the most famous and widespread tales in the Europe and North America. In many countries such as Finland, Russia, and Siberia, it is a fox that plays the major role as animal helper, as is the case in most Sicilian tales. In the literary tradition the best known versions are those of Straparola, "Constatino Foruntato," *Le Piacevoli Notti*; Basile, "Gagliosa," *Lo cunto de li Cunti*; Perrault, "The Master Cat, or Puss in Boots," *Histoires ou Contes du temps passé*. The Brothers Grimm published a version of "Puss in Boots" ("Der gestiefelte Kater") in the 1812 first edition of *Kinder- und Hausmärchen*, but they deleted it because it was too similar to Perrault's tale. For Sicilian and Italian variants, see Gonzenbach, "Count Piro," *Sicilianische Märchen*; Schneller, "Graf Martin von der Katz," *Märchen und Sagen aus Wälschtirol*; Imbriani, "Re Messemi-gli-becca-'l-fumo," *Novellaja Fiorentina*.

10. MAMMA-DRAGA THE OGRESS (*LA MAMMA-DRÀA*)

Tale Type ATU 480: The Kind and the Unkind Girls. This tale was widespread in both the oral and literary tradition throughout the world since the fifteenth century, largely because of its simple moral statement. The dissemination of the tale and its various versions in folklore have been studied meticulously in Warren E. Roberts' significant book, *The Tale of the Kind and*

Unkind Girls (1994). Almost all the tales follow the same plot: a good-natured, beautiful stepsister is compelled, like Cinderella, to do all the work around the house, and at one point she loses a spindle or some article necessary for her household chores. In order to retrieve this object, she descends into a well or a hole and finds herself in a strange land. During her journey in this realm she meets three animals or things and kindly helps them. Because she behaves so well in this realm, she is rewarded by an old woman, witch, fairies, or a powerful spirit. The good girl returns home, and when she speaks, jewels and precious stones fall from her lips, or she finds that the box is filled with gold. The stepmother sends her ugly, nasty daughter to this same realm, but because she is mean, she returns and spits out vipers and toads. The bad girl is generally punished by death or madness.

The major literary versions include: Basile, "The Three Fairies," *Lo Cunto de li Cunti*; Marie-Jeanne Lhéritier, "Les Enchantements de l'éloquence, ou Les Effets de la Douceur," *Oeuvres meslées*; Perrault, "The Fairies," *Histoires ou contes du temps passé*; Grimm, "Mother Holle," *Kinder-und Hausmärchen*. There were numerous folk and fairy tales about friendly and unfriendly witches or old women after the Grimms published their *Kinder- und Hausmärchen* in Germany, and the most popular and didactic rendition was Ludwig Bechstein's "Die Goldmaria und die Pechmaria," *Deutsches Märchenbuch (1845)*.

Pitrè's "Mamma-draga the Ogress" is a close variant of the Grimms' "Mother Holle" and "The Three Little Gnomes in the Forest." This is a widely diffused tale in Sicily; Mamma-draga (Mamma-dràa in Sicilian) appears in many of these tales, sometimes purely menacing but at other times acting with benevolence toward the heroine or hero (like her counterpart Baba Yaga in Russian folk tales).

11. PRETTY POOR GIRL (*POVIRA BEDDA*)

Tale Type ATU 891: The Man Who Deserted His Wife. The sparring in verse between heroine and prince is a brief version of the exchanges developed at great length in "The Pot of Basil."

Similar tales can be found in Boccaccio's, "Giletta di Nerbona," *Decameron*; Straparola's "Ortodosio Simeoni," *Le Piacevoli Notti*; Basile's "La Sapia Liccarda," *Lo cunto de li cunti*; and Marie-Jeanne Lhéritier's "The Discreet Princess, or The Adventures of Finette," *Oeuvres meslées*. See also Pitrè's "Catarina the Wise," and other variants listed in Lo Nigro's *Racconti popolari siciliani*.

The prince's desire for revenge is also the desire to control a woman. When he finally does try to kill her, he licks the "blood" from the sword because, according to Sicilian folklore, this gesture will prevent him from being tormented by remorse or from being discovered. Of course, the sugar or honey makes him regret his actions even more, and all his efforts to control Sorfarina are frustrated.

12. THE POT OF BASIL (*LA GRASTA DI LU BASILICÒ*)

Tale Type ATU 879: The Basil Maiden (The Sugar Puppet, Viola) and ATU 891: The Man Who Deserted His Wife. This tale, like "Catarina the Wise," features a spunky and independent heroine, a commoner, who repeatedly gets the better of a prince in a contest of wits and strategy, before she finally marries him. Such heroines seem to have been favorites with Agatuzza Messia, Pitrè's major informant. The tale stands out for its steady repetition of witty verse in escalating units of length, as each character momentarily gains the upper hand.

Pitrè says this tale more often goes under the name "La Bedda Majurana," and he also mentions a version from Polizzi titled "Lu Zu Ninu" (where the rhyme names parsley rather than basil). He cites a precise parallel for the teasing exchange in verse in Basile's "Viola" and a more general plot parallel in "Sapia Liccarda," *Lo Cunto de li Cunti*, as well as in Imbriani's "La Stella Diana," *Novellaja Milanese*, and "La Verdea" and "La Bella Giovanna," *Novellaja Fiorentina*. The story of the doll is also paralleled at the end of Gonzenbach, "The Daughter of Prince Cirimimminu," and "Sorfarina," *Sicilianische Märchen*, and in Bernoni's "Il Diavolo," *Fiabe Popolari Veneziane*. The prince licking the blood off his sword has traditional Sicilian overtones as I have explained in the previous note

13. THE COUNT'S SISTER (*LA SORU DI LU CONTI*)

Tale Type ATU 1419E: Underground Passage to Lover's House and ATU 926: Judgment of Solomon.. This story can be traced back to the late Middle Ages and is found in the anonymous *Seven Wise Men* of the thirteenth century among other works. The traditional plot concerns adultery, not virginity. Generally speaking, it is not a brother who protects the chastity of his sister and is deceived. Rather, it is a husband who is deceived by an adulterous wife, who manages to meet her lover through an underground passage. This theme is common in many of *The Lais of Marie de France* from the late twelfth century. Variants of "The Count and his Sister" were widespread in India, Turkey, Greece, and Italy.

Pitrè noted that this tale was widely diffused in Sicily. Calvino observed that this tale has elements of novelistic romance often found in Sicilian folktale tradition but largely avoided in the tales collected from Messina. Gonzenbach published an important version "The Count and his Sister," in *Sicilianische Märchen*. Calvino had high regard for this tale type, which is also more erotic than most of the Sicilian tales. In the variants quoted below, there are references to nudity, rarely mentioned in many versions.

Pitrè provided summaries of two Sicilian variants, "Lu Cannileri" (The Candlestick) from Vallelunga and "La Lampa d'oru" (The Golden Lamp) from Noto, as follows. Here is the first variant:

The Candlestick (Lu cannileri)

The girl protagonist, alone in a room of her palace, always eats meat with no bones. One day her mother sends her a piece of meat with a bone in it, and she uses this new tool to bore a hole in her wall and pass directly to a room of the royal palace. There she finds an enchanted candlestick and asks it:

> "Candlestick of gold, candlestick of silver,
> What is my lord doing, sleeping or active?"

And the candlestick answers:

> "My lady, you may pass safely within,
> The prince is sleeping in the nude."

For three nights she sleeps with the prince, who cannot learn her identity despite various devices (such as using saffron or placing nails on the floor). Nine months later he wakes to find the girl has left a baby at his side. To find out who the mother is, he has the baby exposed in the palace as if dead, with funeral music. Dressed as a peasant woman, the mother arrives to mourn, crying:

> "Son of a worthy mother,
> Her feet pierced with nails;
> Son of a vain mother,
> Her clothing stained with saffron."

After she confesses, the prince takes her as his wife, and she is recognized as: sister of a count, and wife to a king.

Collected in Vallelunga

14. THE TALKING BELLY (*LA PANZA CHI PARRA*)

This story, which has no tale type, was first published by Pitrè as tale seven in *Fiabe e Leggende Siciliani* (Palermo: Lauriel, 1870).

Pitrè wrote: "I don't know any Italian stories that can compare with the present one." The motif of dispatching the painters to draw a picture of the most beautiful woman and to provide a prince with a bride because he is not content with the women in his kingdom is also in Laura Gonzenbach's "The Story about the Daughter of the Sun," *Sicilianische Märchen* (Tale Type ATU 898—The Daughter of the Sun).

15. MANDRUNI AND MANDRUNA (*MANDRUNI E MANDRUNA*)

Tale type ATU 425D: The Vanished Husband. This tale's opening incident—the boy mischievously throwing and breaking the old woman's jug and receiving her curse—also opens Tale Type ATU 408, The Three Oranges. This motif is frequently seen elsewhere—e.g. in "Snow-White, Blazing Red." Gonzenbach's "The Princes and King Chiccheriddu," "The Beautiful Maiden with the seven Veils," and "Beautiful Innocenta," *Sicilianische Märchen*; as well as in the frame tale of Basile's *Lo Cunto de li Cunti*. Also in Basile, "Penta Mano Mozza" (Penta without Hands) has a magician who publicly announces a reward for whoever comes and relates the greatest misfortune, a parallel to what Mandruna does as innkeeper.

16. THE KING OF SPAIN (*LU RE DI SPAGNA*)

Tale Type ATU 313: The Magic Flight and ATU D2003: Forgotten Fiancée (Bride). For interesting variants, see: Schneller, "Die drei Tauben," *Märchen und Sagen aus Wälschtirol*; and Imbriani, "El Re del Sol," *Novellaja Milanese*.

17. THE KING OF LOVE (*LU RE D'AMURI*)

Tale Type ATU 425A: The Animal as Bridegroom. This is one of many versions of the Cupid and Psyche story first recorded by the Roman novelist Apuleius in *The Golden Ass*, mid second century AD. In the Cupid and Psyche pattern, a sub-type of 425A, the husband keeps his appearance a mystery because he visits only at night; the heroine's sister(s) convince her to try to see his face; she does so with a candle or lamp and accidentally awakens him by dripping hot wax or oil on him, and he abandons her. Then she undergoes a series of trying ordeals to discover and reunite with him.

Pitrè indicated that there were many parallels to this tale: Gonzenbach, "The Story about the Merchant's Son Peppino," *Sicilianische Märchen*; Schneller, "Die Heirat mit der Hexe," *Märchen und Sagen aus Wälschtirol*; Basile, "Lo Catenaccio," *Lo Cunto de li Cunti*.

18. THE THIRTEEN BANDITS (*LI TRIDICI SBANNUTI*)

Tale Type ATU 956B: The Clever Maiden Alone at Home Kills the Robbers. There are many different versions in Sicily. The motif of the doll made of sugar and honey, used as a protective trick by the heroine, is found in several other Sicilian tales. Other versions of this tale can also be found in Ser Giovanni's *Pecorone*, Gonzenbach's *Sicilianische Märchen*, Imbriani's *Novellaja Fiorentina*, and Pitrè's *Otto Fiabe e Novelle popolari siciliane*.

19. THE SILVERSMITH (*L'ARGINTERI*)

Tale Type ATU 567A: The Magic Bird Heart and the Separated Brothers. Elements and motifs of this tale can be found in Straparola, "Adamantina figliuola di Ragolina Savonese, per virtù du una poavola, di Drusiano Re di Boemia moglie diviene," *Le piacevoli Notti*; Basile, "La papara," *Lo Cunti de li Cunti*; and Imbriani, "Coa," *Novellaja milanese*.

20. PEPPI, WHO WANDERED OUT INTO THE WORLD (*PEPPI, SPERSU PRI LU MUNNU*)

Tale Type ATU 400: The Man on a Quest for his Lost Wife, ATU 302: The Ogre's (Devil's) Heart in the Egg, and ATU 566: The Three Magic Objects and the Wonderful Fruits (Fortunatus). There are not too many versions of this tale type to be found in Sicily. Two close variants can be found in Gonzenbach's *Sicilianische Märchen*: "The Story about the Merchant's Son" and "The Story about Ciccu."

21. THE MAGIC PURSE, CLOAK, AND HORN (*LA VUZA, LU FIRRIOLU E LU CORNU 'NFATATU*)

ATU 566: The Three Magic Objects and the Wonderful Fruits (Fortunatus). There are other variants in: Gonzenbach, "The Story about Ciccu," *Sicilianische Märchen*; Imbriani, "Coa," *La Novellaja Milanese*; Coronedi-Berti, "Fola del Nan," *Novelle popolari bolognesi*; and Widter-Wolf and Wolf, "Der arme Fischerknabe," *Volksmärchen aus Venetien*.

22. KING ANIMMULU (*LU RE D'ANÌMMULU*)

Tale Type ATU 425: The Search for the Lost Husband and ATU 425E: The Enchanted Husband Sings Lullaby. This tale is a sub-type of the Cupid and Psyche story. Pitrè said it could have been placed next to "The King of Love" and that the opening motifs are similar to those of "Rosemary." A distinctive attraction of this tale is the charming lullaby sung by the prince, which appears in several other places in Italian folk-tale tradition. Compare Basile, "Lo catenaccio," *Lo Cunto de li Cunti*; Imbriani, "Ombrion," *La Novellaja Milanese*; Gonzenbach, "Prince Scursuni," *Sicilianische Märchen*; Hahn, *Albanische Märchen*.

23. TRIDICINU (*TRIDICINU*)

Tale Type ATU 328: The Boy Steals the Ogre's Treasure. This is a fine example of the tale type familiar to English readers as "Jack and the Beanstalk" or "Jack the Giant Slayer." The various Italian versions have the sequence of successful thefts that reach a perfect climax in the task of stealing the ogre himself, a feature found also in Gonzenbach's "The Story about Ciccu" and "Caruseddu," *Sicilianische Märchen*. Pitrè summarized a tale from Bisaquino in which Tredicinu, on his way to stealing the ogre's golden curtain, meets an eagle, a lion, and an ant who ask him to arbitrate their dispute over some prey. Tredicinu's division finds such favor that they each give him a gift: respectively, a skin, a feather, and a foot, which aid him in carrying out his thefts. He concludes by stealing the ogre's ring and finally the ogre himself.

Among other variants, Pitrè cited Imbriani's "Tredesin," *Novellaja Milanese*, in which Tredesin is a father of thirteen sons and succeeds in having the sorcerer's thirteen sons killed in place of his own, then steals his bird, his bedcover full of little bells, and finishes his tricks by shutting the sorcerer up in a chest; and Widter-Wolf and Wolf's "Der listige Knecht," *Venetianische Märchen*, in which Tredesin is the thirteenth son who manages to steal a blanket, an enchanted bird, and an enchanted horse. Several motifs in "Tridicinu" are familiar in folk tales, such as the rivalry with brothers who think they can get rid of the hero by sending him on a dangerous mission.

24. THE STORY OF A QUEEN (*LU CUNTU DI 'NA RIGGINA*)

Tale Type ATU 327 B: The Brothers and the Ogre, ATU 328: The Boy Steals the Ogre's Treasure, ATU1119: The Ogre Kills his Mother (Wife),

and ATU 531: **The Clever Horse.** This tale bears many similarities to "The Enchanted Horse," except here the protagonist is a cunning woman, who manages to trick a sorcerer and his wife.

25. THE HERB-GATHERER'S DAUGHTERS (*LI FIGGHI DI LU CAVULICIDDARU*)

Tale Type ATU 707: The Three Golden Children. There is another version of this tale, "Re Sonnu" in Pitrè's *Nuovo Saggio di Fiabe e Novelle*. Moreover, it has many other important oral and literary sources: Fiorentino, *Il Pecorone*; Foriano Pico, *Historia della Regina Oliva, figlia di Giuliano Imperatore e moglie del Rè di Castiglia. Ad istanza, et esempio delle persone divote e timorate di Dio. Data in luce*; Straparola, "Ancilotto, re di Provino," *Le Piacevoli Notti*; Basile, "Cerva fatata," *Lo Cunto de li Cunti*; Mme d'Aulnoy, "La Princesse Belle-Étoile et le Prince Chéry," *Suite des Contes Nouveaux ou des Fées à la mode*; Gozzi, *La 'ngannatrice*; Galland, "Histoire de deux soeurs jalouses de leur cadette," *Les Milles et une nuit*; Grimm, "De drei Vügelkens," *Kinder- und Hausmärchen*; Comparetti, "L'uccellino che parla," *Novelline Popolari Italiane*; Gonzenbach, "The Banished Queen and her Two Abandoned Children," *Sicilianische Märchen*; De Gubernatis, "I cagnolini" and "Il Re di Napoli," *Novelline di S. Stefano*.

Though this fairy tale may have originated in the Orient, the source is not clear. Straparola's version was widely known by the French writers at the end of the seventeenth century, and it is certainly the source of d'Aulnoy's and Le Noble's tales. However, it may have even influenced Galland's version. His tale of "The Two Sisters Who Envied their Younger Sister" was told to him in Paris by a Maronite Christian Arab from Aleppo named Youhenna Diab or Hanna Diab. There was no Arabic manuscript for this tale, and Galland created it from memory after listening to Diab and may have introduced elements from the European tales he knew. His tale of "The Two Sisters" in his translation of *The Thousand and One Nights* and d'Aulnoy's tale of "Princesse Belle-Étoile" had an influence through the French and German eighteenth-century chapbooks (*Bibliothèque Bleue* and *Blaue Bibliothek*) in Europe and in England.

26. ROSEMARY (*ROSAMARINA*)

Tale Type ATU 407: The Girl as Flower. Similar to Giambattista Basile's "Mortella," *Lo Cunto de li Cunti*.

27. THE MAGIC BALLS (*LI PALLI MAGICHI*)

Tale Type ATU 432: The Prince as Bird. This tale is probably of Arabic origin, and once the vain king dies, it follows the traditional plotline that can be found in Apuleius's "Cupid and Psyche": the queen falls in love with the prince; her chambermaid causes her to betray him; the prince vanishes with his wounds; she travels to cure him; they are reunited in the end.

For other variants, see Bernoni, "El re de Fava," *Fiabe Popolari Veneziane*, and Imbriani, "Petru lu massariotu" and "El pegorée," *Novellaja Milanese*.

28. THE BEAUTY OF THE SEVEN MOUNTAINS OF GOLD (*LA BEDDA DI LI SETTI MUNTAGNI D'ORU*)

Tale Type ATU 400: The Man on a Quest for his Lost Wife. Other interesting versions are: Gonzenbach, "The Wasteful Giovanninu," *Sicilianische Märchen*; De Gubernatis, "La fanciulla e il Mago," *Novelline di S. Stefano*; Imbriani, "Impietrito," *Novellaja Fiorentina*; and Schneller, "Der Todenarm," *Märchen und Sagen aus Wälschtirol*.

29 . THE FIG-AND-RAISIN FOOL (*LU LOCCU DI LI PÀSSULI E FICU*)

Tale Type ATU 675: The Lazy Boy. This tale has a significant literary tradition. The most important early versions are: Straparola, "Pietro the Fool," *Le Piacevoli Notti*; Basile, "Pervonto," *Lo Cunto de li Cunti*; Marie-Catherine d'Aulnoy, "Le Dauphin" (1698) in *Suite des Contes Nouveaux ou des Fées à la mode*, 2 vols. (Paris: Théodore Girard, 1698); Brothers Grimm, "Simple Hans," first published as Nr. 62 in *Kinder- und Hausmärchen* (1812). It was omitted in the following editions either due to its French origins or similarity to a poem by Christoph Martin Wieland.

The mysterious pregnancy of a daughter was a real concern for many noble families and commoners as well. A woman's body was regarded as a possession of the male, and any violation of a female body was a violation of patriarchal authority. At stake were the legacy and honor of a family. In the cycle of tales that involve a fool, often called Peter or Hans, who seeks his luck by wishing that a princess becomes pregnant, there are other motifs that recall King Lear's harsh treatment of his innocent daughter as well as the cycle of tales that deal with a proud princess or noblewoman who needs to learn humility. Christoph Martin Wieland, one of the most gifted German writers of the eighteenth century, wrote "Pervonte" (1778/79), a remarkable verse rendition of Basile's "Peruonto," which concerns a poor simpleton, whose heart is so good that he is blessed by the fairies and thus rises in society. Another interesting German tale written during the romantic period was Heinrich von Kleist's "Die Marquise von O" (1810–11). Though not a fairy tale, it raises all the same pertinent questions about a mysterious pregnancy that the tales in this cycle pose.

30. THE HAUGHTY KING (*IL RE SUPERBO*)

ATU 874: The Proud King is Won. Several Sicilian tales include this plot: a young woman, generally a princess and youngest daughter, falls in love with a king, whom she has never met. She writes to him or has a messenger deliver a letter. The king scorns her or rejects her. When she tells him that she weeps for him, he sends her a handkerchief. When she tells him that she will hang herself, he sends her a cord. When she tells him that she intends to commit suicide, he sends a knife. Consequently, she decides to humiliate him and arranges to become one of his slaves. After he falls in love with her, she resists his affection and frustrates him by showing him the objects that he had sent to her one by one. In the end, they are reconciled, and he marries her.

31. THE HAUGHTY QUEEN (*LA RIGGINA SUPERBA*)

ATU 900: King Thrushbeard. There are many tale types that include a haughty princess or queen, and the most famous is "King Thrushbeard," which is primarily known through the Grimms' *Kinder- und Hausmärchen*. In this tale type, a haughty princess refuses to wed all the suitors who come to her because she feels none of them are good enough for her. Her father commands her to wed the first man who comes to the palace, and it is a beggar (a disguised king). This king takes her to his realm and humiliates her until she is docile. Then the king forgives her for her haughtiness and marries her. In Pitrè's version, the introduction of magical transformation and a magician who transforms the queen into the wife of a tripe dealer is original as is the theme of mistaken identities that makes the tale more humorous than others do in this tale type.

32. THE LITTLE BIRD (*L'OCIDDUZZU*)

ATU 720: The Juniper Tree, also called My Mother Slew Me, My Father Ate Me. In the "classical" version of this tale type, a mother dies after giving birth to a baby boy. The father remarries, and his new wife has a baby girl. The stepmother is jealous of the father's son and murders him.

Then she serves him in a stew to his father. Her daughter, however, refuses to eat him and buries his bones beneath a Juniper tree, associated with the boy's mother. Then a bird (the dead boy transformed) flies from the tree and sings a song of how his stepmother murdered him. The bird brings gifts to the father and stepsister, but drops a millstone on the stepmother, who is killed. Then the boy is resuscitated. This tale type, which reflects the intense relations in families that involve stepmothers and stepfathers and their children is widespread in Europe. One of the major verions, "The Juniper Tree," was published by the Brothers Grimm in 1812.

33. GIUFÀ AND THE PLASTER STATUE (*GIUFÀ E LA STATUA DI GHISSU*)

ATU 1643: The Broken Image. There is a Neopolitan version, "Vardiello," in Basile's *Lo Cunto de li Cunti*. See also "Giacomino e la pianta dei fagiuoli" in *Cinque Storie della Nonna* (Turin, Paravia).

34. GIUFÀ AND THE PIECE OF CLOTH (*GIUFÀ E LA PEZZA DI TILA*)

ATU 1642: The Good Bargain. This is a variant of "Giufà and the Plaster Statue."

35. GIUFÀ AND THE JUDGE (*GIUFÀ E LU JUDICI*)

There are similar anecdotes in: Imbriani, "La frittatina," *Novellaja Fiorentina; Bertoldo, Bertoldino e Cacasenno* (Venice, MDCCXCI); *Piacevoli e Ridicolose Semplicità di Bertoldino* (Milan, 1871). Bertoldino chases after the flies and attacks them. But he is not able to defeat them and calls upon his mother Marcolfa for help. There is also a short episode in the thirteenth night about a fool named Fortunio in Straparola's *Le Piacevoli Notti*.

Here is a variant that Pitrè included in his collection:

Giufà Goes to the Judge (*Giufà nni li Judici*)

Some flies began irritating Giufà and stung him. Therefore, he went to the judge and filed a complaint. However, the judge laughed and said, "The next time you see flies, hit them with your fist."

Just at that moment, while the judge was talking, a fly landed on his face, and Giufà quickly hit him with his fist and broke the judge's nose.

Told by an anonymous person in the district of Denisinni and recorded in Palermo

36. "EAT, MY FINE CLOTHING" ("*MANCIATI, RUBBICEDDI MEI!*")

37. "GIUFÀ, PULL THE DOOR!" ("*GIUFÀ, TIRATI LA PORTA!*")

This tale is imilar to the first anecdote, "Sdirrameddu" in the *Novella di Cascasenno* (Milan, 1870) and to "Patalocca" in Coronedi-Berti's *Novelle Popolari Bolognesi*. See also De Gubernatis, "Leggende dei popoli comparati: Lo scicco" in *Civlità Italiana*.

38. GIUFÀ AND THE HEN (*GIUFÀ E LA HJOCCA*)

ATU 1218: The Numskull Sits on Eggs to Finish the Hatching.

39. FIRRAZZANU'S WIFE AND THE QUEEN (*LA MUGGHIERI DI FIRRAZZANU E LA RIGGINA*)

The same version, "The Story about Firrazzanu," can be found in Laura Gonzenbach's *Sicilianische Märchen*.

40. FIRRAZZANU AND THE SWINEHERD (*FIRRAZZANU E LU PURCÀRU*)

41. THE TWENTY PERCENT (*LU VINTI PIR CENTU*)

42. THE HUNDRED BEATINGS (*LI CENTU LIGNATI*)

For other another variant, see Laura Gonzenbach, "Ferrazzanu," *Sicilianische Märchen*.

43. COLA PESCE (*COLA PISCI*)

44. PESCECOLA (*LU PISCI COLA*)

45. PESCECOLA (*LU PISCI COLA*)

46. BRANCALIUNI! (*BRANCALIUNI!*)

Tale Type ATU 125B: Contest between Donkey and Lion. This story can be found in Straparola's *Le Piacelvoli notti*, tenth night, second tale, and the name of the ass is the same: Brancaleone. In this tale, an ass flees a monastery (monaio) and arrives on top of a mountain. There he meets a lion and asks what his name is. The lion tells him that he is called lion, and the ass says his name is Brancaleone. Challenged to prove that he really is the "lion's claw" (Brancaleone), the ass eventually triumphs over the lion.

The basis for the variants can be found in *Brancaleone, historia piacevole et morale, dalla quale può ciascun avere utilissimi documenti per governo di se stesso e d'altri, scritto già da Latrobio filosofo et hora dato in luce da Ieromino Triultio* (Milan: Giovanni B. Alzato, 1610). Editions were also published in Venice, 1607; Pavia, 1612; and Milan, 1682. In one version by Giorgio Besozzi, the ass is adorned splendidly, and when the lion approaches and asks the ass who he is, the ass is stiff and standoffish and demands on the contrary to know the name of the lion. Therefore, the lion states his name, and the ass replies, "If you are the lion, then I am Brancaleone." Then the plot continues as in the other versions of this tale.

47. THE MAN, THE WOLF, AND THE FOX (*L'OMU, LU LUPU E LA VURPI*)

Tale Type ATU 155: The Ungrateful Serpent Returned to Captivity. Normally the major "protagonist" of this fable is a snake, and it is one of the oldest fables in the world. Its origins can be traced back to the *Panchatantara* (c. 100 BC), which began circulating in Europe in the eleventh century and was also known under the name *The Fables of Bidapi*. There are also versions in *Disciplina Clericalis* by Petrus Alfonsi, the *Roman de Renart*, and the *Gesta Romanorum* (Deeds of the Romans, fourteenth century).

There is another version in Laura Gonzenbach's *Sicilianische Märchen* with the title "Lion, Horse, and Fox." In this tale a lion falls into a hole. A horse frees it, but the lion wants to eat it. They appeal to a fox to decide what should be done. The fox wants to see how the situation was when the lion was in the hole and freed by the horse. When the lion returns to the hole and descends, the fox throws a rock on top of him and kills him.

48. THE KING OF THE ANIMALS, THE WOLF, AND THE FOX (*LU RE DI L'ARMALI, LU LUPU E LA VURPI*)

This is one of the oldest stories in Europe and can be found in the works of Carlo Gozzi, Carlo Casalicchio, and Venerando Gangi.

49. THE FOX (*LA VURPI*)

Tale Type ATU 32: The Wolf Descends into the Well in One Bucket and Rescues the Fox in the Other. There is a variant in *Novella di Cacasenno, figlio del semplice Bertoldino* (Milan: Fr. Pagnoni, 1870). A fox falls on top of a bucket in a well in which there are many fish, and the other bucket (there are two, one that has fallen and the other that was already lowered down) rises up. The fox cannot get out of the well and moans and groans until a bear comes and asks him why he is lamenting.

"Because I can't get the fish out of the well, and I can't eat them," the fox replied. "Why don't you come down here and eat them?"

The bear lowers himself down in the other bucket, and the fox rises in his bucket, and this is how he gets out of the well.

There is another version in Coronedi-Berti's *Fola dèl Corov*, in which a fox gets revenge on a wolf that has eaten his fox cubs. He ties the wolf to a cord and lowers the wolf into a well to drink. When the wolf is down in the water, the fox lets go of the rope. Then the wolf drowns in the water.

50. THE WOLF AND THE CARDINAL (*LU LUPU E LU CARDID-DUZZU*)

Tale Type ATU 20 D*: Pilgrimage of the Animals, ATU 130: The Animals in Night Quarters, and ATU 210: Rooster, Hen, Duck, Pin, and Needle on a Journey. This story not only mocks the rooster's vanity, but it also makes fun of his illiteracy and those of his companions. The tale is a pastiche of different fables which can be found in the works of the Brothers Grimm, Korn, Vernaleken, Haltrich, Waldau, Grundtvig, and Campbell. Laura Gonzenbach published a Sicilian variant, "The Rooster Who Wanted to be Pope," in *Sicilianische Märchen*.

Index of Titles